The Justice of Visual Art

In the aftermath of mass conflict, how is it possible to address violent and traumatic pasts, reconcile divided nations, and strengthen state institutions? This study explores the connections between transitional justice and visual art in order to answer that question. Garnsey argues that art can engage and shape ideas of justice. Art can be an inquiry into, and an alternative experience of, justice. Art embeds justice on different political levels – both local and global. Art becomes a radical form of political participation in times of transition. Arising out of extensive fieldwork at the Constitutional Court of South Africa and the South Africa Pavilion at the Venice Biennale, which included 130 interviews with key decision makers, the book provides the first substantive theoretical framework for understanding transitional justice and visual art, and develops novel conceptions of visual jurisprudence and cultural diplomacy as forms of transitional justice.

Eliza Garnsey is a British Academy Postdoctoral Fellow in International Relations at the University of Cambridge and is a Junior Research Fellow at Wolfson College Cambridge. She was previously awarded the 2017 Lisa Smirl PhD Prize for best thesis in Politics and International Studies, University of Cambridge.

The Law in Context Series

Editors: William Twining (*University College London*), Maksymilian Del Mar (*Queen Mary, University of London*) and Bronwen Morgan (*University of New South Wales*).

Since 1970 the Law in Context series has been at the forefront of the movement to broaden the study of law. It has been a vehicle for the publication of innovative scholarly books that treat law and legal phenomena critically in their social, political and economic contexts from a variety of perspectives. The series particularly aims to publish scholarly legal writing that brings fresh perspectives to bear on new and existing areas of law taught in universities. A contextual approach involves treating legal subjects broadly, using materials from other social sciences, and from any other discipline that helps to explain the operation in practice of the subject under discussion. It is hoped that this orientation is at once more stimulating and more realistic than the bare exposition of legal rules. The series includes original books that have a different emphasis from traditional legal textbooks, while maintaining the same high standards of scholarship. They are written primarily for undergraduate and graduate students of law and of other disciplines, but will also appeal to a wider readership. In the past, most books in the series have focused on English law, but recent publications include books on European law, globalisation, transnational legal processes, and comparative law.

Books in the Series

Acosta: *The National versus the Foreigner in South America*
Ali: *Modern Challenges to Islamic Law*
Alyagon Darr: *Plausible Crime Stories: The Legal History of Sexual Offences in Mandate Palestine*
Anderson, Schum & Twining: *Analysis of Evidence*
Ashworth: *Sentencing and Criminal Justice*
Barton & Douglas: *Law and Parenthood*
Beecher-Monas: *Evaluating Scientific Evidence: An Interdisciplinary Framework for Intellectual Due Process*
Bell: *French Legal Cultures*
Bercusson: *European Labour Law*
Birkinshaw: *European Public Law*
Birkinshaw: *Freedom of Information: The Law, the Practice and the Ideal*
Brownsword & Goodwin: *Law and the Technologies of the Twenty-First Century: Text and Materials*
Cane & Goudkamp: *Atiyah's Accidents, Compensation and the Law*
Clarke & Kohler: *Property Law: Commentary and Materials*
Collins: *The Law of Contract*
Collins, Ewing & McColgan: *Labour Law*
Cowan: *Housing Law and Policy*
Cranston: *Legal Foundations of the Welfare State*

Darian-Smith: *Laws and Societies in Global Contexts: Contemporary Approaches*
Dauvergne: *Making People Illegal: What Globalisation Means for Immigration and Law*
Davies: *Perspectives on Labour Law*
Dembour: *Who Believes in Human Rights?: Reflections on the European Convention*
de Sousa Santos: *Toward a New Legal Common Sense*
Diduck: *Law's Families*
Estella: *Legal Foundations of EU Economic Governance*
Fortin: *Children's Rights and the Developing Law*
Ghai & Woodman: *Practising Self-Government: A Comparative Study of Autonomous Regions*
Glover-Thomas: *Reconstructing Mental Health Law and Policy*
Gobert & Punch: *Rethinking Corporate Crime*
Goldman: *Globalisation and the Western Legal Tradition: Recurring Patterns of Law and Authority*
Haack: *Evidence Matters: Science, Proof, and Truth in the Law*
Harlow & Rawlings: *Law and Administration*
Harris: *An Introduction to Law*
Harris, Campbell & Halson: *Remedies in Contract and Tort*
Harvey: *Seeking Asylum in the UK: Problems and Prospects*
Hervey & McHale: *European Union Health Law: Themes and Implications*
Hervey & McHale: *Health Law and the European Union*
Holder & Lee: *Environmental Protection, Law and Policy: Text and Materials*
Jackson & Summers: *The Internationalisation of Criminal Evidence: Beyond the Common Law and Civil Law Traditions*
Kostakopoulou: *The Future Governance of Citizenship*
Kreiczer-Levy: *Destabilized Property: Property Law in the Sharing Economy*
Kubal: *Immigration and Refugee Law in Russia: Socio-Legal Perspectives*
Lewis: *Choice and the Legal Order: Rising above Politics*
Likosky: *Transnational Legal Processes: Globalisation and Power Disparities*
Likosky: *Law, Infrastructure and Human Rights*
Lunney: *A History of Australian Tort Law 1901-1945: England's Obedient Servant?*
Maughan & Webb: *Lawyering Skills and the Legal Process*
McGlynn: *Families and the European Union: Law, Politics and Pluralism*
Moffat: *Trusts Law: Text and Materials*
Monti: *EC Competition Law*
Morgan: *Contract Law Minimalism: A Formalist Restatement of Commercial Contract Law*
Morgan & Yeung: *An Introduction to Law and Regulation: Text and Materials*
Nicola & Davies: *EU Law Stories: Contextual and Critical Histories of European Jurisprudence*
Norrie: *Crime, Reason and History: A Critical Introduction to Criminal Law*
O'Dair: *Legal Ethics: Text and Materials*
Oliver: *Common Values and the Public–Private Divide*
Oliver & Drewry: *The Law and Parliament*
Picciotto: *International Business Taxation*
Probert: *The Changing Legal Regulation of Cohabitation, 1600-2010*
Reed: *Internet Law: Text and Materials*

Richardson: *Law, Process and Custody*
Roberts & Palmer: *Dispute Processes: ADR and the Primary Forms of Decision-Making*
Rowbottom: *Democracy Distorted: Wealth, Influence and Democratic Politics*
Sauter: *Public Services in EU Law*
Scott & Black: *Cranston's Consumers and the Law*
Seneviratne: *Ombudsmen: Public Services and Administrative Justice*
Seppänen: *Ideological Conflict and the Rule of Law in Contemporary China*
Siems: *Comparative Law, 2nd Edition*
Stapleton: *Product Liability*
Stewart: *Gender, Law and Justice in a Global Market*
Tamanaha: *Law as a Means to an End: Threat to the Rule of Law*
Turpin & Tomkins: *British Government and the Constitution: Text and Materials*
Twining: *Globalisation and Legal Theory*
Twining: *Rethinking Evidence: Exploratory Essays*
Twining: *General Jurisprudence: Understanding Law from a Global Perspective*
Twining: *Human Rights, Southern Voices: Francis Deng, Abdullahi An-Na'im, Yash Ghai and Upendra Baxi*
Twining: *Jurist in Context*
Twining & Miers; *How to Do Things with Rules*
Ward: *A Critical Introduction to European Law*
Ward: *Law, Text, Terror*
Ward: *Shakespeare and Legal Imagination*
Wells & Quick: *Lacey, Wells and Quick: Reconstructing Criminal Law*
Zander: *Cases and Materials on the English Legal System*
Zander: *The Law-Making Process*

International Journal of Law in Context: A Global Forum for Interdisciplinary Legal Studies

The *International Journal of Law in Context* is the companion journal to the Law in Context book series and provides a forum for interdisciplinary legal studies and offers intellectual space for ground-breaking critical research. It publishes contextual work about law and its relationship with other disciplines including but not limited to science, literature, humanities, philosophy, sociology, psychology, ethics, history and geography. More information about the journal and how to submit an article can be found at http://journals.cambridge.org/ijc

The Justice of Visual Art

Creative State-Building in Times of Political Transition

ELIZA GARNSEY
University of Cambridge

CAMBRIDGE
UNIVERSITY PRESS

CAMBRIDGE
UNIVERSITY PRESS

University Printing House, Cambridge CB2 8BS, United Kingdom

One Liberty Plaza, 20th Floor, New York, NY 10006, USA

477 Williamstown Road, Port Melbourne, VIC 3207, Australia

314–321, 3rd Floor, Plot 3, Splendor Forum, Jasola District Centre, New Delhi – 110025, India

79 Anson Road, #06–04/06, Singapore 079906

Cambridge University Press is part of the University of Cambridge.

It furthers the University's mission by disseminating knowledge in the pursuit of education, learning, and research at the highest international levels of excellence.

www.cambridge.org
Information on this title: www.cambridge.org/9781108494397
DOI: 10.1017/9781108637701

First published 2020

Printed in the United Kingdom by TJ International Ltd, Padstow Cornwall

A catalogue record for this publication is available from the British Library.

Library of Congress Cataloging-in-Publication Data
Names: Garnsey, Eliza, author.
Title: The justice of visual art : creative state-building in times of political transition / Eliza Garnsey.
Description: 1. | New York : Cambridge University Press, 2021. | Series: Law in context | Includes bibliographical references and index.
Identifiers: LCCN 2019037036 (print) | LCCN 2019037037 (ebook) | ISBN 9781108494397 (hardback) | ISBN 9781108714518 (paperback) | ISBN 9781108637701 (epub)
Subjects: LCSH: Law and art. | Transitional justice. | South Africa. Constitutional Court–Art collections.
Classification: LCC K3778 .G37 2021 (print) | LCC K3778 (ebook) | DDC 344.68/097–dc23
LC record available at https://lccn.loc.gov/2019037036
LC ebook record available at https://lccn.loc.gov/2019037037

ISBN 978-1-108-49439-7 Hardback

For Philippa and John

Contents

Figures

Acknowledgements

I would like to express my sincere gratitude to Duncan Bell for his guidance, support, and encouragement. I am privileged and feel fortunate to have been able to work with such an astute academic. He has been able at all times to provide me with expert critique as my work developed and infallible advice on academic life. I could not have imagined having a better mentor.

Many thanks to Charles Jones, Duncan Kelly and Mihaela Mihai whose detailed and insightful feedback and guidance at various stages of drafting this book has been invaluable.

I would like to express my thanks and appreciation to the Constitutional Court of South Africa, in particular to Stacey Vorster, and to the National Arts Festival, in particular to Tony Lankester, Ismail Mahomed and Brenton Maart, for welcoming and supporting my research into their collection and exhibition, respectively. Many thanks are due to the numerous people associated with these institutions who assisted me in the research. Special thanks go to the friends I made through these institutions, particularly to Pops Mahlangu, Ruth Morgan, Toni Morkel, Mxolisi Mthombeni, Bié Venter and Nelisiwe Xaba, who were all so kind to me while I was in Johannesburg and Venice.

I am especially grateful to the 130 people I interviewed, who embraced the research and shared with me their stories, their thoughts, their time and their homes. The need for anonymity means that I cannot individually thank these many people, but what I can simply say is that without you this research would not be possible. Special thanks to the artists and their galleries for their unique insight and support, and for the use of images.

Thank you to Jade Jacobs, Josephine Matla, Matumelo Ngwenya, Molemo Ramphalile, Shoeshoe Setai and Taryn Woodford for their research assistance.

I am very thankful to the many people who have provided valuable advice at various stages in the research process and who have read and commented on parts of this book or related papers, including Roland Bleiker, Arnaud Kurze, Christopher Lamont, and at: Australian National University, Benjamin Authers and participants in the 'Human Rights, Utopias and Promises' workshop; Centre for Governance and Human Rights, University of Cambridge, Sharath Srinivasan, Thomas Probert and participants in the research seminar; Centre for Human Rights and Institute for Comparative Law in Africa,

University of Pretoria, Christof Heyns, Tshepo Madlingozi, Isolde de Villiers and participants in the research seminar; European Consortium for Political Research, Mihaela Mihai, Cynthia Milton, Mathias Thaler and participants in the 'Imagining Violence' joint session; International Studies Association conventions, Rocco Bellanova, Tahseen Kazi, Simon Robins and participants in various panels; King's College London, Rachel Kerr and the War Crimes Research Group; London School of Economics, Denisa Kostovicova and the Conflict Research Group; University of Cambridge, Diane Barlee, Stephanie Diepeveen, Zenobia Ismail, Annette LaRocco, Nikolay Mintchev, Or Rosenboim and Marcos Zunino; University of Marburg, Mariam Salehi and participants in the 'Spectres of Justice' conference; University of Sydney, Millicent Churcher, Moira Gatens, Danielle Celermajor and participants in the 'Institutional Transformation' workshop; and, University of Witwatersrand, Daryl Glaser, Matthew Evans and participants in the research seminar. Many thanks to the editors of the *Law in Context* series, Maksymilian Del Mar, Bronwen Morgan and William Twining, and the anonymous reviewers of the book for their invaluable guidance. Many thanks also to Tom Randall, Laura Blake and the team at Cambridge University Press for all their help during book production.

This work has been generously supported at various stages by: Australian National University; British Academy grant number PF170086; British International Studies Association; Ca'Foscari University of Venice; Cambridge Political Economy Society Trust; Centre of Governance and Human Rights at the University of Cambridge, and the Centre for Human Rights and the Institute for International and Comparative Law in Africa at the University of Pretoria, through a grant from the David and Elaine Potter Foundation; Centre for Law, Arts and the Humanities, Australian National University; Centre for International Security Studies, University of Sydney; Department of Politics and International Studies, University of Cambridge; European Consortium for Political Research; International Studies Association; Queens' College Cambridge; Smuts Memorial Fund, managed by the University of Cambridge in memory of Jan Christiaan Smuts; University of Sydney; University of Witwatersrand; and, Wolfson College Cambridge.

My heartfelt gratitude goes to my partner James. Your steadfast support, love and belief in me have been the greatest source of inspiration throughout this journey, and your wise counsel and sympathetic ear have been the greatest comfort. *Sulla veranda, AML.* Thank you also to my parents-in-law, Sue and Alan, for your kind encouragement and support.

I would like to thank my parents, Philippa and John. Your support and love have enabled me to thrive and to reach this point. This book is dedicated to you both.

Abbreviations

ANC	African National Congress
ASAC	*Archivio Storico delle Arti Contemporanee* (Historic Archives of Contemporary Arts) (Venice, Italy)
AZAPO	Azanian People's Organisation
Biennale, the	*La Biennale di Venezia* (The Biennale of Venice) / The International Art Biennale in Venice
Court, the	The Constitutional Court of South Africa
DAC	Department of Arts and Culture (South Africa)
DIRCO	Department of International Relations and Cooperation (South Africa)
IR	International Relations
LGBTI	Lesbian, gay, bisexual, transgender, and inter-sex
NAF	National Arts Festival (Grahamstown, South Africa)
SA	South Africa
SAHA	South African History Archives (Johannesburg, South Africa)
TRC	Truth and Reconciliation Commission of South Africa
UAE	United Arab Emirates
UK	United Kingdom
UN	United Nations
USA	United States of America

1

Introduction

> [P]roblems that currently haunt world politics . . . are far too serious not to employ the full register of human intelligence to understand and deal with them.[1]

> Human understanding and the need for human understanding is actually the true link between art and justice.[2]

When transitioning from conflict, divided societies face multiple practical and ideological challenges. Transitional justice seeks to understand and respond to these challenges primarily by providing accountability, establishing truth, and fulfilling victims' rights, as well as meeting a range of other objectives, including resolving conflict, preventing and deterring future conflict, fostering democracy, and promoting reconciliation.[3] These objectives are most commonly sought through legal measures, such as trials and truth commissions. However, no single transitional justice measure can possibly comprehend or respond to the diverse claims of individuals and groups affected directly and indirectly by conflict, as well as the inter-generational trauma, social injustices, and deep grievances which are both the result of conflict and the long-term causes of conflict. A holistic perspective of transitional justice should include legal, social, and cultural measures, within which the arts have an important role.[4]

At the heart of this book lies an urge to better understand the relationship between art and justice in times of transition; how the past shapes the present, how the present shapes the past, and how the present envisages the future

[1] Roland Bleiker, *Aesthetics and World Politics* (Hampshire: Palgrave Macmillan, 2009), 1.

[2] Constitutional Court of South Africa Judge 4.

[3] Rama Mani, 'Women, Art and Post-Conflict Justice', *International Criminal Law Review*, vol. 11 (2011): 545. Transitional justice is most widely associated with a liberalising direction of political change; see Ruti G Teitel, *Transitional Justice* (New York: Oxford University Press, 2000), 5.

[4] Calls for an holistic perspective, include Makau Mutua, 'What Is the Future of Transitional Justice?', *International Journal of Transitional Justice*, vol. 9, no. 1 (2015): 1–9; Tricia D Olsen, Leigh A Payne, and Andrew G Reiter, *Transitional Justice in Balance: Comparing Processes, Weighing Efficacy* (Washington, DC: United States Institute of Peace, 2010), 25; Naomi Roht-Arriaza and Javier Mariezcurrena, eds., *Transitional Justice in the Twenty-First Century* (Cambridge: Cambridge University Press, 2007).

through art. The purpose of the enquiry is to analyse the relationship between visual art and transitional justice; how visual art contributes to, and affects, transitional justice, and vice versa.[5] The primary aim of the book is to demonstrate that there are aesthetic and creative ways to pursue transitional justice – ways which have the capacity to address identity divisions and exclusions. This is achieved through a detailed case study analysis of post-apartheid South African visual art in two major state-sponsored institutions, the Constitutional Court of South Africa (the Court) and the South Africa Pavilion at the International Art Biennale (the Biennale) in Venice. South Africa remains scarred by the physical, structural, and ideological violence and trauma generated by apartheid – scars which continue to circumscribe the political and social interactions between the state and its citizens, and between citizens.[6] The transition remains ongoing.

Analysis of post-apartheid visual art in these institutions is used to explore three areas: the theoretical framing of art and justice; the visual jurisprudence of justice measures developed in and emerging out of transition; and the cultural diplomacy practices of states emerging from conflict. Three broad questions shape the enquiry:

1. How can the meeting point between visual art and transitional justice best be understood?
2. Why should the relationship between visual art and transitional justice be considered?
3. What is the nature and extent of the role played by visual art within state-sponsored institutions emerging out of South Africa's transition?

I argue that art plays an important role in animating and activating the narratives of individuals so that they take on collective importance. In doing so, the past can be shared so that a new political future can be imagined. The Court's art collection is a kind of visual jurisprudence in which the assumptions of justice and what it means to uphold the Constitution in the face of the past are probed. The narratives of transitional justice emanating from the South Africa Pavilion at the Biennale position the state as continuing to heal its internal wounds while constructing itself as an archetype of political transition in order to re-establish its position within the international community. At a broader level, the book is underpinned by the normative argument that an account of transitional justice without aesthetic dimensions is insufficient. Artworks offer insightful visions and experiences which have an afterlife beyond their creation. These need to be

[5] Visual art is understood broadly to include painting, drawing, photography, video art, sculpture, installation, and performance art. I use the term 'transitional justice' rather than 'post-conflict justice' in order to underscore the salience of continuing change captured in transitions and to reflect the 'high currency of the term in the literature' as stated by Mihaela Mihai, *Negative Emotions and Transitional Justice* (New York: Columbia University Press, 2016), 5.

[6] See Lawrence Hamilton, *Are South Africans Free?* (London: Bloomsbury, 2014).

acknowledged and analysed in order to understand the possibilities and limits of justice in the aftermath of conflict.

The book makes an important contribution to the field of transitional justice by providing a theoretical framework for understanding the relationship between art and transitional justice which emerges from extensive empirical research. The book also develops a novel conception of visual jurisprudence (an undertheorised concept in legal scholarship and a non-existent one in transitional justice) in relation to art, and exposes unique and alternative spaces of transitional justice which art creates, especially at an international level. Importantly, the book synthesises disparate bodies of scholarship within transitional justice, International Relations (IR) and art theory, generating new and productive research through a radical transdisciplinary approach. That is, an approach aimed at rethinking rather than reproducing accepted knowledge frames in order 'to create the conditions of possibility for imagining alternative worlds (and thus to be able to recognize the political commitments sequestered in every political imaginary)'.[7] The book also has important implications for people who engage in transitional justice practice and policy-making, whereby drawing on a full range of possibilities, including art, facilitates an understanding of how the past affects the present and the subsequent ability to access and acknowledge feelings of justice.

Transitional justice is broadly understood as the 'conception of justice associated with periods of political change'.[8] It arises after periods of great conflict, where the reform of formal institutions, particularly legal and governmental ones, is necessary in order to prevent further harm. The field of transitional justice largely focuses on this reform. However, emerging scholarship (from diverse areas of study) on transitional justice and the arts seeks to understand how institutional change relates to cultural transformations.[9] Despite this, and despite calls for further investigation into the arts, the consideration of transitional justice and the arts, especially visual art, is in its infancy.

There is a tendency in transitional justice scholarship which does address the arts to privilege civil society arts initiatives over state-sponsored ones.[10] This is primarily because new state institutions are often slow to recognise the

[7] Michael J. Shapiro, *Studies in Trans-Disciplinary Method* (Oxford: Routledge, 2013), xv.

[8] Teitel, *Transitional Justice*, 69.

[9] Pablo de Greiff, 'On Making the Invisible Visible: The Role of Cultural Interventions in Transitional Justice Processes', in *Transitional Justice, Culture, and Society: Beyond Outreach*, ed. Clara Ramirez-Barat (New York: Social Science Research Council, 2014), 13. The diverse areas include socio-legal studies, sociology, literary studies, arts, film studies, and performance studies.

[10] This tendency is evident in both seminal volumes on transitional justice and the arts: Clara Ramirez-Barat, ed. *Transitional Justice, Culture, and Society: Beyond Outreach* (New York: Social Science Research Council, 2014); Peter D. Rush and Olivera Simić, eds., *The Arts of Transitional Justice: Culture, Activism, and Memory after Atrocity* (New York: Springer, 2014).

value of incorporating arts initiatives into transitional justice processes, especially in the face of trying to address urgent human need. It is also because former state institutions are often responsible for committing the violence that is under consideration. When state-sponsored arts initiatives are examined, the predominant focus is on monuments and memorials, prompting the question: What other kinds of arts initiatives are emerging through state institutions in the wake of conflict?

Scholarship on transitional justice and the arts tends to focus on the performing arts (dance, theatre, film, music), leaving the visual arts under-theorised, likely as a result of the existing use of performing arts to examine conflict transformation in related peacebuilding scholarship; also because transitional justice mechanisms are themselves performative.[11] When visual art is discussed specifically in relation to transitional justice, it is most often analysed in relation to a single artwork or an artist's body of work, meaning that discussions about groups of artworks and the spaces they inhabit, such as exhibitions, collections, and arts institutions, remain secondary (or absent).[12] The practice of transitional justice in physical sites of former conflicts (such as the Court of Bosnia and Herzegovina, which is based in a former prison building), in mobile spaces (such as the Truth and Reconciliation Commission [TRC] which travelled throughout South Africa), or in community spaces (such as Rwanda's *Gacaca* courts) has social and political significance.[13] The significance of the space of transitional justice takes on even more importance when coupled with the realm of visual art which has its own spatially significant practices of display and curation. By examining the visual art exhibitions of two state-sponsored institutions – the Constitutional Court of South Africa

[11] See Nadia Siddiqui, Hadi Marifat, and Sari Kuouvo, 'Culture, Theatre and Justice: Examples from Afghanistan', in *The Arts of Transitional Justice*, ed. Peter D. Rush and Olivera Simić (New York: Springer, 2014); Olivera Simić and Dijana Milosevic, 'Enacting Justice: The Role of Dah Theatre Company in Transitional Justice Processes in Serbia and Beyond', ibid. Also see case studies in Ksenija Bilbija et al., *The Art of Truth-Telling about Authoritarian Rule* (Madison: University of Wisconsin Press, 2005). In peacebuilding scholarship, see, for example, Cynthia E. Cohen, Roberti Gutiérrez Varea, and Polly O. Walker, eds., *Acting Together: Performance and the Creative Transformation of Conflict* (Oakland: New Village Press, 2011). Regarding the performativity, see Sanja Bahun, 'Transitional Justice and the Arts: Reflections on the Field', in *Theorizing Transitional Justice*, ed. Claudio Corradetti, Nir Eisikovits, and Jack Volpe Rotondi (Oxford: Routledge, 2015), 160; Catherine M. Cole, *Performing South Africa's Truth Commission: Stages of Transition* (Bloomington: Indiana University Press, 2010).

[12] For example, see the focus on Willem Boshoff at the Constitutional Court in Carrol Clarkson, *Drawing the Line: Toward an Aesthetics of Transitional Justice* (New York: Fordham University Press, 2014), 65–87. Or the focus on two artists in Rosemarie Buikema, 'Performing Dialogical Truth and Restorative Justice: The Role of Art in the Becoming Post-apartheid of South Africa', *Journal of Memory Studies*, vol. 5, no. 3 (2012): 282–293. Or the focus on individual artists in Vikki Bell, *The Art of Post-dictatorship: Ethics and Aesthetics in Transitional Argentina* (Abingdon: Routledge, 2014).

[13] See, for example, Alex Jeffrey and Michaelina Jakala, 'Using Courts to Build States: The Competing Spaces of Citizenship in Transitional Justice Programmes', *Political Geography*, vol. 47 (2015): 43–52.

and the South Africa Pavilion at the Biennale – this book begins to fill these gaps.

The focus on South Africa arises for three reasons. First, South Africa is at the centre of much transitional scholarship because of its modern history. The twentieth century in South Africa was marked by the severe racial, economic, and social discrimination and gross human rights violations (including massacres, killings, forced resettlement, and torture) enacted under apartheid against the country's majority non-white population. The abolition of apartheid in 1994 is hailed as a largely negotiated political transition between the African National Congress (ANC) – fighting against apartheid – and the Nationalist Party – the architects of apartheid. The TRC established in the wake of this transition features prominently within transitional justice scholarship which often accredits it as being the first of its kind and a significant initiative responsible for shaping the field.[14] South Africa's importance in mainstream transitional justice research provides a solid base from which to engage this field, and also from which to explore the more unusual subject of art.

Second, South African post-apartheid visual art provides substantial material to examine its relationship with transitional justice; the 'contemporary art world in South Africa has served as a veritable hotbed for re-articulating the past, and as an important counterweight to the dominant narrative imposed by the TRC'.[15] In particular, the institutions of the Constitutional Court and the South Africa Pavilion at the Biennale are *unique* and *significant* sites to explore the relationship between visual art and transitional justice across national and international levels. Both institutions occupy thought-provoking relationships with the state, being patronised by the state but also being supported by non-governmental entities.

Third, and perhaps most fundamentally, South Africa occupies an important place in my personal connection to the research. Learning about certain South African artworks and arts initiatives has been pivotal in shaping my deep concern for art and justice, and arriving at this research agenda. At a broader level, my interest in South Africa arises from my desire to know more about the state's contemporary approach to race relations, reconciliation,

[14] See, for example, P. B. Hayner, *Unspeakable Truths: Transitional Justice and the Challenge of Truth Commissions* (London: Routledge, 2011), 2; Hugo van Der Merwe and Audrey R. Chapman, *Truth and Reconciliation in South Africa: Did the TRC Deliver?* (Philadelphia: University of Pennsylvania Press, 2008); Claire Moon, *Narrating Political Reconciliation: South Africa's Truth and Reconciliation Commission* (Lanham: Lexington Books, 2008).

[15] Erin Mosely, 'Visualizing Apartheid: Re-framing Truth and Reconciliation through Contemporary South African Art', in *Curating Difficult Knowledge: Violent Pasts in Public Places,* ed. Erica Lehrer, Cynthia E. Milton, and Monica Eileen Patterson (New York: Palgrave Macmillan, 2011), 130. Also see Jill Bennett, *Empathic Vision: Affect, Trauma, and Contemporary Art* (Stanford: Stanford University Press, 2005); Annie E. Coombes, *History after Apartheid: Visual Culture and Public Memory in a Democratic South Africa* (Durham: Duke University Press, 2003).

constitutional recognition, inter-generational trauma, land rights, and colonial legacies of oppression – issues somewhat similar to ones which are of continuing relevance to the political, social, cultural, and economic landscape of my home country, Australia.

Legacies of violence, discrimination, and dominance are of central concern in South Africa. Studying such troubled histories requires a commitment to the ethical concerns which emerge through the process of interpretation and are, in turn, re-embedded through interpretive research.[16] Concerns over ethical questions, implications, and obligations shape the enquiry. Three questions are of central importance: how does this book affect the subjects of the research; what is my responsibility to the subjects of the research in terms of justice and advocacy; and, how do I acknowledge my own cultural embeddedness and institutional privilege in the enquiry?[17] The in-depth case study of South African post-apartheid visual art occurred across two periods of participant observation fieldwork, seven months at the South Africa Pavilion in Venice in 2013 and six months at the Constitutional Court in Johannesburg in 2014. During this time, I undertook visual and archival research and conducted 130 semi-structured interviews with people involved in both institutions, including judges, artists, staff, visitors, and government representatives.[18]

Structure of the Book

Chapter 2 sets out the theoretical framework for the book. I undertake a close visual analysis and narrative investigation of one artwork – *REwind* by Gerhard Marx, Maja Marx, and Philip Miller – in order to unpack four ideas which make art exigent and meaningful to transitional justice, and vice versa.

16 Peregrine Schwartz-Shea and Dvora Yanow, *Interpretive Research Design: Concepts and Processes* (New York: Routledge, 2012), 102.

17 Questions from Bina D'Costa, 'Marginalized Identity: New Frontiers in Research for IR?', in *Feminist Methodologies for International Relations*, ed. A. Brooks, Maria Stern, and Jacqui True (New York: Cambridge University Press, 2006), 129–152.

18 I interviewed seventy-six people associated with the South Africa Pavilion, including: six staff members (including gallery invigilators and Biennale education team members); four curatorial team members (including the curator and members of NAF curatorial committee); thirteen exhibiting artists; seven members of exhibition management (including senior members of NAF and senior Government representatives); and forty-six visitors (including twenty-four women and twenty-two men from fifteen countries). I interviewed fifty-four people associated with the Court: six art committee members; five staff members (including security, library and tour guide personnel); four curators (including former and current curators); fourteen exhibiting artists; six judges (including former and current judges); six law clerks; and thirteen visitors (including legal professionals, tourists, and students). People were selected primarily for their prominent roles within each institution, and then a snowballing technique was employed. Interviewees are anonymised in the reporting of the research. This means throughout the book, quotations are attributed using an arbitrary numbering system attached to general categories, such as Judge 5. Quotations are only attributed to names after seeking written consent of the person to do so.

These ideas are about the circulation of political sentiment, the mediation of political agency, the invitation of political encounters, and the invention of political space. I argue that art plays an important role in animating and activating the narratives of individuals so that they take on collective importance. In so doing, the past can be shared so that a new political future can be imagined.

The book is then divided into two parts in order to highlight the national and international dimensions of transitional justice. Part I explores transitional justice in the nation state through the Constitutional Court of South Africa. Established at the point of transition from apartheid to democracy, the Court was built on the site of several former notorious prisons. The court building is a unique space by international comparison, not only because it has transformed the penal site, but because it also incorporates artworks into the fabric of the building and houses a large visual art collection developed by and for the Court. In Chapter 3 I provide an historical account of the Court as a key institution in the 'new' South Africa. In order to understand the conceptual and concrete transitions of the Court, I trace its development with a particular focus on the unique policies and processes through which the art collection came into being. I argue that art has been a central component of the most significant institution to emerge out of South Africa's transition, and it continues to be so.

Chapter 4 examines the spatial politics of the Court. The Court's architecture and art collection are intended to symbolise the values of the Constitution. I explore five themes critical to justice which are dominant in the discourse of the Court – both in how people speak about the Court and in how the Court portrays itself. Four of these themes refer to values rooted in and fostered by the Constitution (accessibility, equality, dignity, and freedom of expression) while the fifth theme (justice under a tree) relates to a process of South African constitutionalism embedded in regional vernacular and post-apartheid identity formation. I analyse each theme by examining how its material manifestation – specific artworks and architectural features – intervenes in the appearance and performance of the Court, shaping how the Constitution is understood in different ways. These material interventions and the space they create are key to the provision of justice at the Court.

In Chapter 5 I explore three dominant narratives which emerge from the art collection at the Court; narratives which recognise people, community, and time as key to the project of justice and democracy in South Africa. These three narratives play a central role in shaping the Court's larger transitional justice story. They draw attention to how the impossibility of attaining universal justice, is what drives justice practices and the enactment of human rights for particular people and communities at particular times.

Chapter 6 theorises the Court's art collection as a new kind of visual jurisprudence – the philosophy of the visual in law. I analyse the ways in which people, especially judges, talk about the art collection in order to show

how artworks at the Court become central to the bodies of aesthetic knowledge that shape the appearance of justice and how justice is understood. I argue that in such close proximity to the Court, the art collection inhabits a unique position in which the assumptions of justice (and Justices) and what it means to uphold the Constitution can be probed. This creates a visual jurisprudence that reflects both the values which underpin the Court as well as the ways of practicing justice in post-apartheid South Africa.

Part II explores transitional justice on the global stage through the South Africa Pavilion at the Venice Art Biennale. In Chapter 7 I provide an historical overview of South Africa's relationship to the Biennale. In 1968, protests at the Biennale changed how it took place. These changes included banning South Africa from exhibiting – a boycott of the apartheid regime. It was not until 1993, with the prospect of transition from apartheid to democracy, that South Africa was invited back to the Biennale. Through this invitation to exhibit at the Biennale, South Africa was being rewarded for political change. By chronicling South Africa's appearances at the Biennale, the chapter reveals the complex national and international politics and diplomatic negotiations involved in becoming and remaining a member state of the Biennale. I argue that South Africa's participation continues to be deeply affected by international and national politics; its long absence from the Biennale reverberates through the way in which it represents itself to the international community and establishes itself as a member state of this international organisation.

Chapter 8 examines the geo-politics of the Biennale. It begins by mapping how the Biennale transforms the local city space of Venice into a global art-scape. The Giardini and the Arsenale house the majority of the eighty-five national pavilions – established member states own art embassies in the Giardini while probationary member states rent exhibition spaces in the Arsenale. Pavilions become proxies through which states present an image of themselves to the international community. I contrast South Africa's 2013 national pavilion with that of the United Arab Emirates (the two states shared an exhibition space in the Arsenale) in order to show how comparisons between states are forced upon them by virtue of exhibiting in the Biennale. I argue that these art-scapes provide fertile ground for states to offer an image of themselves – images which are not necessarily perceived how states intend.

Chapter 9 explores the exhibition *Imaginary Fact* in the 2013 South Africa Pavilion at the Biennale. Three key narratives about violence emerge from the exhibition: the unresolved violence of apartheid-era crimes; the structural violence of pervasive practices of discrimination; and the physical violence to which people continue to be subjected. I analyse three artworks which epitomise each narrative: David Koloane's *The Journey*, Sue Williamson's *For Thirty Years Next to His Heart*, and Zanele Muholi's *Faces and Phases*. I argue that these three narratives are important actions in South Africa's transition because they warn against the repetition of violence, document the structures of violence, and expose continuing practices of violence in the 'new' South Africa.

Chapter 10 theorises *Imaginary Fact* as a unique instance of cultural diplomacy. *Imaginary Fact* plays a paradoxical role in the process of nation-building because it presents a dual image of a nation struggling with ongoing internal complexities while projecting a collective narrative of a state that has undergone a difficult transition and come out the other side to re-assert itself in the international community. By examining South Africa's conception of cultural diplomacy presented in government white papers, I show how the official image of South Africa as a global competitor (a transitioned nation) sits uncomfortably with the artists' image of South Africa as a transitioning nation circumscribed by ongoing challenges to human rights. I argue that this establishes a *glocal* (global-local) image of the state which is in tension with South Africa's foreign policy agenda.

The conclusion outlines the key implications and contributions of the book. Art is a radical form of political participation in times of transition. In South Africa, visual art creates new critical spaces of political recognition and representation. Art is embedded in creative state-building, both internally and externally. The state uses visual art from the inside out to reconceptualise the South African justice system, and from the outside in to re-engage the international community with the South African state. The conclusion also addresses two potential criticisms facing the book, namely that what is discussed does not count as transitional justice and whether art really matters in post-conflict settings in the face of urgent human need.

2

Art and Justice in Times of Transition

> [P]olitics is the public discussion on matters of justice among speaking people who are all able to do it. But there is a preliminary matter of justice: How do you recognize that the person who is mouthing a voice in front of you is discussing matters of justice rather than expressing his or her private pain?[1]

> [A]rt figures as an aesthetic operation (a way of doing, as opposed to an object of philosophy) that takes as its subject matter the already aesthetic nature of everyday perception.[2]

> [A] philosophy of art is sterilized unless it makes us aware of the function of art in relation to other modes of experience, and unless it indicates why this function is so inadequately realized, and unless it suggests the conditions under which the office would be successfully performed.[3]

Fourteen sets of black headphones hang in a row. Suspended from a great height by long cables, their plastic spines cast haunting shadows on the dusty wooden floor below. The headphones gently twist out of line with the movement of people passing by, picking them up, putting them on. Inside each earpiece are the sounds of singing, orchestral music, sobbing, spoken testimonies, and the sighing of 'verbalised punctuation'.[4] At either end of the line of headphones there is a speaker which projects the distinct screech of a cassette tape rewinding and the sound of a woman's voice lamenting, 'I wish this news could just rewind.' These are the sounds of Philip Miller's operatic cantata, which is based on testimonies given during the public hearings of South Africa's TRC. Miller's compositions present an archive of re-imagined voices in an act of remembering.[5]

In front of the headphones, the glossy rectangles of seven flat-screen televisions float on a dark wall. Each of the screens shows a different stop-frame animation. Time slows down as photographic stills of houses, human shadows, and domestic objects appear and disappear – present and absent. Created by

1 Jacques Rancière, *The Politics of Aesthetics*, trans. Gabriel Rockhill (London: Continuum, 2006).
2 Jill Bennett, *Practical Aesthetics* (New York: IB Tauris, 2012), 3.
3 John Dewey, *Art as Experience* (New York: Penguin, 2005), 10.
4 Brenton Maart, *Imaginary Fact: Exhibition Catalogue* (Grahamstown: National Arts Festival 2013), 19.
5 Philip Miller, 'Artist Statement' in ibid., 74.

Figure 2.1 Gerhard Marx, Maja Marx, Philip Miller, *REwind* (2007-2013), audio-visual installation, monitors and headsets, dimensions variable. Installation view of *Imaginary Fact*, 2013
Venice Art Biennale, photography by Giovanna Zen. Courtesy of the artists and the National Arts Festival

Gerhard and Maja Marx in response to, and in conversation with, Miller's music, these images form the dual component in the collaborative audio-visual installation, *REwind* (Fig. 2.1), as it was exhibited in the South Africa Pavilion at the International Art Biennale (the Biennale) in Venice, Italy in 2013.[6] *REwind* embodies a literal and conceptual meeting point between transitional justice and visual art. The TRC unfolds through *Rewind*, and *REwind* is given form through the TRC.

The following close visual analysis and narrative investigation of *REwind* discursively elucidates four key ideas which make art exigent and meaningful

[6] Sections of *REwind* can be viewed on YouTube: Gerhard Marx, Maja Marx, and Philip Miller, 'REwind: Venice Monitor 2 Rewind HD/Scene for Wawela Awards 2015', 2007–2013, www.youtube.com/watch?v=XzdGruYiTyo; Gerhard Marx, Maja Marx, and Philip Miller, 'REwind: Venice Monitor 6 Mrs Plaatjies & Edward Juqu HD/Scene for Wawela Awards 2015', 2007–2013, www.youtube.com/watch?v=6gya0j3w0PY; Gerhard Marx, Maja Marx, and Philip Miller, 'REwind: Venice Monitor 7 Calata/Scene for Wawela Awards 2015', 2007–2013, www.youtube.com/watch?v= EcDBXvKZ6IA.

to transitional justice, and vice versa.[7] These ideas are about the circulation of political sentiment, the mediation of political agency, the invitation of political encounters, and the invention of political space. Memories and emotions – what I am grouping together as sentiment – circulate in *REwind,* generating an expectation that the 'process of reconciliation begins with the projection of a past worth remembering'.[8] Political agency is mediated through the re-telling of people's stories and through the re-imagining of their testimonies in artistic form. Politics revolves around what is seen and said and who has the ability to see it and say it. *REwind* performs a kind of transitional justice in the openings invited by aesthetic encounters. Through these encounters the artwork becomes an artistic intervention in South Africa's transitional justice narrative emerging in the wake of apartheid. The invented spaces of *REwind* shape South Africa's transitional justice narrative, presenting an image of the state seeking to continue to heal its internal wounds while offering itself as an archetype of political transition.

The theorisation of these ideas frame two central arguments. The first argument arises out of the general meeting of art and transitional justice: an account of transitional justice without aesthetic dimensions is insufficient, precisely because transitional justice 'acknowledge[s] itself as a process inseparable from *feelings* of justice'.[9] Artworks can fill out affective topologies in ways that facilitate or stimulate recognition and feelings of experience. Artworks can 'provoke us to travel into the others' world, thinking and feeling our way into their universe'.[10] This recognition is essential in order to comprehend and respond to the diverse claims of individuals and groups affected both directly and indirectly by conflict. The second argument emerges from the specific focus on *REwind*: that art plays an important role in animating and activating the narratives of individuals so that they take on collective importance. *REwind* shares individual stories of pain and suffering so that they can be affectively accessed and interpreted by viewers. In doing so, the past of one person becomes the present of many people so that together a new political future can be imagined. The importance of establishing a shared collective vision of the past has become 'a trope in the discourse of political transition'.[11]

[7] This chapter contains ideas explored earlier in Eliza Garnsey, 'Rewinding and Unwinding: Art and Justice in Times of Political Transition', *International Journal of Transitional Justice,* vol. 10, no. 3 (2016): 471–491.

[8] Carrol Clarkson, 'Drawing the Line: Justice and the Art of Reconciliation', in *Justice and Reconciliation in Post-Apartheid South Africa,* ed. Antje du Bois-Pedain and François du Bois (Cambridge: Cambridge University Press, 2008), 17.

[9] Eugene McNamee, 'Fields of Opportunity', in *The Arts of Transitional Justice,* ed. Peter D Rush and Olivera Simić (New York: Springer, 2014), 22. Emphasis in the original.

[10] Mihaela Mihai, 'From Hate to Political Solidarity: The Art of Responsibility', in *Hate, Politics, Law,* ed. Thomas Brudholm and Birgitte Schepelern Johansen (Oxford: Oxford University Press, 2016), 205.

[11] Ruti G Teitel, *Globalizing Transitional Justice* (Oxford: Oxford University Press, 2014), 14.

Circulation of Political Sentiment

> Miller's operatic compositions present an archive of re-imagined voices in an act of remembering. In front of the headphones, the glossy rectangles of seven flat screen televisions float on a dark wall. Each of the screens shows a different stop-frame animation. Time slows down as photographic stills of houses, haunting shadows, charred remnants of letter bombs, and domestic scenes, appear and disappear; present and absent.
>
> —Author's note

REwind navigates memory and emotions so that views of the past are circulated; creating a discursive impression of a past worth remembering. Memories circulate throughout *REwind.* The dominant voice in *REwind* – as it was exhibited at the Biennale – is that of Eunice Miya. Miya's voice is reimagined by a performer who speaks and sings the sighs, gasps, pauses, and words of her testimony to the TRC about hearing of the death of her son, Godfrey Jabulani Miya:

> The reason why I am here again is because . . . nobody had come to tell me that Jabulani had passed away. First of all, we were listening to the news, with my daughter. One of the children was shown on TV who had a gun on his chest. Only to find out that it was my son, Jabulani. I prayed. I said, 'Oh no, Lord!' I wished the news could just rewind.[12]

Jabulani Miya was killed in what later became known as the Gugulethu Seven incident, when on 3 March 1986 seven young anti-apartheid activists were shot by members of the South African Police Service.[13] For a long time, the circumstances surrounding their deaths were clouded in controversy, with official narratives contradicting eyewitness testimonies. In 1996, the TRC officer charged with investigating the incident wrote that 'it is our view that these young men were led into an ambush by the security forces after they had been infiltrated by askaris [police informants] . . . who participated in the training of these men and provided them with weapons'.[14] The final report of the TRC details the deaths of the seven men and the involvement of specific police officers:

> [S]hortly after 07h00, seven men aged between sixteen and twenty three were shot dead in Gugulethu. They were Mr Mandla Simon Mxinwa, Mr Zanisile Zenith Mjobo [CT00116/FLA], Mr Zola Alfred Swelani [CT00700/FLA], Mr Godfrey Jabulani Miya [CT00818/FLA], Mr Christopher Piet, Mr Themba

[12] Maart, *Imaginary Fact,* 74. The exact words of Eunice Miya's testimony used in *REwind* differ slightly from the official TRC record; see Eunice Miya, 'Testimony' (Truth and Reconciliation Commission, 1996).

[13] For an overview of the Gugulethu Seven incident, see Cole, *Performing South Africa's Truth Commission*, 18–25.

[14] Zenzile Khoisan, as quoted in Alejandro Castillejo-Cuéllar, 'Knowledge, Experience, and South Africa's Scenarios of Forgiveness', *Radical History Review,* vol. 97 (2007): 1.

> Mlifi [CT00100/FLA] and Mr Zabonke John Konile [CT00108/FLA]. All sustained numerous gunshot wounds to their bodies; all were shot in the head; one had half his face blown away. Police officers involved on the scene or in the investigation thereafter were Warrant Officers Barnard and McMaster, Majors Johan Kleyn, Dolf Odendal and Stephanus Brits, Captains Charles Brazzelle and Leonard Knipe, Sergeants John Sterrenberg, Grobbelaar and Rian Bellingan, and Constable Mbelo.[15]

This matter-of-fact style of reporting stands in contrast to the language Miya uses in her testimony to convey grief.

The official narrative of the TRC – one grounded in fact-finding and reportage – is complicated by a creative, and an emotive, narrative in *REwind*.[16] The sound recording in *REwind* draws out emotion through the repetitive lament of one phrase: 'I wish this news could just rewind', followed by the distinct sound of an analogue cassette tape rewinding, which permeates the sonic register of the exhibition. In doing so, it gives voice to memories: the individual memory of Eunice Miya recalling her grief when she found out her son had been killed; and a collective memory where an individual story 'takes the emotion of traumatic incident and expands it (at least psychologically) into a collective incident of infinite proportions'.[17] This incident became a discursive event in the struggle against apartheid, one later inscribed into the TRC's efforts to reveal the truths of the past which turned it into an 'emblem of reconciliation'.[18]

REwind is both a memorial to past trauma and a memorial to the TRC. It was created to commemorate the tenth anniversary of the TRC: 'Its timing, intention and execution was, in effect, an attempt at monumentalising the monument that was the TRC.'[19] This memorialising is also haunting. Miya's testimony pervades the viewing experience. The ghosts of apartheid are preserved through the re-imagining of her testimony in both musical and visual forms. One of the television screens shows the text of Miya's testimony projected onto a domestic scene: the outline of lace curtains and windowpanes, and the silhouette of an armchair, lamp, and pot plant frame the written words (Fig. 2.2). These words float across the screen, passing by the uncannily familiar objects. The film for Miya's testimony was created by projecting the words of her testimony onto curtains from the inside. 'The filming, in turn, was done from the outside, seeing the interior world projected onto the veiled

15 Truth and Reconciliation Commission, 'Truth and Reconciliation Commission of South Africa Report: Volume Two' (1998).

16 See Robyn Leslie, 'Truth Will Set You Free: Implications of a Creative Narrative for the "Official" Discourse of the South African Truth and Reconciliation Commission', in *Art and Trauma in Africa: Representations of Reconciliation in Music, Visual Arts, Literature and Film*, ed. Lizelle Bisschoff and Stefanie Van de Peer (London: IB Tauris, 2013), 170–191.

17 Maart, *Imaginary Fact*, 19.

18 Castillejo-Cuéllar, 'Knowledge, Experience, and South Africa's Scenarios of Forgiveness,' 2.

19 Maart, *Imaginary Fact*, 19.

Figure 2.2 Gerhard Marx, Maja Marx, Philip Miller, *REwind* (2007-2013), audio-visual installation, monitors and headsets, dimensions variable.
Image courtesy of the artists, Goodman Gallery and Whatiftheworld Gallery

window.'[20] Here the political past has seeped into the domestic and private domain. The ghosts of the past remain linked to the present through their visual connection with everyday domestic objects. In this way memory is condensed; it 'oscillates'[21] between a past remembered (Miya's testimony), a past re-imagined (the performing and filming of Miya's words), and a present re-created (the testimony screened and projected in the exhibition space).

[20] Marx and Marx in ibid., 75.

[21] Regarding time oscillating in artworks, see Vikki Bell, 'Contemporary Art and Transitional Justice in Northern Ireland: The Consolation of Form', *Journal of Visual Culture*, vol. 10, no. 3 (2011), 324–353.

In working with memories, questions concerning processes of selection become particularly important. Marx and Marx talk about their responsibility in translating and transcribing the visual spectacle of the TRC in order to merge one person's past reality with another's present reality.[22] Miller describes how, when listening to hours of TRC audio recordings, he questioned whether he was listening for his own absolution in place of his own confession for being implicated in the structures and everyday modes of apartheid.[23] Miller also sought written permission to re-imagine these testimonies.[24] The question of informed consent is especially pertinent. What are the implications of re-imagining such personal testimonies given during the public hearings of the TRC? How can these testimonies continue to be treated justly? What responsibility do the artists have to the people whose testimonies they reimagine? Are the artists' intentions crucial for the reception of the artwork?

There is an onus on the artists to work respectfully and productively with such personal stories. This is especially so when there is an expectation that the artwork will give back or return something to the people who testified, as in the case of Miya who believes *REwind* will play a didactic role: '*REwind* gives me hope for the future, for our grandchildren. They will be able to see what happened in the past. It would be great for our grandchildren to learn something from our history.'[25] The idea that the artwork might return something to survivors positions it as symbolic reparation which acknowledges the harm suffered under apartheid, and shares this recognition with others.[26] The artists take on ethical accountability for the creative reworking of the past; the process of creation is circumscribed by responsibility, as is the display and dissemination of the artwork. In this way artistic practice becomes an ethical relationship and way of participating in the world.[27]

Each musical and visual story in *REwind* communicates, and intervenes in, a conception of the past so that the ghosts remain and can be treated justly 'in order that they might inform, abstractly (normatively, ethically), the worlds we wish to create and inhabit'.[28] Each of the seven screens in the installation depicts a story which responds to the music played in the pairs of headphones. One screen shows a close-up shot of an envelope; the envelope appears to be

22 Marx and Marx in Maart, *Imaginary Fact*, 75.

23 Miller in ibid., 74.

24 Miller in ibid.

25 Eunice Miya as quoted in 'Giving Voice to the Past, Hope to the Future', *City Press*, 19 May 2008.

26 For a discussion of symbolic reparations in relation to the arts, see Olivera Simić and Zala Volcic, 'In the Land of Wartime Rape: Bosnia, Cinema and Reparation', *Griffith Journal of Law & Human Dignity*, vol. 2, no. 2 (2014): 377–401.

27 Bell, *Art of Post-Dictatorship*, 191.

28 Vikki Bell and Mario di Paolantonio, 'The Haunted Nomos: Activist-Artists and the (Im)possible Politics of Memory in Transitional Argentina', *Cultural Politics*, vol. 5, no. 2 (2009): 159.

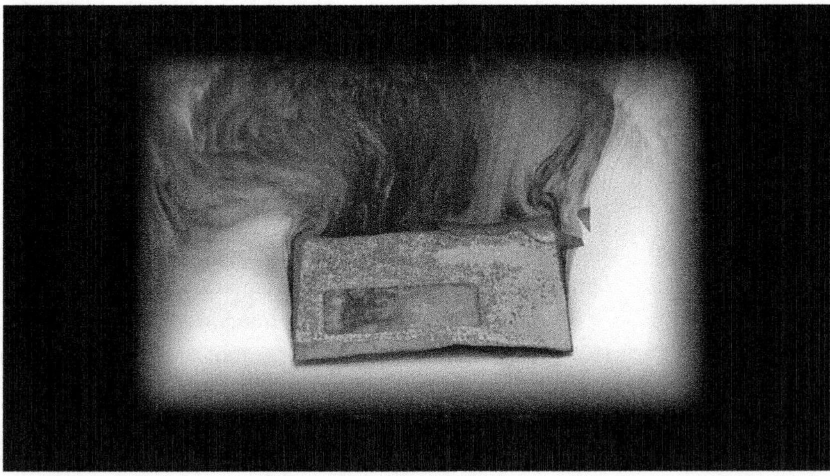

Figure 2.3 Gerhard Marx, Maja Marx, Philip Miller, *REwind* (2007–2013), audio-visual installation, monitors and headsets, dimensions variable.
Image courtesy of the artists, Goodman Gallery and Whatiftheworld Gallery

smoking (Fig. 2.3). What looks like black smoke slowly fills the screen, engulfing the envelope. The film is actually of an envelope which has been impregnated with black dye submerged in water; slowly the dye bleeds into the surrounding water. This film refers to the testimony of Father Michael Lapsley and is accompanied by a musical piece played through pairs of headphones. At the TRC Lapsley testified about the moment when he opened a letter bomb:

> So I came upon this envelope that had been among the accumulated mail. I opened it and it was addressed to me and inside were two religious magazines and they - the magazines were - were wrapped in plastic - sealed in plastic. So I ripped open the plastic and took out the magazines both religious - one in Afrikaans one in English. I put aside the Afrikaans one because my Afrikaans is not very good and I opened the English magazine and the act of opening the magazine was the detonating device for a bomb. I - one of the extraordinary things was that I, and the doctors don't know why, I didn't become unconscious - I didn't go into shock. The ceiling of three rooms blew out and there was a hole in the floor and I can still remember what happened - the actual explosion it still - it's still - it's still something with me.[29]

While the music makes specific reference to Lapsely's testimony, the film is more symbolic. Without knowing Lapsley's story, the visual imagery of a letter bomb brings out references to acts of terrorism which pervade many conflicts. Overarching lines of connection can be drawn between what is seen, what may be known, and what is remembered.[30]

[29] Michael Lapsley, 'Testimony' (Truth and Reconciliation Commission, 1996).
[30] Clarkson argues artworks have 'lines of force' in Clarkson, *Drawing the Line*.

By drawing on emotive sounds and symbols *REwind* engages the 'moral imagination'[31]: the gasps of crying, the screech of a tape rewinding, the silhouette of a chair, the image of an envelope. The artwork creates an affective topology which mediates how it is viewed and how the stories within it reverberate. It reconfigures individual and collective memory by representing multiple memories and encouraging multiple interpretations. This attention to viewers' subjectivity activates an affective register. Archives of familiar sounds and objects offer the potential for viewers to connect with a past worth remembering; a past remembered so that it is not repeated.[32]

The curatorial narrative of *Imaginary Fact* (discussed in Chapters 9 and 10) – like that of *REwind* – emphasised the importance of memory and emotion in coming to terms with the grievances of apartheid. Affects, feelings, and sense impressions flow between artworks. They are not necessarily anchored by a single artwork or object. In *Imaginary Fact*, *REwind* was exhibited alongside several artworks, each of which was intended to examine the use of archives in imagining contemporary South Africa.[33] Opposite *REwind* hung Sue Williamson's forty-nine photographic panels entitled *For Thirty Years Next to His Heart* (Fig. 2.4). Each panel showed two pages from John Ngesi's *dompas* (passbook) which, under the apartheid Pass Laws, black South Africans had to carry. To the left hung David Koloane's *The Journey* – a series of nineteen drawings reconstructing the events which lead to the death of the leader of the black consciousness movement and anti-apartheid activist, Steve Biko, in 1977. The way in which the artworks are hung in the exhibition creates conversations and generates associations. These are shaped and negotiated by the conversation between artworks and the audience which views them. Perspectives journey back and forth, in the eyes and minds of viewers, in the contact between artworks, and in the curatorial narrative of the artworks; this is the circulation of political sentiment.

Mediation of Political Agency

> At either end of the line of headphones there is a speaker which projects the distinct screech of a cassette tape rewinding and the sound of a woman's voice lamenting, 'I wish this news could just rewind'.
>
> —Author's note

People become visible through the re-telling of their stories and through the re-imagining of their testimonies in *REwind*. The emphasis on

31 The term 'moral imagination' comes from John Paul Lederach, *The Moral Imagination: The Art and Soul of Building Peace* (Oxford: Oxford University Press, 2004).

32 For a parallel discussion of how 'the TRC sought to reframe destructive trauma narratives and make new, shared meanings out of past injustice and pain', see Emma Hutchison, *Affective Communities in World Politics* (Cambridge: Cambridge University Press, 2016), 28.

33 Maart, *Imaginary Fact*.

Figure 2.4 Installation view of *Imaginary Fact*, 2013 Venice Art Biennale, photography by Giovanna Zen. Courtesy of the National Arts Festival. (Left) Sue Williamson, *For Thirty Years Next to His Heart* (1990), mixed media, 196 × 262 cm. (Back) David Koloane, *The Journey* (1998), acrylic and oil pastel on paper, each 29 × 42 cm. (Right) Gerhard Marx, Maja Marx, Philip Miller, *REwind* (2007–2013), audio-visual installation, monitors and headsets, dimensions variable.

people – individual stories, testimonies, and experiences – takes on heightened significance in the context of transitional justice. 'Politics revolves around what is seen and what can be said about it, around who has the ability to see and the talent [or space] to speak'.[34] Apartheid epitomised a struggle for rights, a struggle which is at its heart a struggle for equal recognition. *REwind* uses stories of individuals to impart a larger story about humanity, a sharing of personal stories to imagine new political possibilities, a kind of politics of becoming. New shared identities are formed out of past differences.

Although people familiar with modern South African history will invariably draw different connections with the artwork than people who are encountering the subject of apartheid and the TRC for the first time, the musical and visual utterances of *REwind* allow viewers to connect empathetically – to engage the unimaginable. That is, the artwork conveys a sense of shared humanity so that the post-apartheid present becomes accessible for different people with different experiences. *REwind* does this by emphasising people; each soundtrack, each film tells individual stories. Take, for example, one screen which shows a loaf of bread slowly crumbling, and a glass containing milk slowly disappearing (Fig. 2.5). The first image on this screen lists the origin of the testimony – *Interview with Ethel Nobantu Plaatjies, Mother of*

[34] Rancière, *The Politics of Aesthetics*, 13.

Figure 2.5 Gerhard Marx, Maja Marx, Philip Miller, *REwind* (2007–2013), audio-visual installation, monitors and headsets, dimensions variable.
Image courtesy of the artists, Goodman Gallery and Whatiftheworld Gallery

Luthando, Killed, 1986 [from the book] *A Human Being Died that Night* by Pumla G. Madikizela. When the film is viewed while listening to the music in the headphones, the words on the screen connect with the words being sung; the words appear in text in the same rhythmic scansion in which they are heard. The words of the woman singing are directed at the viewer. It is as if Ethel Nobantu Plaatjies is speaking to the viewer: 'At ten o'clock I was sitting, right there where you are sitting'.

The first-person narrative emphasises a personal connection. The performer sing-speaks Plaatjies's story:

> My son was eleven. He came home during school break. At ten o'clock I was sitting, right there were you are sitting. Sitting in that very chair. He walked in dressed in his school uniform. Went to the cupboard, over there. Cut himself a slice of bread. He's doing all this in a rush. He's like that when he comes home during break. He spreads the peanut butter. And then puts the rest of the bread back, leaving the crumbs all over the cupboard. And the knife still smudged with peanut butter. He ran out he's still chewing his bread and holding it in his hand. It wasn't long, I heard shots outside. Some commotion and shouts. Then I am hearing, 'Luthando!' 'Luthando!' 'Nanku Thando!' 'Bamdubele!' Then someone calling out for me, 'Ma Ka Luthando!' Ma Ka Luthando!' I went flying out of this house. Now I am dazed. I ran, not thinking. My eyes are on the crowd that has gathered. Here is my son, my only child. I felt his last breath leave him. Leaving the crumbs all over the cupboard.

As these words are sung, the milk slowly drains from the glass. The glass is empty by the time the words 'leaving the crumbs all over the cupboard' are heard. In the same way that the visuals mirror the words, the music emphasises the text. The film and music are punctuated by affective cues which enable the viewer-listener to access the story being told. As in the film of Miya's testimony, everyday objects, such as a loaf of bread and glass of milk, become markers of the story – familiar points of access. These objects bear witness to the testimony being recounted, but they also help to render these testimonies accessible and memorable.

The subjects of these testimonies are never directly represented, their presence becomes known through narration and through the ghostly embodiment of objects being moved and food being eaten. The body is withheld as a way to resist compounding the injustices suffered and survived. Re-imagining these testimonies raises ethical questions about representation: do 'those who give testimony in public formats before truth commissions fully realize what putting their words into circulation in the public domain means'?[35] Although the artists sought written consent to re-imagine people's testimonies in *REwind*, what does it mean for political agency when these testimonies are truncated, paraphrased, or selectively displayed? Do the performances of these testimonies give them a life beyond their owners? Further still, what does it mean for us as viewers to receive these testimonies in different forms?

Through these acts of artistic interpretation, the agency of people comes to be known. In *REwind* people are visible and become visible through the processes by which the artwork came to be created and exhibited, through the experience of the artwork and its mediated truth, and through the associations the artwork sends out into the world. Plaatjies's words are given voice by a female singer who recites the music composed by Miller; a chorus of singers and musicians share in the performance. This music is given visual form by Marx and Marx, who draw connections between words and objects in order to highlight Plaatjies's experience and make it accessible to viewers both familiar and unfamiliar with the experience of apartheid. The music and film combined share a story with the viewer. This story, and the viewers' experience, is curated by the team responsible for creating and hosting the exhibition; they have selected how the artwork will be displayed and what information – such as labels and accompanying explanatory text – will be imparted. Both named and unnamed people become visible, their effect on the artwork being recognisable in the stages of translation and experience.

While the chain of agency could be extended further to include everyone involved in the production of the artwork (from funding bodies to arts institutions) as well as everyone involved in the events the artwork is referencing (from atrocities committed under apartheid to the TRC), what remains key is the recognition of people and their agency in the processes and experience of

[35] Catherine M Cole, 'Reverberations of Testimony: South Africa's Truth and Reconciliation Commission in Art and Media', in *Transitional Justice, Culture, and Society: Beyond Outreach*, ed. Clara Ramírez-Barat (New York: Social Science Research Council, 2014), 425.

the artwork. *REwind* shows how people can generate political agency through the re-telling of their stories and through the re-imagining of their testimonies in artistic form. For instance, Plaatjies's testimony about the death of Luthando takes on heightened political resonance as it is performed and interpreted by multiple people. Performers re-embody, and viewers re-interpret, her testimony. Her personal narrative becomes connected with other people's personal experiences so that agency ripples between people. This is a political becoming which has the potential to shape new political possibilities and futures.

Invitation of Political Encounters

> The headphones gently twist out of line with the movement of people passing by; picking them up; putting them on. Inside each earpiece are the sounds of singing; orchestral music; sobbing; spoken testimonies; the sighing of 'verbalised punctuation'.[36]
>
> —Author's note

REwind performs its own kind of transitional justice in the openings generated by aesthetic encounters: 'Insight through aesthetic engagement comes through making (creating, producing) connections.'[37] The TRC is aesthetically reworked; its visual spectacle is evoked through the hanging line of headphones at the same time it is questioned through the way testimonies are selectively transposed and received. The artwork embodies a series of critical encounters. It is an encounter between audio and visuals; it is an encounter about sight and sound; it is an encounter with individual and shared stories; and it is an encounter between national and international narratives about the TRC and transitional justice.

Through these encounters the artwork intervenes in South Africa's transitional justice. As an audio-visual installation, *REwind* is sensorially rich. The artwork is an encounter between two artistic mediums under the auspices of a visual art installation. *REwind* requires viewers to engage with the sight of films streaming across the seven television screens, as well as the sound of the music playing from the individual headsets and two loudspeakers on either side of the screens. It is difficult to bypass the moving images on the screens and hard to resist picking up the headphones to hear what is playing inside. The repetitive screech of the analogue cassette tape from the loudspeakers dominates other peripheral sounds in the exhibition space. These audio and visual registers facilitate an experiential opening, allowing the possibility of engagement with the artwork and its content.

36 Phrase 'verbalised punctuation' comes from Maart, *Imaginary Fact*, 19.
37 Bennett, *Practical Aesthetics*, 74.

Just as the physical experience of the artwork is mediated by sight and sound, so too is the conceptual experience of *REwind*. Viewers are not only encouraged to engage physically with the artwork through seeing and hearing it, but they are also confronted by the idea that seeing, speaking, and listening are important actions in transitional justice processes.[38] In one film, excerpts from multiple testimonies – the 'Testimony of Tony Yengeni, political activist, tortured by Jeffrey Benzien 1987'; the 'Testimony of Lucas Baba Sikwapere, Tortured in Detention 1985–1987'; and, the 'Testimony of Mlandeli Walter Mqikela, tortured by police, Cape Town 1985' – draw attention to acts of seeing, speaking, and listening. Towards the beginning of the film, text begins to roll across the screen: 'Yes Mr Yengeni, when you say "demonstration", has he not described it satisfactorily to you?', 'I also want to see it with my own eyes what he did to me'. This testimony is heard spoken by two different male voices; one emphasises the act of describing, the other the act of seeing. As the words continue to roll across the screen, a woman's voice says, 'When I close my eyes, somebody that looked me straight in the eyes.' Another voice follows with 'Apartheid, I don't even want to see it anywhere I go.' A voice then follows saying, 'I feel what, what has brought my sight back, my eye sight back is to come back here and tell this story. But I feel what has been making me sick all the time is the fact that I couldn't tell my story.' Eyes and seeing are recurring motifs throughout these testimonies.

The emphasis on sight unexpectedly occurs through written and spoken words rather than through imagery. The linguistic elements of the testimonial excerpts are privileged over the representation of the people whose words and stories they narrate.[39] Text journeys across the screens as it does on the sound waves. Language both mediates the visual experience and is the visual experience. There seems to be a lurking anxiety about the direct representation of the person speaking. Instead, text and objects become proxies for people; the body is withheld but remains implicated in the visual access points of the first-person narratives. Even the passport-style photographs (Fig. 2.6) which fade in and out of one of the screens are inverted so that images of people are transformed into the shadows of ghosts. This has the effect of stripping down the individuality of the images, dulling personal characteristics, instead emphasising similarities in the shapes and silhouettes; the face of one becomes the face of many. The individual voice becomes implicated in a collective vision.

[38] Theories of sensory democracy offer similar ideas; see, for example, Andrew Dobson, *Listening for Democracy: Recognition, Representation, Reconciliation* (Oxford: Oxford University Press, 2014); Jeffrey Edward Green, *The Eyes of the People: Democracy in an Age of Spectatorship* (Oxford: Oxford University Press, 2010).

[39] This idea of linguistic privileging comes from Mark Reinhardt, 'Picturing Violence: Aesthetics and the Anxiety of Critique', in *Beautiful Suffering: Photography and the Traffic in Pain*, ed. Mark Reinhardt, Holly Edwards, and Erina Duganne (Chicago: University of Chicago Press, 2007), 24.

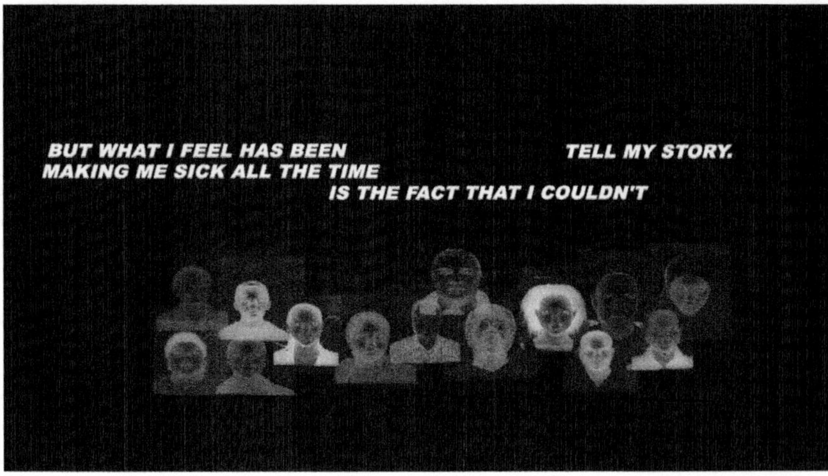

Figure 2.6 Gerhard Marx, Maja Marx, Philip Miller, *REwind* (2007–2013), audio-visual installation, monitors and headsets, dimensions variable.
Image courtesy of the artists, Goodman Gallery and Whatiftheworld Gallery

Towards the end of the film the emphasis shifts from seeing to speaking and listening. A voice repeats, 'Yes I am ready to tell you. I'd like to tell you what happened.' A chorus of voices can be heard layered over one another, speaking in different languages. The choir begins to sing as stringed instruments play music that pulses. A voice says, 'Listen to your stories and make the whole world to know about your stories.' Another voice can be heard saying, 'But we are doing this because we believe that if, if people repeat again all their hurt that they had, as they repeat the stories again, as they repeat the stories again, as they repeat the stories again.' The same text rolls across the screen. It is as if the words on the screen are read in real time by the people whose voices can be heard in the headphones. The film ends with the image of a snow-plagued television screen – an image which has punctuated the film throughout – switching off; the light goes out. The stories have been told.

The excerpts of testimony emphasise sight and sound as restorative actions in the aftermath of apartheid trauma. The journey from sight to sound is made on the screen and in the music – seeing leads to speaking and speaking leads to listening. Each of the three testimonies pertains to acts of torture committed by the apartheid state. Each of the three testimonies talks about seeing in the process of coming to terms with these acts. Each of the three testimonies relays the importance of repeating their stories, speaking their former silences. Testimonial experiences and records are connected in *REwind* to produce a reading of transitional justice based on shared cathartic communication, a direct echo of the TRC.

However, by bringing together these excerpts into the one visible and audible space, the artists provoke a questioning; they use fragments to generate a deliberately open reading of events, experiences, and memories. Ambiguities, anxieties, and uncertainties emerge through the process of creative interrogation. This highlights an inherent paradox within *REwind.* At the same time fragments of testimony are brought together to create a larger narrative – a narrative made up of individual stories which come to stand in for a larger whole – they are pulled apart into their constituent elements. In other words, the claims to individuality which are emphasised by the careful labelling of testimonial origins at the beginning of the films sits in tension with the larger cosmopolitan narrative about shared humanity being offered up by the artwork.

The openings created by the encounters in *REwind* are potentially transformative, facilitating the emergence of different and subjective interpretations in South Africa's transitional justice narrative: '[I]ndividuals and collectives … participate in a culture of feelings or sensibilities and subsequently engage in discursive encounters about what is just.'[40] One encounter leads to another. The encounter between artistic mediums highlights the substantive encounter between seeing and speaking present within the excerpts of testimonies. In turn, the testimonial encounters underscore the meeting and tension between individual and collective stories. What emerges is that these encounters are not simply representative of political change; they also help to construct the political transition and shifting identity of South Africa.

Invention of Political Space

> Fourteen sets of black headphones hang in a row. Suspended from a great height by long cables, their plastic spines cast haunting shadows on the dusty wooden floor below … The South African Truth and Reconciliation Commission unfolds through REwind and REwind is given form through the TRC.
>
> —Author's note

REwind invites and invents physical, symbolic, and affective spaces which shape and reflect how South Africa's transitional justice narrative is performed. It does this through its intrinsic connection to spatial practices of display. *REwind* inhabits the physical space of an art exhibition while evoking the quasi-legal space of the TRC hearings. The invented space of *REwind* is physically and symbolically connected to the transitional justice mechanism it is exploring. The sights, sounds, and symbols of the TRC are referenced in the artwork. The distinct shape of the headphones, the television screens, and the overlapping sounds of language translations transpose the hearing rooms and public screenings of the TRC into the exhibition space. Voices impart sung and spoken testimonies at the same time as the words appear written on the screens. The audience bear witness to these testimonies – testimonies which

[40] Shapiro, *Studies in Trans-Disciplinary Method,* 100.

have travelled from personal depths to public acknowledgement. By creating a physical space in which the symbolic space of the TRC is evoked, it is as if the artwork becomes an extension of the original TRC process.

REwind functions as an alternative archive, 'one based on the "missing" aspects where an inflection is as much a form of communication as an accusation, or a repentance'.[41] Partial testimonies are repeatedly re-performed throughout the artwork so that the idea of justice being achieved through testimonial representation is called into question. In doing so the artwork raises questions about legitimacy. Did the TRC process provide a legitimate process for justice to be served? Is it legitimate for the artists to re-frame the testimonies of others? Does the physical and symbolic connection to the TRC confer a sense of legitimacy onto the artwork? Marx, Marx, and Miller become key interlocutors between the TRC and viewers – taking on the responsibility for doing justice to the deeply personal material with which they are working.

REwind negotiates the in-between spaces – the imaginative and affective spaces – in order to convey different feelings of justice. The artwork invites emotive responses from viewers: on the screens 'mundane household objects become emotional anchors in the emotional turmoil of the [testimonial] moment'.[42] While in the music the gasps, sighs, wails, and pauses punctuate the testimonial sound. Through these emotive connections *REwind* presents a view of the past that is indebted to the present. That is, the past becomes imaginable, knowable through the present experience of the artwork; an experience that is affectively rich. The films are intended to explore these in-between spaces: 'the space between the text (testimony) and the context (the space in which the testimony is received) [i]s a means of negotiating the space between confessor and listener, and the political past and the contemporary (the private present of a post-democratic South Africa).'[43] *REwind* invites these in-between spaces which go beyond the physical and symbolic, into affective and subjective spaces. In doing this, *REwind* opens up a space in which the political possibilities of post-apartheid South Africa can be explored – in which alternative narratives can be imagined and new identities tried out.

The invented physical and symbolic space of *REwind*, coupled with the invited imaginative and affective space of the artwork, performs its own kind of transitional justice in which modalities reconstitute a shared vision of the past. At the same time that focus is given to individual stories and individual testimonies, attention is shifted to the commonalities and similarities between these stories, creating a sense of connection and attempt at a balance of representation. The repetition of like images encourages these connections; reflection on what is seen and unseen, heard and unheard; what is similar,

41 Maart, *Imaginary Fact*, 19.
42 Marx and Marx in ibid., 75.
43 Marx and Marx in ibid.

what is different; what is remembered and what is forgotten; what is present, what is absent. The stop-frame animations shown on the seven screens slow down time, forcing the viewer to see details which might normally flash by unnoticed. A chair disintegrates; a loaf of bread crumbles; black ink bleeds into water. On one screen the facades of different houses pulse past. The front doors and windows of these houses show striking similarities. The architectural features begin to blur together so that the lives of the people imagined to be living in these houses take on a collective appearance. Again the tension between individual and collective is activated.

Each time *REwind* is performed or exhibited, its content is re-presented, re-interpreted, and re-inscribed. Each incarnation of the artwork brings with it different expectations and possibilities unique to particular artistic mediums, but more importantly each incarnation re-inscribes the personal stories and collective transitional justice narrative of South Africa – one that imposes a kind of forgetting of certain stories as much as it does a remembering of others. At the 2013 Venice Biennale *REwind* was exhibited as an audio-visual installation, showing images on television screens and playing recorded music through speakers and headphones. In this installation the images and sounds played over one another. Viewers could enter in and out of the artwork, switching between headphones which played different parts of the cantata; glancing at the screens which showed moving images relating to different parts of the music. The installation was interactive. The audience participation was selective.

In other incarnations in South Africa the work has been performed live with vocal soloists, chorus, musical instruments, and images being projected onto the stage. In these iterations the work follows a narrative progression and is ephemeral.[44] The music is performed sequentially. The images are projected at specific moments. The audience absorbs the work in linear concert format. In yet further iterations the work can be found in digital form; excerpts are hosted by the artists on YouTube, and the entire cantata (without the films) can be purchased on iTunes. The specific spatial locations in which *REwind* is installed, exhibited, performed, and witnessed are of central importance to the way in which the work re-inscribes a vision of transitional justice in South Africa.

As it travels between different sites, *REwind* is responsive to, and constitutive of, a vision of transitional justice in South Africa. The TRC inhabits a unique *glocal* (global-local) narrative.[45] The TRC is inherently connected to

[44] Earlier live performances of *REwind* are discussed in Cole, *Performing South Africa's Truth Commission*, 135–154.

[45] The term 'glocal' is used to refer to something that reflects and intertwines both local and global considerations. In IR, the term tends to be used to refer to phenomena that are sub-state (local) and supra-state (global): the state remains the key analytical unit. See, for example, Neil Brenner, 'Global Cities, Glocal States: Global City Formation and State Territorial Restructuring in Contemporary Europe', *Review of International Political Economy*, vol. 5, no. 1 (1998): 1–37;

the South African context, inwardly focused on reconciling the deep cleavages of exclusion and trauma generated by apartheid. The TRC is also internationally upheld as a model for how to perform transitional justice, whereby its truth-seeking framework is transplanted into other contexts.[46] *REwind* exemplifies this glocal positioning. *REwind* is inward-looking, addressing individual cases of suffering experienced by South African citizens. At the same time *REwind* is outwardly focused, projecting a collective narrative of a nation addressing its past – an important focus in the context of the Biennale.

The spatial organisation of the Biennale (discussed in Chapter 8) raises questions about the political organisation and priorities of the states which exhibit in this global exposition. At the Biennale, *REwind* encountered a space in which national narratives are embedded into international relations. *REwind's* inward focus on the specific experience of the TRC in addressing the legacy of apartheid was projected outward becoming an emblem of the state's liberalising transition. In other words, the deeply personal narratives within *REwind* became a collective narrative of the state coming to terms with its past. The artwork lent itself to being an unusual case of cultural diplomacy, an emerging spatial frontier in transitional justice (explored in Chapter 10).

REwind expands the range of '"what can be seen, what can be said, what can be thought", and . . . what can be done' in times of political transition.[47] The discursive exploration of *REwind* exposes a web of – at times competing – relationships which constitute the bond between art and transitional justice. The four ideas about sentiment, agency, encounters, and space offered in this chapter frame the meeting of transitional justice and art as being rooted in a spectrum of complexities and possibilities.

Examining *REwind* offers aesthetic insight that is both central to understanding South Africa's transition and constitutive of that transition. The artwork functions to produce and maintain the state's transitional justice narrative, but it also opens up spaces for new political thinking, possibilities, and actions in this narrative. Memory and emotion reverberate in *REwind*. The ways in which they inhabit the artwork, and oscillate within it, generate a vision which colours the past and exposes the complexity of the present. There is an expectation that transitional justice begins with this vision of the past. *REwind* uses individual stories to impart a larger story about humanity. The artwork generates a productive tension between individual and collective agencies so that new shared identities are formed out of past differences. The openings invited by these encounters produce connections that are

Taedong Lee, *Global Cities and Climate Change: The Translocal Relations of Environmental Governance* (New York: Routledge, 2014).

46 See Hayner, *Unspeakable Truths*, 124; Marcos Zunino, *Justice Framed: A Genealogy of Transitional Justice* (Cambridge: Cambridge University Press, 2019), 117.

47 Jacques Rancière, *The Emancipated Spectator* (London: Verso, 2009), 103, as quoted in Frank Möller, *Visual Peace: Images, Spectatorship and the Politics of Violence* (Hampshire: Palgrave Macmillan, 2013), 20.

potentially transformative, facilitating the emergence of different and subjective interpretations in South Africa's transitional justice narrative and confronting viewers with ideas about important actions – such as seeing, speaking, listening – in the aftermath of conflict. The narratives that emerge from *REwind* are shaped by spatial practices of display – practices unique to artistic mediums and curated exhibitions. The invented physical, symbolic, and affective spaces of *REwind* shape how South Africa's transitional justice narrative takes on domestic and international significance.

In coming to terms with past conflict and strengthening democratic institutions in the aftermath of state-sanctioned violence, art plays an important role in communicating and creating affective topologies of justice in order to recognise diverse and often competing claims for recognition. This recognition is essential in order to comprehend, and respond to, the claims of people *affected* – both individually and collectively, directly and indirectly – by conflict, particularly when conflict has been centred on struggles for equal rights and acknowledgement as in the context of South Africa. *REwind* exemplifies how narratives of individuals can be activated to take on collective significance, so that shared visions of the past open up possibilities to imagine a new political future. While transitional justice policies and practices have become fundamental to the ways in which states emerging from conflict engage with international institutions and international norm compliance, artistic production has become a radical form of political participation in times of political transition.

Afterword on 'Power', Ethics, and Modes of Display

The creative process is 'enmeshed in both that which it wishes to interrogate and that which it renders possible'.[48] The discussion of *REwind* is embedded in the context of post-apartheid artists working with the TRC as both an archive of material and a process to be explored, where truth can be problematised and gaps filled or exposed. This chapter has largely and intentionally focused on a view of artworks as objects which have the potential to offer, to shape, and to intervene in sentiment, agency, encounters, and space. However, art is not intrinsically emancipatory, nor do I naively believe only in its progressive potential.

Art can equally disrupt conflict resolution, complicating and upsetting narratives of transition. '[A]rt is part of the social world and it is not immune to power constellations.'[49] Art can be co-opted and instrumentalised by various parties – propaganda art has a long history in both liberal and

[48] Leslie, 'Truth Will Set You Free', 172.
[49] Mihai, 'From Hate to Political Solidarity', 212.

oppressive societies.[50] Art can be used and abused, especially in transitional contexts where norms and practices are in flux.[51] These opposing powers of art are always present and need to be kept in mind. What I am concerned with throughout the book are artworks which have emerged in post-apartheid South Africa that are commenting on, and contributing to, transitional justice in some way. The value of these artworks depends on their context and their content, as well as how they are used by various institutions.

In translating material from the TRC into *REwind*, the artists face ethical questions about what it means to work with such personal and traumatic stories.[52] What does it mean for the scope and nature of political agency that the artists selected certain testimonies and not others? What does it mean for the mediation of the personal and public to reinterpret and perform other people's stories? What does informed consent really mean in the context of the artists seeking it from the people whose testimonies they recreated? What does it mean in a post-apartheid context that these three particular artists created this work? Furthermore, what does it mean for me as an author, with my own national and privileged institutional embeddedness, to make a further selection about which artwork I choose to discuss and which stories I choose to highlight? The processes of selection, re-imagination, re-interpretation, and analysis of traumatic events provoke ethical encounters which must be acknowledged and continually reflected upon if representative violence and silencing is not to be re-inscribed. These concerns underpin the book and are returned to throughout it, in an effort to acknowledge the ethical complexities of whose art is in the spotlight, whose story is being told and by whom, and whose justice it is.

Two dominant modes of display emerge from *REwind*: that of figurative and didactic display. Many of the artworks discussed throughout the book also engage these modes of display, suggesting some shared approaches – not to be mistaken for criteria for creation – in how visual art in post-apartheid South Africa addresses issues of justice. *REwind* embodies a figurative style of art. By figurative I mean that it retains strong references to human form and recognisable objects. Photographic images of houses, chairs, envelopes, televisions permeate the artwork. While there are moments of abstraction in *REwind*, these still remain connected to 'real world' objects. For instance, when one film fades into a blurry screen of black and white pixels, the image remains firmly rooted in the malfunctioning television set it is referencing. The figurative style of *REwind* facilitates visual entry points into the artwork which link the ghosts of the past with the present. Everyday objects come to represent people's

50 For example, see Toby Clark, *Art and Propaganda in the Twentieth Century: The Political Image in the Age of Mass Culture* (New York: Harry N. Abrams, 1997).

51 Bahun, 'Transitional Justice and the Arts', 159.

52 Idea also raised by Cole, 'Reverberations of Testimony', 407. Also see Cole's discussion of the public reactions to Miller's use of testimony in the early stages of the cantata's development in Cole, *Performing South Africa's Truth Commission*, 135–154.

stories – objects stand in for people – becoming entwined with deeply personal testimonies.

Despite this emphasis on people, *REwind* avoids displaying the human body in overtly figurative form. In one film, passport-style photographs of people are inverted so the images become shadows; identifying characteristics are removed so the images are no longer of somebody, but could be of anybody. By resisting overtly figurative displays of the human body or direct representations of the people whose testimonies are being performed, *REwind* avoids compounding representational injustice which might otherwise occur through the display of the body of the testimonial subject as art object. That is, the refusal to display the body is a way to avoid compounding oppression.[53]

Many of the artworks discussed throughout the book also reference the real world and resist displaying the body. Figurative artworks feature heavily in the art collection of the Constitutional Court. Judith Mason's *The Man Who Sang and the Woman Who Kept Silent* (Chapter 5) displays the image of a dress in place of the body of Phila Ndwandwe, whose story the artwork is commemorating. Arguably when an artist's own oppression is the subject of the artwork, bodily representation can be achieved. Zanele Muholi's *Faces and Phases* (Chapter 9) deliberately uses photographic portraits to restore black queer visibility in South Africa. Among these photographs is Muholi's self-portrait. Rather than resist the display of the body, *Faces and Phases* intentionally displays the body to achieve its aims of acknowledgement and visibility.

The way in which the human body is displayed or is implied through reference to recognisable objects underscores the central importance of people. It is a reminder that the injustices under consideration actually happened to people. The focus on and reference to individual people in these artworks is always situated within the context of larger communities, such as the victims and survivors of apartheid. This means that individuation is connected to humanness, or a wider shared humanity; a connection which implicates viewers in the subject of the artworks. Figurative displays become a way for people to recognise their relationship to injustice. However, at the same time this focus on people arguably shifts attention away from structural dynamics and institutional forces, meaning that the larger causes of injustice may remain under-acknowledged.

REwind also explicitly references particular events of apartheid and specific people involved. By doing so, it memorialises these events, but also shares information about the history of apartheid and the TRC process. Eunice Miya (whose testimony is re-imagined in *REwind*) suggests the artwork is educational: '[O]ur grandchildren … will be able to see what happened in the past.'[54] By recounting testimonies almost word for word, *REwind* becomes a kind of visual textbook which seeks to impart an understanding about the consequence of such trauma and to warn against its repetition.

[53] Reinhardt, 'Beautiful Suffering', 20.

[54] Eunice Miya quoted in 'Giving Voice to the Past'.

This didactic display occurs in many of the artworks explored in the book. Sue Williamson's *A Few South Africans* (Chapter 5) records the images and names of women involved in anti-apartheid struggles in order to make a lesser-known history more widely known. The overarching instruction in several of the artworks in the book is about the non-repetition of apartheid, warning against conflict. David Goldblatt's *Twenty-Six Punishment Cells and Lavatory. Number Four, Hillbrow, Johannesburg. 31 December 1999* (Chapter 5) functions as a reminder of an abusive penal system; hanging in the judges' private corridor at the Court, it is a caution against a return to this system. David Koloane's *The Journey* (Chapter 9), which chronicles the death of Steve Biko, is intended to convey what happens when governments fail to protect people under their care, warning against a repeat of this failure.

Didactic art is often denigrated in art history for being overly moralising, aesthetically unsophisticated, and for limiting interpretation; it is a term indicating a deficiency of some kind.[55] However, in the context of transitional justice, art which displays didactic properties – being educational and informative – emerges as essential. Rather than being instructive to the point of closing down interpretation about the past, *REwind* and the artworks discussed in the book seem to do the opposite: they open up discussion about the apartheid past so that the present and future may unfold along more just, ethically informed lines. They are suggestive but do not necessarily force an arrival or conclusion. Few artists I interviewed raised didacticism as a negative aspect of a post-apartheid aesthetic. Rather, they saw it as a responsibility and a way to participate in social and political debates: 'I had to come up with creative ways to let people know what I think of democracy and how we can achieve [it].'[56] Didactic displays become a fundamental way of working with the past to show – and shape – a different future, especially in the context of the institutions discussed in this book.

This mode of display draws attention to an important tension in post-apartheid South Africa between how didacticism is used by artists as a form of political participation and how didacticism is used by state-sponsored institutions to negotiate democracy-building. On the one hand, the didactic displays stem from the artists' desire to contribute to democracy and to communicate ideas about democracy. Communicating these ideas through art also opens up opportunities for others to participate in democracy. On the other hand, this mode of display becomes intertwined with how state-sponsored institutions emerging in South Africa's transition shape a democratic identity and narrative. These connections between didactic display and democracy are significant, since they contrast with how didactic art is often denigrated for limiting interpretation – essentially for being non-democratic.

[55] Berys Nigel Gaut, 'Art, Emotion and Ethics', 104.

[56] Artist 5. Artist 19 also raised the point that moving beyond politically focused didactic art was an important freedom in post-apartheid artistic practice.

Part I

Recognising Transitional Justice in the Nation State

The Constitutional Court of South Africa

3

From Prison to Court

> Constitutional courts are the sober conscience of the body politic. They remind us, whenever it is most inconvenient, of the high-minded ideals that we have overlooked.[1]

> The Constitutional Court embodies the history of our future . . . the architectural setting of the Constitutional Court building itself, within the very site of so much misery and suffering, is a strong artistic symbol of the establishing of a viable alternative to the appalling reality of the apartheid era.[2]

> It is a court for people made by people about people judged by people.[3]

> Our rights today acquire a particular value through explorations and physical memorials to the past.[4]

The Constitutional Court of South Africa is a unique space in terms of how it interfaces and integrates with people from its urban surroundings. During one of my first visits to the Court it had been transformed into a film set. Outside the Court's main entrance – the area known as the forecourt or Constitution Square, inhabited by Willem Boshoff's granite anthropomorphic shadows and overlooked by the rainbow façade that displays the name of the Court written in South Africa's eleven official languages – there was a crew with cameras and filming equipment, and in the centre of it all were two actors performing what appeared to be a 'meet cute'.[5] On other days, members of the Awethu Project, an entrepreneurial investment start-up with Google-style offices in the neighbouring former Women's Jail, use the area as a soccer field. Almost every day, the forecourt and its adjoining lane – the entrance point for the hourly red tourist bus and the occasional motorcades of visiting dignitaries, all of which

[1] Constitutional Court of South Africa, *The Constitutional Court of South Africa: The First Ten Years* (Pretoria: Constitutional Court of South Africa, 2004), 69.

[2] Artist 26.

[3] Art committee member 4.

[4] Lauren Segal, Clive Van den Berg, and Churchill Madikida, *Mapping Memory: Former Prisoners Tell Their Stories* (Johannesburg: David Krut, 2006), 4.

[5] A meet cute is a scene in films where two people who are destined to fall in love meet for the first time. The filming at the Court was for *Tell Me Sweet Something*, released in 2015, directed by Akin Omotoso.

are visible from inside the Court's chamber – is a thoroughfare for commuters, particularly children in school uniforms who play in this colourful, sculpture-filled, largely pedestrian zone. On some nights, long after legal proceedings have finished, the Court's concrete verandah, separating the suburb of Hillbrow from the Court's offices, becomes a rehearsal venue for a barbershop group, who stand in the dark, singing into the empty road, their voices echoing down the hill.

This unusual setting for a court precinct is circumscribed by the distinct urban spaces of inner-city Johannesburg – a city described as the 'Venice of the South',[6] an ironic label considering its scarcity of water and parched yellow mine dumps visible on the horizon. On one side of Constitution Hill – the area that houses the Constitutional Court – is Braamfontein, a suburb transforming rapidly through urban renewal where art galleries and design centres sit alongside council offices and nightclubs, adjoining retail stores, coffee shops, and brightly coloured student accommodation. Weekend food markets attract northern-suburb dwellers from gated communities into the city, and organic eateries provide meeting places for academics and political figures alike. Bordered by the University of Witwatersrand, which still maintains its spiky security fences and guarded entry points, Braamfontein retains some signs of its previous apartheid-era incarnation as a commercial and industrial area, the deteriorating remains of which are striking in contrast to the glossy gentrification and the University's crisp modernist white cube art museum with walls of glass which paradoxically allow people to peer in yet still keep them firmly out.

On the other side of Constitution Hill is Hillbrow, a densely populated, abjectly poor, residential suburb filled with gutted but inhabited apartment buildings which are dwarfed under the shadows of the Vodacom tower on one side and the fifty-four-storey Ponte tower on the other. The latter was once described as a 'vertical urban slum',[7] now more an urban panopticon. These landmarks function to both map the path to Hillbrow for the more than 74,000 people who live within its small one-square-kilometre footprint and to steer away others who are too afraid to enter on account of the suburb's enduring violent reputation.[8] Hillbrow is a springboard to the rest of the city with a thriving community of businesses, homes, schools, churches, and a hospital, all within its tight borders, yet it lacks fundamental services, infrastructure, security, and basic housing.

[6] Ivan Vladislavic, *Portrait with Keys: The City of Johannesburg Unlocked* (London: W.W. Norton and Co., 2009), 90.

[7] Carrol Clarkson, 'Photo Essay: Welcome to Our Hillbrow', *Safundi: The Journal of South African and American Studies,* vol. 10, no. 2 (2009): 216.

[8] The 2011 Census listed the population of Hillbrow as 74,130 over one square kilometre. However, this figure is arguably conservative given the high proportion of undocumented immigration in the area. The same census listed the population of Braamfontein as 43,167, over approximately five square kilometres. From South African Government, 'Census 2011 Listing Database', 2011, www.census2011.co.za.

The trees and grassy ramparts of Constitution Hill begin atop a hill (as its name implies) and slope downwards, north towards the parks, wealthier suburbs called Parktown and Parkview. The parks are a green separation from the largely concrete flanking suburbs, reflecting the apartheid-era division of 'quintessentially black and white spaces'.[9]

Constitution Hill is rooted in the centre of this contrasting urban geography and connects, but it also separates the people-thronged landscapes which, like much of Johannesburg and the rest of South Africa, map out extreme economic and social divisions within close proximity of each other.[10] The Hill is similarly circumscribed by distinct spatial differences: once populated by penal institutions which comprised the Johannesburg Fort, the area is now home to the Constitutional Court, along with several other institutions which play a role in safeguarding constitutional freedoms, including the Commission on Gender Equality and the South African History Archive, both with offices in the former Women's Jail. As a consequence, the Hill has been transformed. It is no longer known as a place that violates human rights, but one now known to hold the responsibility of protecting them.

Custody of the Past

The Hill's shift is most evident through the physical and symbolic transformations of the former infamous penal institutions. These have been reformed into a museum – which historicises the site – as well as accommodating governmental and commercial spaces, including the Constitutional Court (Fig. 3.1). The following overview of the prisons introduces these ongoing transformations in order to contextualise the unique development of the Court on this site.

The oldest prison on Constitution Hill is the Old Fort dating from 1893. Built by the *Zuid-Afrinkaansch Republiek* as a high-security jail 'intended to intimidate and keep control of the *uitlanders* (foreigners)', it was used during the Anglo–Boer war first as a military fort and, when the British took occupation of Johannesburg, as a prison to house Boer soldiers.[11] During apartheid the Old Fort was used to house white male prisoners. Today the colonial buildings house offices, venue spaces for hire, and a gastro-pub.

[9] Federico Freschi, 'Postapartheid Publics and the Politics of Ornament: Nationalism, Identity, and the Rhetoric of Community in the Decorative Program of the New Constitutional Court, Johannesburg', *Africa Today*, vol. 54, no. 2 (2007): 37.

[10] See also Zarina Patel and Clinton David van der Merwe, 'Constitution Hill: Just Space or Space for Justice?', in *Architecture and Justice: Judicial Meanings in the Public Realm*, ed. Jonathan Simon (London: Routledge, 2016), 124.

[11] Lauren Segal, *Number Four: The Making of Constitution Hill* (Johannesburg: Penguin, 2006), 11.

Figure 3.1 View of the Constitutional Court of South Africa. The rainbow façade of the Court is behind the trees in the centre. In the left foreground is the former Number Four prison, and in the right foreground is one of the remaining staircases of the Awaiting Trial Block.
Photography by Akona Kenqu, 2014

In 1902, Section Four and Section Five, the isolation cells, collectively known as Number Four, were built to house 'native' male prisoners.[12] Throughout the twentieth century, Number Four housed political prisoners – Mandela was imprisoned there three times (1956, 1958, and 1962) – prisoners who were sentenced for violent crimes, and in the vast majority of cases people criminalised by the repressive colonial and apartheid race laws, such as pass offenders, curfew breakers, and beer-brewers.[13]

Prisoners in these parts of the fort were subjected to brutal and degrading conditions, such as severe overcrowding, food allocated according to apartheid race classifications, and *tausa*, a routine that prisoners were made to perform in front of other inmates to prove they were not concealing anything on their body:

> A naked person leapt in the air, spinning round and opening his legs wide while clapping his hands overhead and then, in the same moment, coming down,

[12] Jonathan Alfred Noble, *African Identity in Post-Apartheid Public Architecture: White Skin, Black Masks* (Farnham: Ashgate, 2011), 115.

[13] Audrey Brown in Segal, *Number Four*, 123.

> making clicking sounds with the mouth and bending his body right forward so as to expose an open rectum to the warder's inspection.[14]

Sections Four and Five (about 20 metres from the Court) are now preserved as a museum.[15] Decades of graffiti remain etched into the walls of the dark isolation cells, rusted barbed wire still hangs overhead, and the dank communal cells are inhabited by displays created by former prisoners.

The Women's Jail, where white and black women, along with their infant children, were segregated, was built around 1910. Like Number Four, the Women's Jail housed political prisoners – including Winnie Mandela on several occasions – people convicted for petty or violent crimes, but again, the majority of prisoners were incarcerated for breaching apartheid race laws. The Women's Jail now houses exhibitions about the prison, including memory installations in which former inmates recount their experiences. It also houses offices and venue spaces for hire. The central atrium, where prisoners describe being hit and kicked for walking through without permission, is now offered for events.[16]

The Awaiting Trial Block was built in 1928 and is particularly significant for two reasons. First, the building helped foster political assembly, the antithesis of its intended use. Many of the black male political prisoners were kept there, including the Rivonia trialists in the 1950s. Political prisoners awaiting trial were held together but separated from the rest of the prison population. This collective separation enabled them to assemble in ways which were prevented on the outside due to political suppression.[17]

Second, the majority of the Awaiting Trial Block was demolished – somewhat controversially – to make way for the Constitutional Court. Unlike the three other prisons (the Old Fort, Sections Four and Five, and the Women's Jail) which were preserved in a largely structurally complete form, only three stairwells remain of the Awaiting Trial Block. One of the stairwells is incorporated into the Court, serving 'as a dramatic reminder of the way in which our courts and criminal justice system were implicated in the daily administration of, and struggle against, apartheid' (see Fig. 5.10).[18] The two other stairwells

14 Indres Naidoo, *Island in Chains By Prisoner 885/63* (Harmondsworth: Penguin, 2012), unpaginated electronic book.

15 See Sarah Longair, 'Unlocking the Doors of Number Four Prison: Curating the Violent Past in Contemporary South Africa', in *Art and Trauma in Africa: Representations of Reconciliation in Music, Visual Arts, Literature and Film*, ed. Lizelle Bisschoff and Stefanie Van de Peer (London: IB Tauris, 2013).

16 From Bella Dlamini's 'worst memory' account in Segal, Van den Berg, and Madikida, *Mapping Memory*, 58.

17 Segal, *Number Four*, 28; Mark Gevisser and Sarah Nuttall, 'From the Ruins: The Constitution Hill Project', *Public Culture*, vol. 16, no. 3 (2004): 326.

18 Wessel Le Roux, 'War Memorials, the Architecture of the Constitutional Court Building and Countermonumental Constitutionalism', in *Law, Memory, and the Legacy of Apartheid: Ten Years after AZAPO v. President of South Africa*, ed. Karin Van Marle and Wessel Le Roux (Pretoria: Pretoria University Law Press, 2007), 66.

are located in the forecourt. One houses the eternal flame of democracy, lit in 2011 to mark the fifteenth anniversary of the signing of the Constitution.[19] It has a reputation for going out – an unintended metaphor for the ongoing struggle to keep democracy alight. The other stairwell is an interactive memorial with speakers which play songs sung by the prisoners, that echo across the paving. These two stairwells are connected by the outline of the original building; the shadow of the Awaiting Trial Block is sketched across the forecourt as a ghostly record of its past footprint.

The Fort 'was a place where everybody locked up everybody. Boers locked up Brits, Brits locked up Boers, Boers locked up Blacks.'[20] In 1964, part of the fort was declared a national monument by the apartheid government. This declaration conferred a sense a state pride onto the site.[21] The prisons remained in use for twenty years after being declared a monument, creating an unsettling relationship between simultaneously celebrating – monumentalising – past Afrikaner battles and the apartheid-era brutality. From the late 1980s, the buildings lay abandoned until the Court was built in the early 2000s. The arrival of the Court signalled a new beginning for the site as a counterweight to the past, becoming a monumental memorial – 'an antidote against forgetting'[22] – to the past rather than a monument celebrating it. This memorialisation draws attention to the dual aspect of memory embodied in the site where during apartheid the prisons and the knowledge of what happened inside them largely remained hidden behind fortified walls. Post-apartheid, the memories of prisoners were uncovered and excavated for public commemoration.[23]

Court Appearance

> We, the people of South Africa, Recognise the injustices of our past; Honour those who suffered for justice and freedom in our land; Respect those who have worked to build and develop our country; and Believe that South Africa belongs to all who live in it, united in our diversity. We therefore, through our freely elected representatives, adopt this Constitution as the supreme law of the Republic so as to: Heal the divisions of the past and establish a society based on democratic values, social justice and fundamental human rights; Lay the foundations for a democratic and open society in which government is based on

[19] See Urban Works, 'Flame of Democracy at Constitution Hill', http://urbanworks.co.za/flame-of-democracy/.

[20] Albie Sachs in Bronwyn Law-Viljoen and Angela Buckland, *Light on a Hill: Building the Constitutional Court of South Africa* (Johannesburg: David Krut Publishing, 2006), 15.

[21] The idea of pride and monuments is raised in Johannes Snyman, 'Interpretation and the Politics of Memory', *Acta Juridica*, vol. (1998): 317. Also see Le Roux, 'War Memorials', 68.

[22] Snyman, 'Interpretation and the Politics of Memory,' 318. Also evident in the description of commemoration in OMM Design Workshop Programme and Process (8 April 1998) 10, SAHA.

[23] Noble, *African Identity in Post-Apartheid Public Architecture*, 116.

> the will of the people and every citizen is equally protected by law; Improve the quality of life of all citizens and free the potential of each person; and Build a united and democratic South Africa able to take its rightful place as a sovereign state in the family of nations.[24]

The preamble to South Africa's Constitution set out above underscores the importance of acknowledging the past in creating the post-apartheid nation. It does so by intentionally positioning itself as two-sided: focusing the nation's efforts on the past – healing, protecting, improving, and freeing – while simultaneously focusing on future efforts – establishing, laying, and building.[25] The former reflects the paradigm in legal scholarship of transitional constitutionalism which engages history in order to heal the past, while the latter reflects the paradigm of transformative constitutionalism which engages history in order to effect change.[26] Together the implication is that the Constitution transcends the past by remaining firmly rooted in it; this is the paradigm of memorial constitutionalism where memory begets opportunity.[27]

The Court embodies this retrospective-prospective philosophy, reflected in the orientation video shown to visitors of Number Four Museum, that says: 'at Constitution Hill we build our freedom with the bricks that once imprisoned us.' On the one hand, the transformation of the site from a prison to a court establishes a physical precedent for memorialising the past – an ending. The Court is built on and from the past. The main wall inside the Court's chamber is constructed from the recycled bricks of the Awaiting Trial Block, their exposed earthiness dominating the space (see Fig. 4.3). Similarly, the Great African Steps which wind up the hill towards the Court were built from the same recycled bricks. On the other hand, as the apex institution of South Africa's new legislative system, the Court establishes a symbolic precedent for creating change – a beginning. The Court symbolises the transition from

[24] Constitutional Assembly, 'The Constitution' (1996).

[25] Teitel describes this kind of two-sidedness as the 'dual optics of justice: the partially backward-looking aims of transitional justice linked to the largely forward-looking constitutional process'; Ruti G Teitel, 'Transitional Justice and the Transformation of Constitutionalism', in *Comparative Constitutional Law*, ed. Tom Ginsberg and Rosalind Dixon (Cheltenham: Edward Elgar Publishing, 2011), 60. Elsewhere Teitel discusses this optic as transitional constitutionalism, not only 'constituted by the prevailing political order but also . . . constitutive of political change'; Teitel, *Transitional Justice*, 191.

[26] Le Roux, 'War Memorials', 89.

[27] See Lourens Du Plessis, 'Affirmation and Celebration of the 'Religious Other' in South Africa's Constitutional Jurisprudence on Religious and Related Rights: Memorial Constitutionalism in Action?', *African Human Rights Law Journal*, vol. 8, no. 2 (2008): 378–379; Karin van Marle, 'The Spectacle of Post-Apartheid Constitutionalism', *Griffith Law Review*, vol. 16, no. 2 (2007): 411–429. This idea of memory and promise also arises in discussions about political reconciliation, which is seen as 'both retrospective (in coming to terms with the past) and prospective (in bringing about social harmony)' in Andrew Schaap, 'The Time of Reconciliation and the Space of Politics', in *Law and the Politics of Reconciliation*, ed. Scott Veitch (Oxford: Routledge, 2007), 15.

apartheid to constitutional democracy. Like the Constitution, the Court transcends the past by remaining firmly rooted in it: 'every decision that we make in this Court is informed by the history of apartheid.'[28]

The court building is a unique space by international comparison, not only because it has transformed the penal site but because it also incorporates artworks into the fabric of the building, and houses a large visual art collection developed by and for the Court. In order to understand the conceptual and concrete transitions of both the institution of the Court and its building, the following timeline provides an original overview of its development with a particular focus on the process through which the art collection came into being. This is in contrast to much of the literature on the Court's building, which tends to concentrate on the development of the architecture. The aim of the timeline is to introduce the origins of, as well as contextualise, some persistent ideas about the Court and its art, which resurface throughout the book. While two early 'making of' accounts of the Court exist – one on the Court's architecture and another on the art collection – they are largely art books which include descriptive accounts written by the people involved in the development of the Court (judges, architects, consultants) at the time of its opening.[29] These provide valuable first-person insight and visual impressions; however, they do not analyse the decision-making involved in relation to the art collection and have also been criticised for their overly celebratory tone.[30] By contrast, the following timeline analyses key early policy documents as well as recent challenges and initiatives, which are relevant to the development of the art collection, and which are yet to be examined elsewhere.[31] Furthermore, it incorporates recent reflections from key people involved in the initial development of the Court, alongside reflections by people who currently inhabit and manage the Court, providing new and valuable insight into how art has been a central component of this justice institution from its inception and how it continues to be so.

[28] Law clerk 3 from South Africa.

[29] Law-Viljoen and Buckland, *Light on a Hill*; Bronwyn Law-Viljoen and Ben Law-Viljoen, eds., *Art and Justice: The Art of the Constitutional Court of South Africa* (Johannesburg: David Krut, 2008).

[30] See Wessel Le Roux, 'Book Review: Linda Mulchay: Legal Architecture: Justice, Due Process and the Place of Law', *Feminist Legal Studies,* vol. 21 (2013): 109.

[31] These documents include curatorial policy documents, art committee meeting minutes, and funding proposals. While several authors provide brief histories and analysis of the architectural development of the Court, discussion of the art collection policies are largely absent or subsumed under discussions about architecture; see, for example, Noble, *African Identity in Post-Apartheid Public Architecture*; Freschi, 'Postapartheid Publics and the Politics of Ornament'; Judith Resnik and Dennis Edward Curtis, *Representing Justice: Invention, Controversy, and Rights in City-States and Democratic Courtrooms* (New Haven: Yale University Press, 2011); Segal, *Number Four*; Wessel Le Roux, 'Descriptive Overview of the South African Constitution and Constitutional Court', in *Transformative Constitutionalism: Comparing the Apex Courts of Brazil, India and South Africa*, ed. Oscar Vilhena, Upendra Baxi, and Frans Viljoen (Johannesburg: Pretoria University Law Press, 2013).

1994 At the point of South Africa's official political transition, the Constitutional Court was established by the interim constitution as the court 'of final instance over all matters relating to the interpretation, protection and enforcement of the provisions of this Constitution'.[32] In other words, the idea behind the Court was:

> to establish a very visible apex court that dealt with high level issues; constitutional issues and rights issues that had a broad impact on society, and to do it in a way that would immediately be seen as a factor of the new dispensation.[33]

The intention of the Court was in part to be a visible element of a new South Africa, to be immediately distinguishable from the other courts (supreme, high, magistrates) which functioned under apartheid to impose its various oppressive policies and may retain a perception of 'justice being skewed'.[34]

The interim constitution stipulated that the Court was to be made up of eleven judges whose decisions bind the state's legislative, executive, and judicial branches.[35] It also stipulated that the Court had to be located in Johannesburg. As the most populous city in South Africa, Johannesburg was to be accessible to a greater number of people while also distinguishing the new Court from the apartheid-era seats of power located in Pretoria.[36] Both these stipulations about structure and location are indicative of the Constitution being characterised by an appeal and access to humanity which goes beyond the nation-state.[37]

The Court's first home was in an office building in Braamfontein, across the road from its current site. Justices Yvonne Mokgoro and Albie Sachs were charged by Chief Justice Arthur Chaskalson to decorate this rented space and make it 'reasonably functional and not too inelegant'.[38] They used the entire budget to commission one artwork, *Humanity* by Joseph Ndlovu, with the intention that it would reflect 'the humanity and social interdependence that underlay the [first South

32 Chapter 7, point 98.2 in Constitutional Assembly, 'Interim Constitution', (1994).

33 Art committee member 2.

34 Art committee member 2.

35 Chapter 7, point 98.4 in Constitutional Assembly, 'Interim Constitution'. For an overview of the structure of the Constitutional Court, see Le Roux, 'Descriptive Overview of the South African Constitution and Constitutional Court'.

36 See Freschi, 'Postapartheid Publics and the Politics of Ornament.'

37 Idea mentioned in Bronwyn Law-Viljoen and Karel Nel, 'Art and Justice', in *Art And Justice: The Art of the Constitutional Court of South Africa*, ed. Bronwyn Law-Viljoen and Ben Law-Viljoen (Johannesburg: David Krut, 2008), 113.

38 Law-Viljoen and Buckland, *Light on a Hill*, 17.

African] Bill of Rights'.[39] This selection signaled early on the key place for art in the justice institution: 'We were not looking for denunciatory or triumphalist works of art, but [for] works of a high aesthetic quality that represented the spirit of human dignity in all its varied manifestations.'[40]

The story about this seedling origin of the artworks features heavily in how people at the Court speak about the collection as something that grew out of nothing: 'the collection that collected itself'.[41] It draws attention to three key aspects about the collection's development. First, the role of judges in the art collection is paramount. Were it not for Mokgoro and Sachs advocating the importance of art – Sachs in particular is a collector and patron of the arts – it is uncertain whether the collection would exist in its current form. Despite the collection having its origins under the décor banner, it has evolved into a major public art collection – a venture largely driven by judicial personalities and which continues to be driven by a small number of Constitutional Court judges, namely Justice Edwin Cameron and Justice Johann van der Westhuizen.

Second, that the budget was exhausted by the purchase of one artwork foreshadowed the ongoing struggles to fund and manage the collection:

> I suppose the proper way, if you want to build an art collection is: A) you secure the funding; B) you establish a procurement committee; C) you lay down certain criteria; D) you ensure that there's an appropriate curatorial environment for the works. None of those applied. Everything was done in inverted sequence.[42]
>
> [T]he Court had a strict policy of not accepting any support from private firms or individuals who could one day be litigants before it. In the end we received support from the cultural departments of various European governments (the Netherlands, Flanders, Norway and Sweden) and from North American philanthropies (the Ford Foundation, Tides, the Flora Family Foundation, The Shelley and Donald Rubin Foundation and others).[43]

The directional flow of funding from external governments and organisations established from the outset a tenuous relationship between the art collection and the art market but also embedded the collection in a funding dynamic common in post-conflict settings.

39 Law-Viljoen and Law-Viljoen, *Art and Justice*, 19.
40 Albie Sachs in ibid., 20.
41 Albie Sachs, 'Interview', 2011.
42 Judge 2.
43 Sachs in Law-Viljoen and Law-Viljoen, *Art and Justice*, 23.

Third, by extension, the lack of funds resulted in the collection largely being donated by artists, patrons, and gallerists. The organic way in which the collection developed disrupted the established conventions associated with developing public art collections. It has also resulted in a collection that is eclectic and of varying quality.

1995 In the same year that the TRC was established, the Court was inaugurated: the former looked back while the latter looked forward. At the inauguration of the Court, President Nelson Mandela said: 'Today I rise not as an accused, but on behalf of the people of South Africa, to inaugurate a court South Africa has never had, a court on which hinges the future of our democracy.'[44] Mandela's statement clearly identifies the Court as a symbol of the new democracy – an institution uniquely belonging to the future and breaking with the past. As was the case in the preamble to the Constitution, there is an emphasis on temporality *and* transformation in this statement. In both instances, the past is broken with, and at the same time its existence is integral to the journey forward: transitional South Africa looks back to look forward. In Chapter 5, I suggest that this temporal precedent – a recurring idea in transitional justice discourse – is a key narrative in the art collection.

The new logo of the Court was introduced at the inauguration. The logo depicts the outline of a tree with eleven branches, symbolising the eleven Constitutional Court judges. Underneath the tree are eleven human silhouettes, reflecting the eleven official languages of South Africa. The branches of the tree appear supported by the people and vice versa – a visual metaphor for the Constitution being both for the people and belonging to the people: 'The tree . . . is intended as a counter-symbol, one which dethrones more conventional iconography of power, be it imposing classical facades . . . or aloof, blindfolded women balancing scales.'[45] In other words, the logo broke with the European convention of taking Lady Justice as an appropriate symbolic representation – a symbol both outdated for its gendered objectification of women and unsuitable for its references to the visual imagery of colonising powers. The logo is also intended to reflect a specific 'Africaness' of the Court, referencing customary lore delivered by elders under a tree.[46] This idea of justice under a tree (discussed further in Chapter 4) was deeply influential in shaping the design

[44] Nelson Mandela, 'Speech by President Nelson Mandela at the Inauguration of the Constitutional Court', 1995, www.constitutionalcourt.org.za/site/thecourt/mandelaspeech.html.

[45] Noble, *African Identity in Post-Apartheid Public Architecture*, 120.

[46] Segal, *Number Four*, 50.

of the new court building which opened in 2004: it was 'the little acorn from which the whole project began'.[47] Both these points about the Court's distinctly African and non-European identity feature heavily in how the Court portrays itself.

The day after inauguration, the Court heard its first case, a question of the constitutionality of capital punishment. The Court later unanimously ruled that the death penalty was unconstitutional.[48]

1996 The permanent site for the Court was chosen at the Old Fort prison complex. The Constitutional Court Judges – in conjunction with the Department of Public Works and the Johannesburg City Council – selected the site in order 'to juxtapose the new system of justice with the old site of cruel inhumanity'[49]: 'We [the judges] felt excited by the symbolism of the old prisons, whose function had once been so oppressive, becoming, under the Constitution, a place representing freedom and human rights'[50]; 'Some of us had personal associations with the suffering that was experienced at this place [the Old Fort] ... my father was jailed here for pass law offences.'[51] The central role of the judges in choosing the new site for the Court reflects their involvement in the symbolic and aesthetic development of the Court, in addition to its jurisprudential one: an acknowledgement that the judicial remit extends beyond the courtroom.

The National Monuments Council and the judges disagreed about where the Court should be located within the Old Fort complex. The judges wanted to demolish the Awaiting Trial Block to make way for the building, while the National Monuments Council opposed its demolition, even though they did not have the funds to conserve the site which had been derelict for several years.[52] This debate between preservation and re-construction highlights an important tension in the aftermath

[47] Judge 2.

[48] Constitutional Court of South Africa, 'The State v T Makwanyane and M Mchunu', in *Case no. CCT3/94* (1995).

[49] 'Architectural Artworks for the New South African Constitutional Court Building,' (2002) Court Archive.

[50] Pius Langa as quoted in Segal, *Number Four*, 56.

[51] Yvonne Mokgoro as quoted in ibid., 53. Noble suggests the site was chosen because it was already state-owned land in Noble, *African Identity in Post-Apartheid Public Architecture*, 118.

[52] Segal, *Number Four*, 57–59. This disagreement also reflects the policy of the South African government to preserve past sites rather than demolish them, discussed in Mihaela Mihai, 'Democratic 'Sacred Spaces': Public Architecture and Transitional Justice', in *Theorizing Transitional Justice*, ed. Claudio Corradetti, Nir Eisikovits, and Jack Volpe Rotondi (Oxford: Routledge, 2015); Lynn Meskell, 'Trauma Culture', in *Memory, Trauma and World Politics*, ed. Duncan Bell (Hampshire: Springer, 2006).

of conflict about how best to deal with sites where past abuse has occurred or what to do with monuments of former regimes.[53] The case of the Awaiting Trial Block is particularly significant because from one view, the existence of the Block would have perpetuated the 'symbolic humiliation'[54] of prisoners who had been unjustly incarcerated and subjected to degrading treatment. The demolition of this building helped purge the site of the abuse perpetrated by the former regime. From the other view, however, the Block occupied an important place in the memory of the resistance, particularly because it housed so many political prisoners. As such, the erasure of the Block arguably detracted from the sacrifice made by the people and groups involved.[55]

The decision was made that the Block could be demolished but needed to be commemorated in the new building which replaced it: '[T]his decision has been very seriously criticised by many people, particularly ex-prisoners, who feel that that particular building had a very important place.'[56] The architects of the new court building argued that demolishing the Block enabled an openness of the site to contrast its past incarnation: '[I]n the context of a history in which laws at times forbade people to congregate, it was very important to make a freely accessible public space at the centre of Constitution Hill that celebrated the rights to gather.'[57]

1997 In the same year that the National Arts Council was established, the Cabinet approved an international competition for the design of the new court building. At its launch, the Minister for Public Works, Jeff Radebe, outlined the normative objectives of the project, saying it should

> acknowledge local human needs and social values; recognise a symbiosis between natural and cultural/historic landscapes, with an appreciation of climatic and environmental factors; excellence with limited resources; assert the interaction of technology and local labour resources; and promote the ultimate inspiration of innovation ... This is the first such competition which has been approved by government as an alternative way for the state to engage the design of important sites that reflect our legacy.[58]

53 For a discussion of different approaches to these sites, see Mihai, 'Democratic "Sacred Spaces"'.
54 Phrase 'symbolic humiliation' from ibid.
55 Discussed in Gevisser and Nuttall, 'From the Ruins,' 515–516.
56 Segal, *Number Four*, 60.
57 Paul Wygers in Law-Viljoen and Buckland, *Light on a Hill*, 21.
58 Jeff Radebe, 'Speech on the Occasion of the Launch of the Architectural Competition for the Design of the Constitutional Court of the Republic of South Africa,' (1997) SAHA.

Radebe's statement emphasises how the building of the new court was an opportunity for the state to create its public image; it also reflects an important idea about the state handing control of their architectural legacy to others, including from outside South Africa. The first major post-apartheid building was conceptualised outside of government (by as yet undetermined architects), although the winning design would still be selected by government representatives. This shift is significant because it lends a populist element to the development of the Court while also giving the state 'breathing room' to conceptualise their architectural legacy. Although the Court is a state institution, its aesthetic development was not completely controlled by the state – an important distinction when considering the ideas about human rights and national identity which emerge from the building and its art. Radebe's speech also places an emphasis on humans at an individual level and society at a collective level, which are two recurring themes in the art collection.

The competition brief emphasised the new court as an opportunity to express a transformed system of governance: '[A]ppropriate architectural expressions are required to reflect new democratic institutions and profound changes in society and culture.'[59] The brief focused on change, departure, newness, national memory, and publicness as important ideas to be reflected in the building's design.[60] While requirements for some rooms were outlined in detail in the brief – for instance, the court chamber needed to have a double height ceiling and natural light from above – the requirement for space for the art collection was stipulated in one short and rather unspecific sentence: '[T]here should be an area that can serve as an exhibition gallery and that can be used to accommodate other cultural activities.'[61] This brief stipulation is significant given that art plays such an integral part in establishing the character of the final building.

1998 The winning design for the Court was by Andrew Makin and Janina Masojada from OMM Design Workshop (Durban), and Paul Wygers from Urban Solutions (Johannesburg). The selection jury (comprised of government representatives, court judges, and architects) chose this design because it had

[59] 'Competition for the New Constitutional Court Building of South Africa,' ed. Department of Public Works (1997), 1, Court Archive.

[60] 'Competition for the New Constitutional Court Building of South Africa,' ed. Department of Public Works (1997), 14, Court Archive.

[61] 'Competition for the New Constitutional Court Building of South Africa,' ed. Department of Public Works (1997), 118–119, Court Archive.

'the potential to express a new architecture which is rooted in the South African landscape, both physically and culturally'.[62] The design presented a focus on art far greater than envisaged in the competition brief – including a large exhibition wing to house the art collection and plans to incorporate the work of artists into the fabric of the building. This is a critical inclusion because it became 'a way for other authors, particularly black artists, to provide contesting visions of public space and subjects within a space set out largely by white professionals'.[63] The symbolic intentions of the design and the resulting material interventions in the building are addressed in Chapter 4.

2000–2002 An art committee was established to oversee the development of the artworks programme across three areas: the artwork collection, the architectural artwork, and the public art around Constitution Hill.[64] 'A few days later he [Albie Sachs] said to me "ok I love your work . . . [but] I am not allowed to just accept [art]-work anymore", they had formed a committee to stop him . . . because he is so un-judgmental'.[65] The aims of the 'Art Project', as it was initially called, were to:

- promote 'the inclusion of alternative methods of construction and materials in the formal building industry' and 'the inclusion of cultural expression, tradition and rural skills';
- empower the process of 'skills appreciation, promotion, and transfer'; educate 'the public through visual imagination'; and
- attract 'international support for the development of human rights and culture in South Africa'.[66]

These aims were later expanded to include:

- creating '*a building of the highest ideals for the humblest of persons*', through a respectful and integrated representation of diverse forms of cultural expression, including contemporary, traditional, urban and rural forms of high art and popular craft; and

[62] Competition Jury, 'Statement by the Jury' (1998), 1, SAHA. The members of the jury were: Isaac Mogase (Mayor of Johannesburg), Arthur Chaskalson (Chief Justice, represented by Justice Albie Sachs), Gerald Damstra (from the Department of Public Works), Thenjiwe Mtintso (from the South African Gender Commission), Willie Meyer (South African architect), Charles Correa (architect from India), Geoffrey Bawa (architect from Sri Lanka), and Peter Davey (editor of *The Architectural Review*). For an overview of the other entries into the architecture competition, see Noble, *African Identity in Post-Apartheid Public Architecture*, 113–151.

[63] Hannah Le Roux, 'Hell/Whole: The Inversion of Constitution Hill', *Art South Africa*, vol. 2, no. 4 (2004): 5.

[64] 'Document 4: Basic Procurement Document,' (2002) Court Archive. Quote by Artist 9. To note, three of the original members still remain on the Art Committee.

[65] Artist 9.

[66] 'The Architectural Artworks Programme for the New South African Constitutional Court Building' (2000) Court Archive. Emphasis in the original.

- inviting and working with 'artists from other parts of the world to contribute to help memorialise international support for ending apartheid'.[67]

From the outset the artworks were embedded in ideas about education and diplomacy, as well as construction and skills transfer, ideas which point to the importance placed on art at the Court to not only to reflect the spirit of the new Constitution but to enact it.

The artworks are involved in both the physical and conceptual shaping of the Court, primarily by generating encounters among people involved in the development of the Court, such as designers, engineers, and people with 'different cultural and educational backgrounds'.[68] These encounters position the artworks to play an active role in negotiating post-apartheid relationships. Furthermore, the artworks are embedded in processes of memorialisation within South Africa, and unusually, this is extended to include memorialising the role of the international community in opposing apartheid. The focus on encounters is extended beyond the internal to the external. This dual focus of the art collection reflects the glocal transitional justice narrative (discussed throughout the book) emerging in various discourses around post-apartheid art. It also further embeds the Court's artworks in the cultivation of South Africa's diplomacy, beyond the international funding of the art collection mentioned previously. Despite these aims of the Committee being documented on funding proposals, it is interesting that the list does not include specific mention of the responsibility for generating funds to conserve and manage the artworks – an important omission in light of the current funding issues facing the collection (discussed below).[69]

An early iteration of the collection's procurement policy specified the criteria for the Art Committee to follow when selecting artworks. These criteria are based on principles of diversity, knowledge transfer, innovation, quality, and function:

1. Diverse forms of cultural expression will be represented, including contemporary, urban and rural forms of high art and popular craft. . .
2. Artists will be selected in a manner that creates the possibility for skills transfers and interaction. . .

[67] 'Architectural Artworks Programme for the New South African Constitutional Court Building: Funding Proposal' (2002) Court Archive.

[68] 'The Architectural Artworks Programme for the New South African Constitutional Court Building' (2000) Court Archive.

[69] 'Architectural Artworks Programme for the New South African Constitutional Court Building: Funding Proposal' (2002) Court Archive.

3. Artists will be selected where appropriate in a manner that allows for an innovative mix of forms and styles…
4. The Artworks Committee will attempt to locate artists and crafters who can achieve the highest standards of excellence in their art form.
5. The architects will ensure that the artworks commissioned are appropriate to the functional requirements and aesthetics of the building and its environs.
6. The Artworks Committee will supervise the process of procurement and ensure that the work is of acceptable quality…
7. The Artworks Committee will liaise with the future users of the building with regard to the artworks which will have a direct impact on the environment in which such users will work (for example: the Court Chamber and the judges' chambers)…[70]

At this early stage, these criteria are focused more on practical considerations than the conceptual content of artworks with a greater emphasis on process rather than meaning. This focus contrasts with some of the aims of the Art Committee listed above, which include normative assertions about the role – creating ideals and memorialising the past – that the artworks should play.

The procurement document also stipulates how artists should be paid for their work, as many are in need, but recognises others may wish to donate work.[71] This stipulation points towards a split in the collection between integrated artworks which appear to have largely been funded and loose artworks which seem to have largely been donated. This split indicates that the loose artworks were largely donated by established 'big name' artists, while several of the integrated artworks were created by lesser-known artists. While both these categories of artworks fall under the one art collection – and under the remit of the Art Committee – there were often slippages in how the different parts of the collection are spoken about by people involved with the artworks. This included differing views over the correct use of the terms 'integrated' versus 'loose', and even of the use of phrases such as 'art collection' versus 'artworks programme' – divisions which arguably create problematic hierarchies in how the artworks are perceived as craft versus fine art, or how collectively the artworks form a static group versus an ongoing project.[72]

[70] Architectural Artworks Committee, 'Documents for Procurement and Payment of Artists,' 3, Court Archive.

[71] Architectural Artworks Committee, 'Documents for Procurement and Payment of Artists,' 4, Court Archive.

[72] During interviews, several judges and members of the art committee commented on the terminology used to describe the artworks; the Court's website and most members of the art

In 2000, the Court ruled that the State must provide access to housing, stating that '[h]uman dignity, freedom and equality are denied to those without food, clothing or shelter'.[73] This statement underscores the importance of human dignity as a right in the Court's decisions foreshadowing the normative emphasis on human dignity in the art collection and the idea that the artworks should not be 'repellent to people coming to court to defend their fundamental rights'.[74]

The building of the new Court began in October 2001; 'Each section of the building was discussed with the relevant people – not only the judges but members of the library staff, [and] the administrative staff.'[75] The involvement of people who would inhabit the building in the consideration of its construction reflects an important collaborative element which returns in the art collection through the recognition of communities (discussed in Chapter 5).

2003 A National Artworks Competition for the Court was launched. The competition asked artists to submit proposals to create objects – from functional objects such as drinking fountains and security doors to decorative objects such as wall tiles – for thirty-one sites on the Hill, the majority of which were in the Court building: 'The art competitions ... defined the requirements of each of the artworks in terms of its location and performance (structure, security, sun-control, visibility etc), and in the broader context of the ideals of the Constitution.'[76] These parameters meant the competition was largely concerned with integrated artworks which resulted in a focus on functional craft and design work as opposed to other forms of art.

The intention of holding a competition for the integrated artworks was to 'represent the post-apartheid spirit of the emerging nation in all its diversity'.[77] In other words, the competition was both a way for the people of South Africa to participate in the physical building of this new justice institution and to make the Court a reflection of this participation.

committee use the terms 'loose' and 'integrated' to distinguish between types of artworks. One early architect report also uses the terms 'free standing' and 'intrinsic' in draft report OMM submission (18 August 1998) 6, SAHA.

73 Constitutional Court of South Africa, 'Government of the Republic of South Africa and Others v Irene Grootboom and Others', in *Case No. CCT 11/00* (2000), 19.

74 Albie Sachs quoted in Sean O'Toole, 'The Hanging Judge', *Sunday Times Lifestyle*, 22 February 2004.

75 Justice Kate O'Regan as quoted in Segal, *Number Four*, 94.

76 Janina Masojada in Law-Viljoen and Law-Viljoen, *Art and Justice*, 38.

77 Architectural Artworks Committee, 'Documents for Procurement and Payment of Artists', 4, Court Archive.

2004 At the inauguration of the new Constitutional Court building on Human Rights Day, 21 March, President Thabo Mbeki said:

> The Court represents the conversion of the negative, hateful energy of colonialism, subjugation and oppression into a positive, hopeful energy for the present and the future; a celebration of the creative potential of our people that has given us an architectural jewel.[78]

This statement again underscores the ideas of transition, transformation, and temporality which have become permanently associated with the Court and its narrative of justice, and in particular with its art collection. The aesthetic dimensions of the new building – in which art plays a central role – also became associated with physical, conceptual, and judicial innovation, important associations taken-up in the discussion of visual jurisprudence in Chapter 6.

The initial public reaction to the new court building was largely favourable: 'No other Constitutional Court or its equivalent has dared to incorporate so many images of the past abuses of its former legal system. It inspires great confidence to know that multiple systems of human thought can coexist, complement and embellish each other in this judicial context.'[79] This optimism filters through into academic scholarship which analyses the building (mainly focusing on the architecture, not the artworks) in terms of: being a 'physical signpost of a democratic post-apartheid theory of law'[80]; its memorial capacity to counter constitutional interpretation[81]; and its capacity 'to reimage and reimagine new South African public spaces'.[82]

2013 Initially conceived as the final appellate court for all matters relating to the Constitution, the Court became the apex court for all legal matters in South Africa – the implication being that the Constitution is at the heart of all cases.[83] This judicial restructure is significant for two reasons. First, as the highest court in the country, the Constitutional Court is bestowed with a renewed sense of prominence; under 'the apartheid court system ... the

[78] As quoted in Segal, *Number Four*, 199.

[79] Carol Becker, 'The Art of Law', *In These Times*, 15 March 2003. In 2006, the South African Institute of Architects awarded the architects an Award of Excellence – the highest award for architecture in South Africa – for the Constitutional Court building; see Cara Snyman, 'Constitutional Court wins again', 2006, www.artlink.co.za/news_article.htm?contentID=2271. Reaction also outlined in Freschi, 'Postapartheid Publics and the Politics of Ornament.'

[80] Wessel Le Roux, 'Designs of the Times: The Remaking of South African and Dutch Courtroom Architecture during the 1990s', *Fundamina: A Journal of Legal History*, vol. 13, no. 2 (2007): 70.

[81] Le Roux, 'War Memorials'.

[82] Freschi, 'Postapartheid Publics and the Politics of Ornament,' 45.

[83] South African Parliament, 'Superior Courts Act' (South Africa 2013).

parliament was the ultimate authority whereas now . . . in the new dispensation the Constitution is the ultimate authority'.[84] Second, the Court's elevation of status increases its political influence, not in the sense that the judiciary is political, but rather in the sense that some presidents in South Africa have an unsettled relationship with the Constitutional Court. For instance, during his time in office, former President Jacob Zuma was regularly named in cases before the Court and was also publicly critical about the role of its judiciary.[85] Zuma faced intense political scrutiny after the Court ruled he failed to uphold, defend, and respect the Constitution in regards to the misuse of state funds.[86]

2014 In twenty years the collection grew from one artwork to 402 artworks – not including the artworks built into the fabric of the building – valued at around 5 million US dollars.[87] It is now considered to be a major public collection in South Africa; however, the collection continues to suffer from a lack of funding to conserve and maintain the artworks and to employ full-time staff to undertake this work. This is in part because the Court cannot accept funding from within South Africa, as 'there is always a likelihood that any one of these entities could find themselves appearing before the Court as part of some litigation thus their involvement in other activities of the Court such as the Art Collection could be a reputational risk'.[88] Further, because while 'the global support for South Africa coming through [the transition] was really fundamental . . . [but now] it's really hard because people are like, "Well we've already given money to South Africa, you should be fine."'[89]

The Foundation for Society, Law and Art in South Africa was established in 2014 to address these issues and to support the art collection in raising funds to 'develop and expand the outreach of the Collection, while maintaining its rich history of promoting justice, human rights and reconciliation through artistic expression'.[90] This renewed funding campaign draws attention to a revitalised concern for the preservation of the art collection as

84 Visitor 1, lawyer from South Africa.

85 See, for example, Gary Pienaar and Judith February, 'Twenty Years of Constitutional Democracy', in *State of the Nation 2014: South Africa 1994–2014: A Twenty-Year Review*, ed. M Nkondo et al. (Cape Town: HSRC Press, 2015).

86 Constitutional Court of South Africa, 'Economic Freedom Fighters v Speaker of the National Assembly and Others and Democratic Alliance v Speaker of the National Assembly and Others', in *Case CCT 143/15 and CCT171–15* (2016), 13.

87 'CCAC Inventory List 20140331,' (2014) Court Archive; field note, 21 May 2014.

88 Art Committee, 'Art Committee Meeting Minutes 12 November 2012,' Court Archive.

89 Curator 3.

90 'Constitutional Court Art Collection: Foundation', 2014, https://ccac.org.za/foundation/.

a significant element of the Court: '[W]hen we're fighting for the artworks, we are also fighting for the underlying project of making a viable democracy in South Africa.'[91] It also highlights an issue which arises from the art collection: while the Court is acting with integrity by not accepting money to fund the collection from internal donors who may appear as litigants before it, it is circumscribed by the liberal democratic agenda of the external organisations which support the art collection.

This timeline signals key stages in the development of the Court, and its art collection, in order to introduce and contextualise four persistent ideas which resurface throughout Part I of this book. The first idea is the physical and symbolic precedents established by the Court in being embedded in the past in order to shape the future. The proximity of the Court to the prison points to the limits of the past and possibilities going forward. This reflects how the project of nation building is oriented towards the future.[92] Second, the artworks have a role in both memorialising the past and monumentalising the new Constitution. They simultaneously commemorate past abuse and open up possibilities for democratic inclusion. Third, the artworks play an active role in how the Constitution is shaped at the Court. They offer physical and symbolic encounters between people and ideals. Finally, there is a significant relationship between the Court and the international community which both funds and contributes to the art collection, a point which takes on heightened significance in the context of human rights discourse. The artworks are central to establishing the Court as one which is simultaneously engaged in creating a global civic identity and a national identity – a paradox between a utopian vision striving towards human rights and a state ideology reinventing the 'new' South Africa.[93] While each of these ideas are discussed in detail in the following chapters, what emerges at this point is that art has been a central component of this justice institution from its inception and it continues to be so. When establishing the most significant institution to emerge out of South Africa's transition, judges were not on the side line as mere future inhabitants of the courtrooms; rather, they were on the front line pushing and prioritising art to be at the heart of the Court.

[91] Edwin Cameron and Albie Sachs, 'Celebrating Transition: Apartheid to Democracy', World Policy Blog, 2014.

[92] Meskell, 'Trauma Culture', 162.

[93] See Bill Ashcroft, 'Constitution Hill: Memory, Ideology and Utopia', *Tydskrif vir letterkunde,* vol. 51, no. 2 (2014): 94.

4

Shaping 'Legal' Space

> The building is brimming with art and art is now permanently associated with the idea of this (new) justice.[1]

> Art is as dynamic as the constitution is. . . it means different things at different times.[2]

> Judges wanted a space where people could see that their rights were protected, and they had to use art to do that.[3]

> The physicality of how the building is both constructed and organised, planned, is directly connected to our understanding of the Constitution . . . it manifests itself . . . in the introduction of . . . art and craft integrated into the building fabric as opposed to artistic contribution only hung onto walls.[4]

> The Constitution can be a means to healing and the artworks at the Court can do the same . . . if we lived in what I call a 'stuck-up court', which is a court stuck up with pillars, a pediment, and steps – the worst, most incriminating example being the United States Supreme Court – if we worked in that sort of building, our mindset in this Court may have been different.[5]

The provision of toilets emerged as an unexpected topic at the Constitutional Court of South Africa. During tours of the art collection, the curator regularly mentioned the many toilets in the building – included in the design to reflect a level of human dignity in the new court building which had been severely lacking in the site's former life as a prison. Toilets were scarce in the site's former incarnation as a prison. Overcrowding and lack of sanitation resulted in horrific conditions.[6] Similar conditions persist in prisons across South

[1] Artist 26.
[2] Judge 4.
[3] Court staff member 4.
[4] Statement made in an interview with the author, attributed here with the consent of Janina Masojada, Court Architect and Art Committee Member.
[5] Judge 5.
[6] Evident in the displays and information provided during tours of the Number Four museum. Also see Lauren Segal, *Number Four: The Making of Constitution Hill* (Johannesburg: Penguin, 2006).

Africa, the most notable being Pollsmoor Maximum Security Prison in Cape Town, where one toilet – often broken – services around sixty inmates in a cell originally designed to house less than half that number.[7] Mikail Subotzky's photograph of an overpopulated cell inside Pollsmoor, entitled *Cell 508a, Pollsmoor Maximum Security Prison, 2004 – Panoramic,* that hangs outside the central administration wing of the Constitutional Court, in an area only accessible by staff, is a reminder of this fact.

The right to adequate sanitation continues to plague South Africa, as the South African Human Rights Commission outlines:

> Who is valued and who is not is reflected in decisions by both DA [Democratic Alliance] and ANC [African National Congress] led municipalities to build unenclosed toilets in open public spaces. It is reflected in the rape of children and women who have to use open fields as toilets. It is reflected in the pit in the ground in which six-year old Michael Komape died.[8]

Lack of sanitation is not only a problem in the prison system, but it is also an indicator of extreme poverty, compounded in both instances by the failure of political leadership to deliver adequate services, or to deliver services which meet basic health and safety standards. Toilets – and access to toilets – are baseline indicators of economic wellbeing and human dignity.

The court building is (in theory) open twenty-four hours a day. Any member of the public can enter at any time of the day or night to use the public toilets and/or to view the public art collection which hangs outside these bathrooms.[9] In practice, however, access is deterred by the closure of the main entrance doors at night and their surveillance by security guards. Given the legacy of apartheid, especially in Johannesburg, this sends a clear signal to stay away. While the Court advocates access to sanitation, there are practical limits to its realisation, even within its own building.

During interviews with judges, toilets appeared as an example of the equality ethic of the Court. In other courts in South Africa, judges have private toilets attached to their chambers, while at the Constitutional Court, each chamber has a toilet shared by the judge, secretary, and law clerks, located within a central corridor. The first generation of Constitutional Court judges

7 Edwin Cameron, 'Report: Pollsmoor Correctional Centre – Remand Centre and Women's Centre' (2015). Constitutional Court judges are allocated a number of prisons to visit and report on each year.

8 Pregs Govender quoted in South African Human Rights Commission, 'Report on the Right to Access Sufficient Water and Decent Sanitation in South Africa' (2014). 'Michael Komape drowned in excrement in a pit latrine at his school in Limpopo in January 2014, just a week after he had started his school career', after falling into the pit toilet when the corroded iron sheet – serving as a toilet seat – on which he was sitting collapsed. See Bobbie Louton et al., 'Exploring the Issues around Rural On-Site School Sanitation in South Africa' (2015).

9 The idea that the Court is open twenty-four hours a day is emphasised on tours as a reflection of the accessibility of the Court. It is also implied in the mention of the community's twenty-four-hour use of Constitution Hill in Draft report OMM submission (18 August 1998) 5, SAHA.

(in consultation with the architects) decided that this communal arrangement was important as an embodiment of a daily resistance to hierarchies: 'The judges didn't want to have their own ensuite bathrooms, they thought it was unnecessary, excessive, exclusive ... against their belief of how the Court and country should operate.'[10]

Subsequently, toilets have become a point of concern among successive generations of judges:

> We've [the judges] had issues on small things like why does every office not have its own toilet; in most of the new court buildings that is the case ... it's a kind of comfort that one becomes used to, not only because it's a toilet but ... it's that little bit of privacy.[11]

The symbolic proposal of Constitutional values – in this case, shared toilets – is complicated by the material embodiment of these values. What was intended as a challenge to power has become an encroachment on dignity: one judge's choice for communal living is another judge's invasion of personal privacy.

Toilets are an obvious example of the tension between – what I am calling – the symbolic intentions of the original design and the material interventions of the resulting building. At times there is a gap between the symbolic and the material whereas at other times they are in synergy. Over time, these relationships also shift: '[T]he court building is in a very challenging environment because it's ... constantly being pushed at, in exactly the same way that the Constitution is, and what it stands for.'[12] These tensions and changes at the Court are important in shaping the space of justice. At the same time, they also implicate spatial concerns in the provision of justice.

The title of this chapter is a reference to the changing relationship between space – legal space – and those who inhabit it at the Court. It connects back to apartheid where space was denied, restricted, and made illegal: 'Apartheid was a politics of space more than anything ... much of the Apartheid legislation was denying people the right to move.'[13] It also refers to creating the new Court; building a space of law in which symbolic intentions and material interventions – with a particular focus on art – reflect a departure from the past: 'Claiming art is also reclaiming space.'[14] The legal spaces implicated are

[10] Statement made in an interview with the author, attributed here with the consent of Janina Masojada, Court Architect and Art Committee Member.

[11] Judge 6.

[12] Art committee member 5. For an overview of the need to study both the spatial and temporal dynamics of architecture, see Stewart Brand, *How Buildings Learn: What Happens after They're Built* (London: Pheonix Illustrated, 1994).

[13] David Koloane quoted on the cover of Debbie Hardin and Migs Grove, 'Claiming Art Reclaiming Space: Post-Apartheid Art From South Africa', ed. National Museum of African Art (1999).

[14] Ibid.

conceptual as much as physical; reclaiming space is about physically inhabiting that space, as well as believing in the right to that space.

The original submission by the architects to the design competition proposed 'Building the Constitution' – in a building which would be the embodiment of constitutional values and a beacon of 'justice and human rights to Africa and the world',[15] a proposal guided by the competition brief.[16] The architects highlighted civic participation, the protection of rights, the physicality of dignity, the vision of justice, and connections to the wider community as important ideas reflected in their proposal:

> *The Constitution belongs to us all.* The building shows of our right to participate in the debate. The Court Chamber is on the street, transparent, accessible, integrally a part of the public urban space. *The Constitution protects our Human Rights.* A prominent building made by rational ordering systems, ranges in scale, refinement and site prominence, expresses respect for the power of the Court. The building extends dignity and grace. By the extension of 'shelter' beyond its envelope, opportunity results for diverse and pleasurable experience. The Court has privacy without isolation from life around. The public seating to the Court is in the path of the public open space, a piece of street furniture, public property. The seating of council is an amphitheatre to the public open space. The constitutional debate is thus a public event. *The Constitution is responsive, its vision serves every man, woman and child.* The building allows easy and pleasurable use by the public. The opposite of intimidating and repressive architecture descriptive of previous government.[17]

Through its architectural and artistic features, the court building was intended to '*exteriorise* the Constitution, serving as point of reference for all that the Constitution sought to describe and achieve, while the art woven into its fabric and displayed in its spaces [was intended to] *explicate* the Constitution'.[18] The proposed location, scale, and use of the building are grounded in rights and values which are embedded in the Constitution. The linkage between symbolic intentions and material interventions is evident in this early conceptual stage of the court building.

The relationship between symbolic intentions and material interventions arises out of a process of transposition: 'about the way in which an initial concept is translated from idea to plan, from plan to drawing, from drawing to building, from building to use, and from use to interpretation by users and viewers'.[19] The meanings of this legal space emerge through these

15 Draft report OMM submission (18 August 1998) 3, SAHA.

16 Andrew Makin, Janina Masojada, and Paul Wygers, 'The New Constitutional Court Building of South Africa: Part 1' (1997).

17 Andrew Makin, Janina Masojada, and Paul Wygers, 'The New Constitutional Court Building of South Africa: Part 2' (1997). Emphasis added.

18 Law-Viljoen and Nel, 'Art and Justice', 113. Emphasis in the original.

19 William Whyte, 'How Do Buildings Mean? Some Issues of Interpretation in the History of Architecture', *History and Theory*, vol. 45, no. 2 (2006): 172.

transpositions. This chapter examines five key symbolic intentions of the Court's design and the corresponding material interventions, exploring the values of justice which the art and architecture are intended to create and represent, and how these manifestations intervene in their appearance and performance; how they are transposed and interpreted by the people who inhabit the Court. Four of the symbolic intentions refer to values rooted in and fostered by the Constitution (accessibility, equality, dignity, and freedom of expression) while the fifth symbolic intention (justice under a tree) relates to a process of South African constitutionalism embedded in regional vernacular and post-apartheid identity formation. These intentions respectively relate to different material interventions at the Court, including specific artworks and architectural features. The porous distinctions between integrated artworks and architectural features, in addition to the loose artworks, are reinforced by the conflation and slippages of these symbolic–material pairings which arise from recurring claims made and examples given by people interviewed, as well as dominant ideas reflected in the discourse of the Court, including policy and planning documents.

Accessibility

The most common claim made by interviewees about the new court building is that it is accessible – accessible in both a physical and a conceptual sense. The original design principles of the building – outlined in the initial submission by the architects to the design competition – emphasised '[v]isual and physical public accessibility'.[20] This focus arose from the characterisation of the Constitution as accessible 'in its careful delineation of the rights of all citizens'.[21] From the perspective of the architects as well as the original judges, the building had to appear accessible as much as it had to be physically accessible in actuality:

> Albie [Sachs] was always confident that the Court must be friendly, that ordinary people must walk in and not feel awed, they should rather feel – certainly the dignity and largess of this, the highest court in the land – but must also feel at home, and that colour and a bit of . . . diversity would make people feel that it was their court.[22]

The link in this statement between mind-sets (feeling at home and a sense of belonging) and means (using colour and diversity to achieve connections) is characteristic of the five recurring reasons given by people interviewed as to

20 Makin, Masojada, and Wygers, 'The New Constitutional Court Building of South Africa: Part 1', 2.
21 Law-Viljoen and Nel, 'Art and Justice', 113.
22 Art committee member 4.

why the Court building is perceived as accessible in terms of its form, its feeling, and its function.[23]

First, the building is perceived to be accessible because it is welcoming: 'The Court is welcoming and engaging and you feel like you want to see more. It's not the sort of place where you walk in and think gosh let me get out of here.'[24] This sense of welcome is achieved by a combination of the art and architecture creating an environment that is not intimidating:

> One of the Constitutional Court strengths is it's got some very, very good names like Paul Stopforth and William [Kentridge] and Kim [Berman] and people who really changed the [art] game in South African terms on the walls. And it's got lesser stuff that, some of it is beautiful and some of it is technically mediocre, but ... it all persuades that one runs in a building that isn't going to threaten you. I'm easily threatened by architecture and that building has never made me feel that I wasn't entitled to be there, and I feel welcome being there ... the Constitutional Court has never made me feel small; I've always felt I was the right size in that building.[25]
>
> The art takes away what would become a rather austere and nervous feeling if you are going to the Constitutional Court either to give witness or to bring a case against somebody, and there is an immediate sense of not relaxation, but familiarity ...[26]
>
> When you look at the pictures, you're in a relaxing environment, you feel relaxed ... and you look forward to the [Court] hearing. But if it's in a dirty place, noisy, nowhere to think about other things, you'll be too nervous and end up answering what you're not supposed to answer, or saying what you are not supposed to say.[27]

This idea that the art and the architecture – taken together and not separately – facilitate a welcoming environment was consistent among almost every person interviewed: 'The public approach to the Court is a very user-friendly type of approach, lots of glass and lots of colour.'[28] The distinction between good art and mediocre art in the above statement indicates the eclectic nature of the art collection, which members of the art committee claimed reflected diversity of South Africa on a broad level and, on a specific level, the diversity of the collecting process, the loose artworks being largely donated and the integrated artworks realised through competitive tender.[29]

[23] Whyte argues that architecture is unique because it is instrumental, ornamental, and symbolic in Whyte, 'How Do Buildings Mean?'
[24] Curator 2. This view was also reflected by visitor 9, businessperson from South Africa.
[25] Artist 8.
[26] Curator 4.
[27] Visitor 12, university student from the Democratic Republic of Congo.
[28] Art committee member 2. While almost every person interviewed – from judges to artists to visitors – believed the Court to be welcoming because of its aesthetic, one artist stated the opposite: 'I found that the precinct of the Court just does not excite me, it does not invite me...', Artist 4.
[29] Art committee members 3, 4, and 5 and Judge 1.

Figure 4.1 The façade of the Constitutional Court of South Africa displays the name of the court in South Africa's eleven official languages, in a font based on the graffiti of the former prisons on the site and the handwriting of the first generation of constitutional judges.
Photography by Akona Kenqu, 2014

In addition to the idea that art and architecture – particularly the Court's rainbow façade (Fig. 4.1) – create a welcome environment, the sense of welcome arises from a sense of difference, that the Court does not look like other courts:

> The Court is fundamentally a very different place to most courts around the world and that's not just because of the art collection but because of the architecture . . . because of the broader aesthetic function within the Court . . . For instance, there's a Constitutional lawyer . . . she said to me that before she speaks to the judges . . . she looks out the ribbon window, and it's like a ritual for her . . . it suggests that the symbolic functions . . . are not just fluff, it's not just a pretty space, it really does deeply affect people. You can see it by the way people feel in the space; they feel comfortable. There's awe, it's a beautiful space but it feels like a very low-key, down to earth beautiful space, it doesn't feel serious, formidable, intimidating.[30]
>
> I always say to my guests . . . 'people, when you enter into this room, do you feel like you're inside a court?' . . . most would say while they are still in the Court's foyer or in the gallery they'd say 'no, we don't feel like we're in a court'.[31]
>
> The Supreme Court of Appeal, I mean it's so closed off and it's fenced and hectic . . . it feels so monumental and you don't feel like you can enter that

30 Curator 3.

31 Court staff member 2.

> building. Whereas this building [the Constitutional Court] is just like anyone can walk past it, anyone can enter; it feels like a door to a house, it's not an entrance to a court.[32]

Through difference – created by art and architecture – the Court is seen as welcoming and not threatening. The Constitutional Court building is visually welcoming, in marked contrast to other court houses, such as the Magistrates Court or High Court in Johannesburg, which utilise the iconography of neo-classical facades and the symbolism of Lady Justice. The implication here is that through art and architecture, the Constitutional Court established a new material precedent in how the space of justice can be welcoming or even familiar, while still being respected.

Second, the building is perceived to be accessible because it is public: 'The chamber in which the values of our society are debated sits confidently at the heart of the most public space.'[33] This publicness occurs on two main levels. The Court is public because anyone can enter the building:

> . . . the way one can just walk in. I've walked once or twice into the Court itself when the judges were sitting, and you just walk in and walk out. The honour and respect given to ordinary people by letting them realise they can do that. I wanted to run in and out and around the building just to keep getting that feeling that I'm welcome here.[34]

While members of the public are able to enter the Court, the Court also uses this as an opportunity to interact with members of the public. For instance, at the end of proceedings on 12 August 2014, Deputy Chief Justice Moseneke addressed the crowd of people sitting in the public gallery. He asked them questions about how they were feeling about the case – an unusual practice in a court. This direct acknowledgement of the people there to listen to and see the case – other than the legal professionals involved in the case – changes the dynamic of the court chamber, making it more informal and less intimidating.[35] The Court is also public because it is located at the centre of South Africa's major metropolis:

> It was essential to us [the architects] that you be able to walk from Hillbrow across to Braamfontein, stop for ten minutes to listen to the discussions going on

32 Visitor 8, university student from South Africa. Also reflected in statements made by visitors 4, 5, and 6, lawyers from South Africa.

33 Makin, Masojada, and Wygers as quoted Segal, *Number Four*, 207.

34 Artist 8.

35 The case being heard was about the failure of a municipality to comply with the Court's previous orders to 'provide the applicants with suitable temporary accommodation and to engage meaningfully with them in identifying alternative land' after the Court found in 2011 'that the Municipality violated the applicants' rights to dignity and access to adequate housing following their forced removal from, and the demolishment of, their homes in the Bapsfontein Informal Settlement', in Constitutional Court of South Africa, 'Pheko and Others v Ekurhuleni Metropolitan Municipality (No 2) Media Summary', in *Case No. CCT 19/11* (2015).

> at the Constitutional Court, and move on. The building needed to be that accessible ... We wanted it to be like you could go in there, you could eat your sandwiches, listen to your elders talking about principles that affect your everyday ... and that's how it stayed.[36]

This dual publicness – open to the public and being central in the public realm – is perceived as fostering accessibility.

Despite these claims, the publicness of the Court is conditional on entering through security measures – a body scanner, a bag scanner, and signing the security log. These measures negatively impact the freedom of movement envisaged in the statements above. Being made to sign the security log upon entering the Court has uncomfortable connotations given the legacy of apartheid, where freedom of movement was restricted and monitored. While security measures do not prevent the Court from being public, they do circumscribe how those public interactions occur, in effect tying the Court to the unwelcoming measures commonly imposed in other government buildings – especially the other courts in downtown Johannesburg. This detracts from the sense of difference and accessibility that the Court is trying to cultivate.

The tension between public accessibility and security reflects the inherent tension in architecture between form and function. The Court is designed to symbolically reflect accessibility and is largely perceived to do so, but it is also a high-profile legal institution which carries with it risks to personnel, especially to judges whose decisions may at times be unpopular and subject to protest. It is significant therefore that some of the security measures were not integrated into the design of the building from the outset. For instance, the security gates to the judges' private chambers were each designed by artists and are aesthetically integrated into the building. In marked contrast, the metal detector and x-ray scanner at the Court's entrance are a later addition imposed onto the space. The detector's compact grey plastic frame squats uncomfortably amidst the soaring heights of the entrance hall, a reminder that the ideals of the Constitution – even when they are reflected in the building – remain circumscribed by the evolving security threats which result from ongoing political and socio-economic struggles. Adding to this tension between public accessibility and security is the inclusion of a large private area of the Court – for judges' chambers, administration offices, clerks' offices – which is restricted to judges and court staff. Visitors can only enter this private zone if accompanied by court personnel. While the exclusion of the public from these areas enables the sensitive deliberations of the Court to happen in private, it also arguably reflects a movement in court architecture 'towards

[36] Statement made in an interview with the author, attributed here with the consent of Janina Masojada, Court Architect and Art Committee Member. Also reflected in OMM Design Workshop Programme and Process (8 April 1998) 3, SAHA.

exclusive zones outside the courtroom to which the public have no access [being] fuelled by an overwhelming fear of an unruly and disruptive public'.[37]

It is surprising that the artworks do not especially feature in the reasons given by people interviewed for the court building being public. This is an unexpected absence because the discourse surrounding the Court emphasises the public nature of the art collection, in the sense that the building has a designated *public* art gallery housing a major *public* art collection.[38] So while the building is perceived to be accessible to the public because it is central and anyone can enter it, the artworks do not appear to be associated with the same sense of civic ownership; their narrative is less clear, perhaps because the art collection tends to emphasise the personal over the public (discussed in Chapter 5).

Third, the building is perceived to be accessible because it is transparent: 'The Court has fruitfully achieved transparency and accessibility and ... it would never have achieved it without the art pieces that we have as a collection and without the architectural design itself.'[39] The architects sought 'the power of a preeminent building without the monumentality'.[40] They intended this to be achieved through open space and light: 'light reinforces access: one moves toward light . . . light = transparency = truth'.[41] The connections made between light, transparency, and truth – although a little trite – in the original design submission embeds the building in a post-apartheid narrative where everything new was constructed to be the antithesis of anything associated with apartheid: from a justice system built around containment to a justice system built around transparency – at least in a rhetorical and metaphorical sense.

The Court is perceived as transparent for two main reasons. On the one hand, the building itself is open plan and filled with light:

> We chose to break ranks quite seriously, and one of the ways we did it was to create a lot of open spaces; courts were generally seen to be congested spaces which do not permit a lot of natural light and which actually are constricted in many ways. I've gone around the world and looked at chambers of other judges, they really, truly will be paneled with wood and they would have rolling maroon carpets . . . I think the word is stuffy. We chose a very airy, very open, interactive space, that sought to speak to . . . the normative considerations that one finds in our Constitution – like openness, like transparency, like being prepared to account in an open, public place.[42]

37 Linda Mulcahy, 'Architects of Justice: The Politics of Courtroom Design', *Social and Legal Studies*, vol. 16, no. 3 (2007): 398.

38 See, for example, Law-Viljoen and Buckland, *Light on a Hill*; Law-Viljoen and Law-Viljoen, *Art and Justice*.

39 Court staff member 2.

40 Makin, Masojada, and Wygers, 'The New Constitutional Court Building of South Africa: Part 1', 1.

41 Ibid., 12.

42 Judge 1.

Figure 4.2 Public entrance foyer of the Constitutional Court of South Africa.
Photography by Akona Kenqu, 2014

> There is a lot of light coming through . . . to show the transparency of what they are trying to create here [at the Court].[43]

The open, light-filled spaces (Fig. 4.2) of the building are intended as an intervention in the historical emphasis of borders and defined territories ubiquitous in South Africa and in apartheid-era buildings where 'you cross through a front door, you go through security, you go through very clear levels of definition' and separation; but at the Court, even when the judges are in the private space of their chambers, they still 'have views through to the public or to Hillbrow'.[44] While the open spaces of the foyer, gallery, and court chamber fulfil this intention, reaching these spaces still remains circumscribed by the security paraphernalia described, interrupting the openness by imposing defined territories of security.

On the other hand, certain material interventions are implicated in an idea of transparency:

> Some of the South African judges were very alarmed at seeing the bricks [the recycled bricks from the former prison building] up in the Foyer and the Courtroom and they thought we had run out of plaster. It took some convincing to persuade them that in fact the lack of veneer, if you like, was not only important from a conservation point of view, it was saying something about the openness and the honesty of the justice that was to be dispensed.[45]

[43] Visitor 2, disability care worker from South Africa.
[44] Art committee member 5.
[45] Albie Sachs quoted Law-Viljoen and Buckland, *Light on a Hill*, 70.

Figure 4.3 Main chamber inside the Constitutional Court of South Africa, featuring recycled bricks from the former Awaiting Trial Block (back) and a long horizontal 'ribbon' window (right), as well as woven acoustic panels (left).
Photography by Akona Kenqu, 2014

> It's a building of light, of openness, of enhancing volumes, of liberating capacities . . . all of the art is enhanced by that and in turn enhances it, so I see the interaction between the building and the art collection as being symbiotic, intensely symbiotic.[46]

In the first statement this transparency is literal: exposed brickwork using recycled bricks from the former prison. In the second statement, transparency is symbolic: art contributes to the relational sense of openness. The emphasis on the combination of art and architecture contributing to the transparency and thus accessibility of the Court connects to similar claims made about the welcoming feel of the building.

The most often cited example of transparency was the ribbon window (Fig. 4.3) in the court chamber. The thin window runs along the northeast wall of the chamber, parallel to the judges' bench, at eye level to the judges. The window looks out onto the pavement. When people walk by, it is possible to see their legs through the window: 'The transparency of the window creates an awareness that we work with people.'[47] The window creates a literal connection with the outside and it is a direct intervention into the central space of justice. The window is a symbol of what the Court aspires to achieve in the transparency of the justice system. However, the existence of the

[46] Judge 5.
[47] Judge 6.

window does not *ipso facto* mean that the justice enacted inside the courtroom is accessible, as was often claimed by interviewees as well as tour guides. Seeing the footsteps of people does not mean that it is possible to see the steps of the judges' decision-making processes: 'Despite legal and rhetorical commitments to access ... despite the invocation of transparency by the deployment of glass ... [neither] contemporary courthouses nor the rule regimes they shelter make accessible many of the processes and practices of judges.'[48] The ribbon window makes the chamber appear to be accessible rather than being unapproachable or isolated, but it does not mean there is transparency in decision-making or in the justice processes.

Accessibility through transparency is complicated by the exposure of the chamber to the gaze of the outside. Passers-by can kneel down and peer through this narrow window into the Court. While glass windows 'may signal a powerful metaphor about the transparency of justice [it] can have the opposite effect for users of the courthouse who suffer from the constant threat of inspection'.[49] In the case of the Court, the narrowness of the window is an important intervention that arguably decreases the transparency of the court chamber, because the transparency is really only one-sided, for the people inside to be able to look out.

Fourth, the building is perceived to be accessible because it is engaging: 'The art informs whoever comes into this building about where we come from and the present ... you don't have to go and buy a book ... By coming here you will understand why... it is necessary to have a constitution.'[50] The original intention was for the court building to be an 'accessible democratic form, [with] spatially integrated environments that invite interaction and exchange'.[51] The Court is perceived as achieving these interactions and exchanges specifically through the artworks:

> The artworks play a part in bringing issues pertaining to our past, issues pertaining to our aspirations, issues pertaining to the types of issues that the Court would be dealing with to the public in a far more visible, accessible, tangible sort of way ... it plays an enormous part in making the Court space a place where people feel they have contact with the type of issues that the Court deals with ...[52]

48 Judith Resnik, Dennis Curtis, and Allison Tait, 'Constructing Courts: Architecture, the Ideology of Judging, and the Public Sphere', in *Law, Culture and Visual Studies*, ed. Richard K Sherwin and Anne Wagner (Dordrecht: Springer, 2014), 538. However, Mulcahy outlines that 'research and judicial opinion suggests that courtrooms with an external aspect and natural light help to deliver much better trial outcomes'; Linda Mulcahy, *Legal Architecture: Justice, Due Process and the Place of Law* (Oxford: Routledge, 2010), 155.

49 Mulcahy, 'Architects of Justice,' 399. In the context of the Court, this concern is expressed by Sachs in Law-Viljoen and Buckland, *Light on a Hill*, 75.

50 Judge 3.

51 Makin, Masojada, and Wygers, 'The New Constitutional Court Building of South Africa: Part 1', 11.

52 Art committee member 2.

> There's so many levels to the artworks that you can walk in and think, oh this is pretty. And then you stand in front of the artwork of the little shoes that is just so powerful because it's such a beautiful piece but its message is so horrific [refers to *Every Three Minutes* (2009) by Rose Shakinovsky which references child rape statistics in South Africa] . . . that's how people become engaged in it and then want to look further and learn more about the Constitution, because why is this artwork here? It helps you to engage with what's happening.[53]
>
> The fact that they have incorporated artwork into the architecture makes it more real . . . everything that you look at there is symbolism . . . it is interactive and any kind of person that walks in can identify with at least one part.[54]

These statements acknowledge that because the artworks are engaging, they serve as a means of education, not only by enabling access to the past, but by showing why the Constitution is necessary. It is significant that the artworks are seen as inviting an exchange rather than forcing information on visitors: the implication is that the invitation to engage is less off-putting than overt didacticism.

Finally, the building is perceived as accessible because it is humanised: 'The combination of art and also the architecture enabled a mirror of seeing us in the Court, as a nation. So the citizens of South Africa are able to reflect much better with the structure.'[55] The idea of humanisation arises out of the artworks being seen to facilitate a personal connection:

> You move into that space; and although it is somewhat – in terms of its scale and in terms of what it represents – it is overwhelming, but there is something very intimate and very human through the provision of objects and images that people can relate to on . . . a personal level.[56]
>
> Artwork humanises that space, it softens that space, it makes it less concrete, less cold, less formal . . . the artworks in the Constitutional Court definitely go some way in enabling the Court to have a human face because ultimately the Constitution itself is engendered with those kinds of humane qualities.[57]

The implication is that the Court becomes accessible through personal connection, beyond being engaging and promoting interaction. The art collection is perceived to soften the Court so that the Constitution appears tangible, real, and able to be grasped. The court building then assumes 'the imagined place of nationhood, as it grants the visitor the thrill of what it might mean to "belong"'.[58]

The artworks feature most prominently in three out of the five main reasons given for the court building being accessible. The idea that art makes the space

[53] Curator 2.
[54] Visitor 5, lawyer from South Africa.
[55] Court staff member 2.
[56] Artist 13.
[57] Art committee member 6.
[58] Freschi, 'Postapartheid Publics and the Politics of Ornament,' 33.

welcoming, engaging, and humanised is significant in understanding how the symbolic dimension of accessibility materialises through artistic interventions. The considerable overlap between architecture and artwork in the perceptions about the accessibility of the Court – because of how some of the artworks are embedded into the architecture – means that the art collection often becomes subsumed into the myth-making of the architecture which exerts a deliberate narrative about the civic identity of the Court being 'for the people by the people',[59] an idea which is countered in the distinct visual jurisprudence of the artworks (discussed in Chapter 6).

Equality

Reflecting equality through architecture is at the centre of the original design proposal for the court building. Two positions emerge from this proposal. First, that diversity, or pluralism, is a uniting influence in attaining equality; the first title on the first page reads 'Unity in Diversity / The individual: the collective'.[60] This position reinforces the rainbow nation narrative – 'rainbow nationalism' – that South Africa has become well known for and which was particularly strong at the time the design for the Court was proposed.[61] Second, that participation, and the opportunity to participate, fosters democracy: 'The richness of our world arises from multiplicity . . . opportunity is the basic generator of democratic form.'[62] Further, in the proposal the architects elaborate on 'informal and alternative building technologies and materials' (multiplicity) and creating employment for 'unskilled labour' as well as 'local crafts people and artists' (opportunity).[63] These two positions point towards a justice-based cosmopolitan conception of equality which holds that, on the one hand, all persons are equal (have the same fundamental worth) and therefore should be treated equally and have equal human rights, especially before the law. This is a civic perspective on human life. On the other hand, in a democratic system, all persons should be able to participate equally and should be given equal opportunity to do so. This is a political perspective on governance. Further, a third perspective on economic distribution arises where artistic labour at the Court creates employment opportunities which contribute to both civic and political participation.[64]

59 Visitor 4, lawyer from South Africa.

60 Makin, Masojada, and Wygers, 'The New Constitutional Court Building of South Africa: Part 1', 2.

61 Term 'rainbow nationalism' is taken from Martha Evans, 'Mandela and the Televised Birth of the Rainbow Nation', *National Identities,* vol. 12, no. 3 (2010): 309–326.

62 Makin, Masojada, and Wygers, 'The New Constitutional Court Building of South Africa: Part 1', 2.

63 Ibid., 14.

64 For an overview of these three aspects of 'justice-based cosmopolitanism', see Simon Caney, 'Cosmopolitanism', in *Ethics and World Politics,* ed. Duncan Bell (Oxford: Oxford University Press, 2010), 151–153.

These views of equality which are articulated by the architects are especially reflected in the thinking about the Court's art collection, where the artworks are considered to be key to the *outcome* of unity in diversity: 'The combination of materials ... is like a reflection of Johannesburg, we're a mish mash of people and culture.'[65] They are also considered to be the *process* of participatory democracy: 'Justice for the people by the people; the art gives that sense when you walk in.'[66] This idea of justice for the people by the people is also reflected in the spatial design of the court chamber, where the seating for members of the public and media is elevated above that of the judges – an unusual arrangement for courts where the judges' bench is more often than not elevated to symbolise their judicial power.

The concern for unity in diversity arises from two dominant claims about the art collection. First, the eclecticism of the art collection is spoken about – particularly by the people who work at the Court – as a reflection of South Africa's social and cultural diversity:

> The art pieces are varied ... they speak to the core diversity of our society ... as a people we do cherish our unity in diversity, and as we differ, as we fall apart, we always see ourselves as all together, this notion of a rainbow nation, of a dream nation, of having had a dream transition ... in many ways we see ourselves as almost a wondrous people, and the art is varied, it has many sources ... they're predominantly South African.[67]

In this instance the collection is perceived as varied because it incorporates many sources: sources being implicated as both artistic mediums (paintings, sculptures, tapestries) as well as artists, craftspeople, individuals, and groups. The rainbow nation narrative again resurfaces where, despite degrees of difference, all the artworks are considered worthy of equal treatment. The Court is often used as a venue for corporate team-building exercises. Employees visit the Court as a group and use this experience to discuss issues of diversity, rights, and leadership in post-apartheid South Africa. A visitor on one such exercise noted: 'The last two days have focused on diversity, and how can we influence, how do we see it within ourselves and how can we change things when we're at work. It's been a bit of an emotional trip at the Court.'[68]

The importance of the variety of artworks carries over to the second claim relating to unity in diversity; the work of well-known artists sits alongside the work of 'people who don't even know they are artists'.[69] The collection's eclecticism is considered to be an equalising force. The hierarchies of fine art versus craft, and good versus bad art, are dissolved by being given equal status in the collecting and display practices of the art collection:

[65] Visitor 7, university student from South Africa.
[66] Visitor 4, lawyer from South Africa.
[67] Judge 1.
[68] Visitor 9, businessperson from South Africa.
[69] Sachs quoted in Segal, *Number Four*, 108.

> The idea of art from a street trader which he [Albie Sachs] bought in Ethiopia and he thinks is great – you know it really is – anybody would buy that as a tourist going through Ethiopia . . . but it is part of that whole idea of democracy and a flattening of hierarchies. People instinctively sense – although they may not be art specialists, they may not even be art lovers – that and there is something that most people can relate to when they come to the Court because some of it is . . . ordinary street art which anybody would buy; some of it is great art. There is that distinction. That is one of the strengths of the collection, which you would not find in a museum or a corporate collection. You would only really perhaps find a mix like that in a private collection, which is really where it [the Court's art collection] started.[70]

This statement reflects a recurring theme among people interviewed: that the variety of artworks in the collection – from artists with high-profile reputations such as Marlene Dumas, who was at one time the 'world's most expensive living female artist',[71] to unknown artists who create unsigned works sold to tourists – is a reflection of everyday people who attend the Court:

> It's [the art collection] an aspect [of the Court] which indicates a sort of restorative historical justice being done to the memories of the people who had nothing except themselves to rely on really, in their last moments . . . in general Albie's [Sachs] buying – or hitting people over the head with a sock full of sand and saying 'thanks I'll take that' – was a very beautiful one, because I find a lot of the [art] work, you think 'what's that doing here?' and then you realise that if you go and sit in the foyer, you're not seeing a whole lot of well-clothed clients or legal types; you're seeing anybody who wants to come into the building there, and that's what they're [the artworks] doing there . . . they resemble people and [are] for people who are not ok with the niceties of art.[72]
>
> Although in some ways any art collection is an elitist undertaking, compared to the imposingness of huge Doric columns and high staircase[s], the very variedness and plurality of the collection does demonstrate in a physical way a wish for the Constitutional Court to be grounded in people's expectations and aspirations, and not seen as something so remote hovering far above the collected wisdom of the legal profession.[73]

As these statements suggest, the Court presents an opportunity for people to view an important art collection outside the confines of a conventional art gallery. The modern space of a white cube gallery – where art is reified as autonomous and genius – is traded for an encounter with art in an unexpected legal space.[74]

[70] Curator 4.
[71] Rachel Cooke, 'The Daring Art of Marlene Dumas: Duct-Tape, Pot Bellies and Bin Laden', *The Guardian*, 11 January 2015.
[72] Artist 8.
[73] Artist 6.
[74] See Brian O'doherty, *Inside the White Cube: The Ideology of the Gallery Space* (University of California Press, 1999).

The claim that the art collection is equalising because it includes works of mixed quality and breadth merges into the claim that the art collection enables participation:

> The sculptures, the paintings, the beadwork and other visual art pieces … encapsulate the notion that this is a collaborative, collective place, not unlike our constitutional enterprise, which is meant to basically collect people that are very talented, to bring together the oppressed men and women who have been oppressed in different ways … when we changed apartheid, we targeted many forms of oppression, many forms of exclusion; it never was just about race … you can see how expansive is our notion of equality, of freedom … the artwork feeds into those themes, and reassures us that those are valuable themes.[75]

The artworks are seen as bringing people together in two ways: by being born out of collaborative practice – many of the integrated artworks were made by collectives – and by being a reflection of wider constitutional themes. So while 'a building must not just look good; it must also serve a purpose'[76] (in this case the purpose is a legal one), the same can be said of the artworks at the Court, which are not only aesthetically important but also reinforce moral and political ideas of equality.

However, the Court's art collection inhabits a tension between inviting different voices to be expressed and selecting which voices are heard or seen. On the one hand, parts of the collection were formed primarily by donations from artists, collectors, and patrons. The idea that the collection collected itself was often stated in interviews as a way in which the art collection inhabits a democratic energy of the immediate post-apartheid period. Those with the financial or artistic ability to donate gave artworks to the Court, the majority of which were accepted in the early stages of the collection's development. This open practice of collecting means the Court's art collection is diverse and eclectic; artworks are treated equally regardless of the artistic status of their makers.

On the other hand, the evolving curatorial policy of the collection focuses on the need for artworks to be connected to human dignity. In recent years this policy has been more closely followed than in earlier days: 'As new donations are offered it is about saying "is this filling an important gap? Is this something we really cannot say no to?" … it is really trying to slowly grow this collection until we can say yes it is broadly representative which we cannot say right now.'[77] In practice this means that some donations are not accepted on the basis that the artworks do not fit with the Art Committee's ideas of human dignity or the funding is not available to care for the artworks – therefore, participation is limited. While this practice adheres to the curatorial rigour and business case required to responsibly sustain and manage large art

[75] Judge 1.
[76] Whyte, 'How Do Buildings Mean?', 158.
[77] Art committee member 4.

collections (especially since the maintenance of impartiality of the Court is paramount and leads to a situation where funding cannot be accepted from many sources), it is worth noting the tension it generates in the context of a discussion of participation and equal access to opportunity pitted against the need to shield against dominance.

Dignity

The third symbolic intention which emerges from claims about the art collection and the space of the Court relates to dignity. The architects' intention for the Court was to use familiar materials and recognisable form to extend dignity to people who inhabit the space.[78] They proposed that 'colours of the earth, [and] traditional patterns', such as the ones found in the undulating path of the great African steps, would mean that people from rural environments would feel at ease when at the Court – thus retaining their sense of human dignity.[79] Groups of people were also considered to create artworks as structural elements of the Court, such as the carved entrance doors (Fig. 4.4). This augmented notions of dignity, where the labour of the people – handcrafting foundations of the Court – recognises and acknowledges their value, role, and eminence in sustaining justice (for all):

> It is certainly a place of dignity and a place of authority, but it is also a place where you come and have your day in court, where you are encouraged and welcomed as a citizen, to come and say, this institution is for me. There is something about the building itself; the colour, the vibrancy, the fact that many people recognise a cultural element that resonates where they come from, it makes it ours.[80]

This belief of the architects – linking dignity to recognition and existence and effort – is arguably indicative of their shared intellectual path having all studied architecture at the University of KwaZulu-Natal in Durban in the early 1990s at a time when the arts were being used to reflect and support social conscience.[81]

Dignity was perceived by interviewees through both presence and absence. That is, the physical existence of certain objects and forms at the Court was understood to return a sense of dignity (denied under the former regime) to both the makers and viewers of those objects, while the nonappearance

[78] Makin, Masojada, and Wygers, 'The New Constitutional Court Building of South Africa: Part 1', 17.

[79] Ibid.

[80] Statement made in an interview with the author, attributed here with the consent of Janina Masojada, Court Architect and Art Committee Member.

[81] Masojada also studied architecture at the Massachusetts Institute of Technology where she says social conscience was 'the basis of all of their theoretical teaching'; Janina Masojada, 'Interview', 2012.

Figure 4.4 Entrance doors to the Constitutional Court of South Africa by Andries Botha, Smanga Madlala, Richard Maphumulo, Jabulani Mthethwa, Lindelani Ndinisa, Musa Ngcobo, Richard Shange, and Andrew Verster, carved wood. The doors depict the Bill of Rights in sign language.
Photography by Akona Kenqu, 2014

(absence) of other objects simultaneously conferred dignity. Dignity was seen to be achieved by the material intervention of particular artworks into the space:

> People who had been jailed all their lives and were currently in jail . . . They [the Art Committee] specifically went to that sort of disempowered person and asked them to make an artwork that went into a place as powerful as the judges'

> deliberation room. Just to say that humanity is valued no matter where you are. What I find so amazing about those pieces in particular, is some of the women [who created them] have just put their prison number [on the artwork], they wouldn't even put their own names down, because their dignity had been degraded to such an extent . . . those kind of images are so good for us to say the Constitution is trying to stop those kind of issues from happening, and in that way the artwork is incredibly powerful.[82]

The idea that dignity is restored to people who have had it taken away, by virtue of their hand being present in the Court, was a recurring claim: 'They're part of the court because they brought something with their own hands.'[83] The above statement also raises an interesting point about credit and identity which is pertinent to the idea of conferring dignity: '[A]rt production can provide a public platform to restore the dignity of individuals and groups.'[84] The importance of crediting makers at the Court was often spoken about. For instance, the woven acoustic panels in the main chamber are signed by their makers (see Fig. 4.3). The curator and tour guides suggest that this is as indicator of their dignity, respected in the recognition that they made those objects.

In contrast to the idea of the presence in the Court of artworks instilling dignity, one judge and one curator raised an important idea about the absence of certain objects furthering dignity:

> The Art Committee could never invite a performance artist, for instance, to do a performance piece in the courtroom. It just would never happen because they fundamentally have to . . . respect the Court as a space for justice . . . The Court is the highest court in the country, it's well respected but it's also got a particular kind of reputation to uphold.[85]

In this sense, the dignity of the art collection also emerges in part from a kind of self-censorship about what kind of artworks should be in the space, and what kind of artworks appear to support, rather than complicate, the work of the Court. Dignity in this way is established through consensus rather than dissent.

This sentiment poses a tension as to the purpose of the artworks: to uphold the reputation of the Court or to uphold the Constitution. The suggestion that certain types of art are not suitable for the space of the Court because they may inspire debate and controversy undermines the commitment to pluralism of the Constitution. If the point of silencing the artworks at the Court is to prevent the undermining or offending of human dignity and adding controversy to an institution which is already the subject of political contestation,

82 Curator 2.
83 Quote by Court staff member 4. View shared by Judge 2.
84 Bahun, 'Transitional Justice and the Arts', 157.
85 Curator 3. View shared by Judge 6.

then surely the inverse can also true. Not to foster debate similarly undermines dignity: restricting deliberation on what human dignity and a respect for justice means and entails in the 'new' South Africa. The reality of attracting controversy to the art collection has ramifications not only for the reputation of and respect for the Court in politically turbulent times but for its ability to attract funding from international donors to maintain the collection and, in so doing, find good reasons why the Art Committee would choose *not* to exhibit artwork which may complicate 'the Court as a space for justice'.[86]

However, given that the function of the Court is to protect and uphold the Constitution, putting aesthetic limits on how this function occurs may slide towards the silencing of artworks which do not subscribe to a narrow politically neutral agenda (if such a thing can exist) or which might offer banality in the place of engaging or inspiring thought – which until this point has been the key purpose of the art collection. By censoring the artworks, the Court is trying to uphold a conception of human dignity based on the liberal agenda of the new constitutionalism. However, if this agenda is to be fully upheld to its logical fulfilment, then dissent and debate need to be publically fostered by the art collection to the same degree that consensus and solidarity have already been: '[I]n order to facilitate a pluralistic radical democracy, it is essential to acknowledge multiple and often conflicting pasts [and presents], and the intrinsically power-infused and tension-ridden nature of communal mythological construction'[87] – in this case, the construction of a constitutional aesthetic. This is a conundrum for pluralist approaches to democracy versus the protection of human dignity which speaks to the very heart of the Court's project, not only in its art collection.[88]

In the private part of the collection – only accessible to staff members – there are several artworks which are deliberately hung away from public view because of their potentially controversial or divisive subject matter. One such artwork is Michael Meyersfeld's *Repentance* (2007). A photograph which depicts a man lying inside an isolation cell. The photograph is deliberately bleak and confrontational in its own uncovered nakedness and hyper-real vulnerability. For this reason, it is hung 'out the back', in the private office spaces and is often the subject of requests that it be moved. There is a divide then between the dignity narrative of the art on public display and the dignity of the art restricted to private display. The implication of this is that the public are not able to 'handle' certain artworks, while the Court staff are required to.

[86] Curator 3.

[87] Duncan Bell, 'Agonistic Democracy and the Politics of Memory', *Constellations,* vol. 15, no. 1 (2008): 149.

[88] This conundrum manifests in other exhibitions at Constitutional Hill (outside of the Court) where art is often the subject of contestation, such as the case of Muholi's artworks (discussed in Chapter 9) or the depictions of President Zuma on display at the Hill; see Amanda Khoza, 'I am going to throttle Ayanda Mabulu – Edward Zuma', 2016, News24.

Dignity therefore rests on a highly curated narrative in the art collection and one which at times is in tension with the dignity narrative generated by the Constitution itself. Both of these narratives are based on the idea that the Court is transformative because it simultaneously restores and recognises dignity. However, in the art collection these twin elements of dignity are complicated by the presence of some artworks and, to a lesser extent, the absence of others.

Freedom of Expression

The architects envisaged 'constitution square [the forecourt outside the Court's main entrance] as a place for protestation and freedom of expression . . . social gathering previously denied'.[89] However, nowhere in the original policy documents is freedom of expression mentioned in relation to the artworks. It could be inferred from the artworks being implicated in a narrative that they uphold constitutional values – the three founding values of equality, freedom, and dignity – but it is not explicitly communicated in these terms. This is in contrast to how the art collection is now perceived as a direct embodiment of the right to freedom of expression outlined in the Constitution (although, as noted above, this embodiment is complicated):

> The artworks allow people to understand what the constitution is doing because it gives an embodiment of ideas, so when the constitution has lofty ideals of freedom, it's difficult to understand what freedom means because it's different to all of us, and so an artwork can say, well this is what my freedom is, and then you can relate to general concepts of freedom through that. So it's a way of getting the public to understand what the Constitution is trying to do . . .[90]
>
> . . . at that time [the Chief Justice] was Pius Langa and he spoke about how important freedom of expression is in our Bill of Rights. He said how for him it is actually quite something to have this nude man in the entrance of the Court; it would not be his choice but he absolutely respects the fact that it should be there and that it speaks to our Constitution, it speaks to the value we give to that right.[91]

The nude man referred to is an artwork by William Kentridge, entitled *Sleeper-Black* (1997) (Fig. 4.5). People who work at the Court regularly cited

[89] Makin, Masojada, and Wygers, 'The New Constitutional Court Building of South Africa: Part 2', 2. Also reflected in OMM Design Workshop Programme and Process (8 April 1998) 5, SAHA.

[90] Curator 2. The Constitution outlines the right to freedom of expression as: 'a. freedom of the press and other media; b. freedom to receive or impart information or ideas; c. freedom of artistic creativity; and d. academic freedom and freedom of scientific research. The right in subsection (1) does not extend to - a. propaganda for war; b. incitement of imminent violence; or c. advocacy of hatred that is based on race, ethnicity, gender or religion, and that constitutes incitement to cause harm'; Constitutional Assembly, 'The Constitution'.

[91] Art committee member 4.

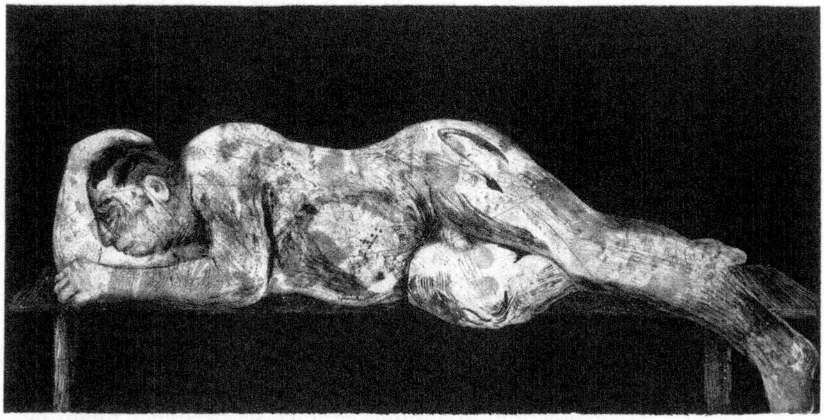

Figure 4.5 William Kentridge, *Sleeper-Black* (1997), etching, aquatint and drypoint on paper. 97 × 193 cm, edition of 50.
Image courtesy of the artist

Kentridge's artwork as an example of the right to freedom of expression. The reason offered for this connection is that the artwork is a self-portrait of a nude man, hung at the *public* entrance to the Court.

The freedom in Kentridge's artwork is seen as twofold. First, the image is of a naked man lying on his side. The provocation is that the image is of a *man.* As one of only two nudes in the art collection – both of them are, unusually, of men, the other is by Meyersfeld (mentioned above) – it challenges the conventional paradigm of female nudity in artworks, a paradigm which has historically objectified the female body.[92] Kentridge's *Sleeper-Black* – the title is a reference to the colour of the art medium but has a particular resonance in relation to racial discrimination – stands in contrast to the conventional images of male judges normally encountered in courts. The man in *Sleeper-Black* appears to be lying in a vulnerable position, cradling his face, which further confounds this undermining of power: images of nude men when they do appear in artworks tend to be in positions of power (for example, in the ancient Greek sculptures of warriors or in the Renaissance depictions of the ideal male body). It is not just that the artwork is of a nude man, it is that the artwork is of a vulnerable nude man which causes *Sleeper-Black* to be the subject of contention and, in turn, the subject of free expression. However, freedom of expression based only on this gendered perception appears to be rather thin. That is, comments by people interviewed imply that if the image were of a nude woman lying in the same vulnerable pose, it would not be unusual because it would confirm gender expectations rather than confound them. Therefore, the freedom of expression which arises from the subject matter of *Sleep-Black* is limited; it is freedom from a narrowly conceived hierarchy of traditional gender roles.

[92] Cameron and Sachs, World Policy Blog.

Second, *Sleeper-Black* is hung in the public foyer and is one of the first artworks encountered in the public gallery. Its position is significant because of its unusual subject matter: 'I wonder if there is any court in the world that has a nude as you walk in; and it's big [the artwork]!'[93] So it is not just significant that the artwork is of a vulnerable nude man (a thin conception of freedom of expression); it is also significant that this large artwork is encountered early, and at the entrance to the public gallery. These two provocations about content and location combine to connect the artwork to the right to freedom of expression, suggesting that this freedom arises from the ability to show an image of a naked man in a civic institution, yet unexpected in the context of the Court, because such legal spaces are conventionally circumscribed by a conservative aesthetic. It is not that the artwork itself is about freedom of expression; in another context *Sleeper-Black* might be considered an innocuous image of a nude man in an impressionistic, cartoon style. However, placed in the Court, the artwork takes on new meaning, and as a result, the justice (institution) affects the art (work), and in turn the art reinforces a notion central to conceptions of justice: freedom of expression.

In the space of the Court, the artwork takes on a heightened relationship to law. On the one hand, it represents the right to freedom of expression which the Court has a responsibility to protect. On the other hand, the artwork reflects why those rights exist, to protect the human body: 'a universal vulnerability in the face of the Constitution and the law'.[94]

That *Sleeper-Black* is almost a self-portrait is also significant. The image is based on the character of Ubu from the play *Ubu and the Truth Commission*, written by Jane Taylor and directed by Kentridge. Ubu not only bears a resemblance to the artist but also appears throughout his work like an alter ego. The self-reflectivity of *Sleeper-Black* resists the layers of complexity which would be present if the portrait was a representation of another nude man and not the artist himself – such as in *The Spear,* a painting by Brett Murray which depicts President Jacob Zuma exposing his genitals. Its exhibition at the Goodman Gallery in Johannesburg triggered much controversy and debate over racialised displays of the body. It also led to the ANC filing a lawsuit for defamation.[95] Kentridge's artwork displays a freedom of expression that is legitimised by autonomy and, arguably, also by his reputation as one of South Africa's best-known artists. While the art collection, mainly through Kentridge, may be implicated in the right to freedom of expression, this sits in tension with the idea raised above, that censorship of certain artworks might be done to complement rather than confound the work of the Court. In this instance the material intervention of art in relation

93 Art committee member 4.
94 Artist 6.
95 See David Freedberg, 'The Case of the Spear', *Art South Africa,* vol. 11, no. 1 (2012): 36–41.

to freedom of expression is limited by the internal considerations about what is respectful, dignified art for the Court.

There was consensus among the interviewed artists that the Court's art collection was an important precedent for a state institution, especially in the wake of the strict artistic censorship under apartheid laws, and the undercurrent of potentially increased censorship under the Zuma government. Many artists expressed concern about the relationship between art and freedom of expression outside of the Court. At the time of conducting interviews in 2014, a new Minister of Arts and Culture was appointed, Nathi Mthethwa. As a former Minister of Police, Mthethwa is implicated in the Marikana massacre in 2012, where forty-four mineworkers were killed by members of the South African Police Service in the deadliest instance of state-sanctioned violence since the end of apartheid.[96] This change in minister coincided with a national election, but it also occurred after widespread and lengthy controversy over *The Spear* – the subject of subsequent legal action related to defamation and debates over pornographic classification.[97]

Many people interviewed – artists in particular – were uncomfortable with the ongoing struggles of censorship and politicisation of artistic freedom in South Africa and the unknown ramifications of a former police minister taking over the arts portfolio: 'They [the government] wish art would stay as a quiet dog in the corner and not bark at anyone.'[98] As one judge put it,

> Unfortunately, the problem is that one senses an approach, even by the post-apartheid government now, which is aimed at thought control; which is aimed at preventing publication of controversial art . . . the sad part is we have taken 20 years in government to start forgetting about the importance of art and about the idiocy of thought control if I can put it that way. And the fact that the majority wants to control thought does not make it more legitimate than if the minority wanted to control thought.[99]

In light of these concerns, the Court has an even greater responsibility to guard against censorship within its own art collection. This means not only exhibiting artwork that is surprising in the context of a court – where there is an expectation of aesthetic conservatism against the backdrop of a legal institution – but that is also surprising and challenging in the context of a political landscape circumscribed by increasing tendencies towards the encroachment of freedom of expression.

[96] See Marikana Commission of Inquiry, 'Report on matters of public, national and international concern arising out of the tragic incidents at the Lonmin Mine in Marikana, in the North West Province' (2015).

[97] See Mike van Graan, '*The Spear* and the Marikana Massacre: Mirroring the Decline of South African Democracy', *African Arts*, vol. 46, no. 2 (2013): 1–4.

[98] Artist 6.

[99] Judge 4.

Justice under a Tree

The final symbolic intention – justice under a tree – is about a specific approach to justice rooted in indigenous South African practices. Unlike the four symbolic intentions captured *in* the art collection (and discussed above), this intention arose in part *from* an artwork by Sandile Goje, entitled *Making Democracy Work* (Fig. 4.6), which depicts a judge, claimants, and reporters deliberating beneath a tree. It reflects the set-up of the TRC where justice was seen to take place in various communal spaces under intense media scrutiny and public spectatorship.[100] As the timeline illustrated (see Chapter 3), this artwork was influential on architectural ideas from the outset – evident from its placement on the cover of the architects' entry in the competition and the repetition of the artwork throughout the submission.[101] Goje's print currently hangs in the Court, in the corridor the judges use to enter the chamber.

Justice under a tree is intended to be reflected in the integrated artworks, such as the slanting mosaicked pillars in the entrance foyer which symbolise tree trunks (see Fig. 4.2).[102] In addition, the woven carpets in the court chamber depict the dappled shadows cast by branches and leaves overhead:

> You walk into that court and there are remarkable pillars, and this concept coming in of seeing them as trees which fitted so beautifully with what the architects had imagined, the concept of justice under the trees coming from deep within African culture.[103]
>
> This building makes it obvious, it kind of goes . . . 'look at the columns they're skew[ed], they're representing a tree' . . . it's in your face and it's showing signs.[104]

A common claim among members of the Art Committee and from judges was the idea that the material interventions of justice under a tree root the Court within 'African culture'. At the heart of these claims is that the Court creates a unique space by communicating concepts of justice by metaphor, and through using recognisable symbols and forms:

> We chose a large traditional African tree and the idea, of course, is to deliberate in the traditional sense, under a tree, under the shade of a tree, and to find resolution of conflict in that situation.[105]
>
> The building is talking about the end of apartheid and the new era and the tree being a symbol of something African . . . So in that way this building, because of its symbolism, it is trying to be an African building . . . it's not

[100] This is described in Cole, *Performing South Africa's Truth Commission.*

[101] Makin, Masojada, and Wygers, 'The New Constitutional Court Building of South Africa: Part 1'; Janina Masojada, 'TedXUmhlanga', 2014, YouTube, www.youtube.com/watch?v=FBEkvSC1sNc.

[102] Law-Viljoen and Law-Viljoen, *Art and Justice*, 91.

[103] Art committee member 4.

[104] Visitor 8, university student from South Africa.

[105] Judge 1.

Figure 4.6 Sandile Goje, *Making Democracy Work* (1996), linocut, 52 x 36 cm, edition 44/100. *Source*: Image courtesy of the artist.

> trying to be Western, it's not trying to adopt symbolisms of justice from anywhere else.[106]

In this sense, the process of justice enacted by the Court takes place within a space deliberately designed to reference justice processes found in nations

[106] Visitor 7, university student from South Africa.

across Africa – that 'breathes South African culture'.[107] However, the metaphor of justice under a tree as something which encapsulates South African culture is complicated by its origins, which do not always reflect the vision and principles espoused by the Court and Constitution. For example, the Constitution is concerned with the equal representation of all citizens, but justice under a tree references patriarchal practices where adult men were the main participants.[108]

The symbolism of justice under a tree is a significant departure from the values of accessibility, equality, dignity, and freedom of expression which emerge out of a global human rights discourse. Justice under a tree speaks to the process of justice. It is embedded in the creation of a national identity distinct from the justice associated with colonising powers (although it should be noted that many European nations also historically associate trees with the deliverance of justice).[109] The Court has adapted a metaphor of South African justice for the purpose of negotiating a new national identity in the post-apartheid state, deriving its newness from the break with the past regime while asserting its authenticity through custom and tradition: '[I]t is a necessary condition of every new nationalism, it seems, to imagine itself as ancient.'[110] This assertion of authenticity perpetuates fictions of nation building. However, it also serves to position the values of justice which emerge out of global human rights as having already been part of South African identity and culture before apartheid. Connecting these values (accessibility, freedom, equality, dignity) to a local process that has existed for a long time (justice under a tree) means that they become claimed by and ingrained into the national imaginary created by this justice institution. The art and architecture of justice under a tree enact an aesthetic vernacularisation of global human rights.[111] That is, they localise the global. This potentially makes it more difficult for future South African governments to envisage violating human rights in the same way as the previous regime, because such abuses would likely be perceived as also violating the national identity embodied by and at the Court.

While scholarship on the architecture of courts is growing, little exists on the art of courts, likely because it is rare for courts to have such a close

107 Art committee member 4.

108 Freschi, 'Postapartheid Publics and the Politics of Ornament,' 42.

109 For a brief overview of the relationship between trees and justice, see Mulcahy, *Legal Architecture*, 17.

110 Freschi, 'Postapartheid Publics and the Politics of Ornament,' 43–44.

111 Vernacularisation is the process of appropriation and local adoption of global human rights; see Peggy Levitt and Sally Merry, 'Vernacularization on the Ground: Local Uses of Global Women's Rights in Peru, China, India and the United States', *Global Networks*, vol. 9, no. 4 (2009): 441–461.

relationship with art.[112] Even literature on the Constitutional Court frequently refers to the artworks as ornament or a decorative programme – problematic references, since they immediately position art as a supplement to, or embellishment of, the architecture of the Court, rather than being fundamental to its development and existence (even if this is not the intention of the authors).[113] The Constitutional Court is unique because of the slippages between art and architecture: the art is deeply embedded into the architecture, but it is also distinct from it. The art collection features heavily in the five symbolic intentions – accessibility, equality, dignity, freedom of expression, and justice under a tree – along with their material interventions; themes which are manifest in justice. What emerges from the analysis of symbolic intentions against material interventions is that spatiality and visuality are key aspects in the provision of justice at the Court.

The art collection is a sign of the Constitution as well as being its material embodiment, although at times the lines between these elements are blurred. While many interviewees claim that the art represents the fulfilment of the Constitution, there is still more to be done, as the example of the Court's self-censorship has shown. Like the Constitution, the art collection should not be perceived as a static entity. Rather, just as the Court is an important conceptual and physical institution emerging out of South Africa's transition, so too its art collection occupies an important symbolic and material presence in that transition, with the ongoing enactment and vision of global human rights in a national imaginary.

[112] Seminal works on court architecture include Mulcahy, *Legal Architecture*; Mulcahy, 'Architects of Justice.'; Resnik, Curtis, and Tait, 'Constructing Courts'; Resnik and Curtis, *Representing Justice*. Also see the database of sources on a diverse range of court architecture kept by the Judicial Images Project which is run by Leslie J. Moran and Linda Mulcahy, 'Judicial Space and Architecture', http://judicialimages.org/resources/publications-key-readings.html#resources_court_room_architecture.

[113] See, for example, the use of ornament and decorative in Freschi, 'Postapartheid Publics and the Politics of Ornament.'; Ashcroft, 'Constitution Hill.'

5

The Art of Recognition

> The collection provokes a series of questions about who we are and where we come from, particularly in South Africa, and it forces us to reconsider the narrative of apartheid in a very different way.[1]

> Giving tours [of the art collection], I am constantly going back to the big picture, I am constantly being reminded of a) the journey that we are going on, why we do this work; and b) the people that it affects.[2]

> There is nowhere in this Court where you cannot see justice, you can always see justice.[3]

Judith Mason's *The Man Who Sang and the Woman Who Kept Silent* (Fig. 5.1) has remained with me since my encounter with an image of it during a lecture in my first year at university. The precise content of the lecture has faded – related to postmodernism and the use of found objects to make political art – but I *do* remember *The Blue Dress* (the commonly used title for the artwork) with its bright blue silhouette pulsing in the dimly lit lecture theatre. This image marked my introduction to South African politics and the TRC through art. The injustices of apartheid became visually recognisable. I have now spent many months looking at the artwork at the Court; talked with the artist; witnessed the Court's curator cry while speaking to tour groups about the dress; listened to judges reflect on the artwork; and read the testimonies from the TRC which inspired the artwork.

This chapter explores three narratives about recognition which arise out of the Court's art collection.[4] These are narratives which recognise people, community, and time as key to the project of justice and democracy in South Africa. Drawing

1 Curator 3.

2 Law clerk from South Africa 1.

3 Visitor 6, lawyer from South Africa.

4 This chapter and Chapter 6 contain ideas explored earlier in Eliza Garnsey, 'The Site and Sights of Transitional Justice: Art at the Constitutional Court in Johannesburg', in *New Critical Spaces in Transitional Justice: Gender, Art, and Memory*, ed. Arnaud Kurze and Christopher K. Lamont (Bloomington: Indiana University Press, 2019); Eliza Garnsey, 'Framing Human Dignity: Visual Jurisprudence at South Africa's Constitutional Court', *Australian Journal of Human Rights*, vol. 22, no. 2 (2016): 81–102 reprinted by permission of Taylor & Francis; Eliza Garnsey, 'South Africa's Blue Dress: (Re)imagining Human Rights Through Art', *Angelaki*, vol. 24, no. 4 (2019): 44–62 reprinted by permission of Taylor & Francis.

Figure 5.1 Judith Mason, 1998, *The Man Who Sang and the Woman Who Kept Silent I-III (The Blue Dress),* found plastic bags, thread, white paint, approx. 200 × 70 × 45 cm; oil on canvas, 190 × 160 cm; oil on canvas, 166 × 122 cm. Constitutional Court Art Collection, Johannesburg. Photography by Ben Law-Viljoen. © Succession Judith Mason | DALRO

on interviews with artists and viewers, I conduct a visual analysis of artworks by Judith Mason, Sue Williamson, the Bambanani Women's Group, David Goldblatt, Dumile Feni, Marlene Dumas, Sipho Ndlovu, Thomas Mulcaire, and Georgia Papageorge. I argue that the three narratives which emerge from the collection play a central role in shaping the Court's larger transitional justice story. They draw attention to how the impossibility of attaining universal justice is what drives justice practices and the enactment of human rights for particular people and communities at particular times.

Recognising Personality

Many artworks within the collection depict or reference important figures in the anti-apartheid struggle. This is a key recognition which simultaneously remembers and reinforces different personalities, building the narrative around South Africa's transition. The most often referenced figure is Nelson Mandela – not surprising, given that he is the most prominent personality in South Africa's recent history. Amos Miller's *Nelson Mandela in New York* portrays a close-up impression of Mandela looking forlorn. The painting was executed at the time of Mandela's travels through the United States. In the background a distant silhouette of the Statue of Liberty seemingly mimics Mandela's famous gesture, the Statue's flame becoming a clenched fist of solidarity. Miller's painting suffers from conservation issues, as it is hung in a semi-exposed public space connected to the Court's open-air courtyard. Most stark are the bird droppings which have affected the canvas – somehow, they look intentional, as they transform into tears running down Mandela's cheeks, adding to the dejected expression already portrayed.

The exposed space of the gallery and consequent conditions of the artworks hung in this area draw attention to the collection's lack of funds and its difficulty in generating ongoing funding, especially for artwork conservation. In 2014, the Court launched a fundraising campaign in the United States – this campaign highlights two significant issues for the collection. First, the campaign was led in the United States by Constitutional Court judge, Edwin Cameron. This senior judicial leadership, coupled with the campaign itself, highlights a renewed recognition by the Court of the value of its collection. Arguably over the preceding years – since the collection's euphoric conception and realisation – the collection has witnessed some deterioration to the artworks owing to a lack of financial support. In a sense, Justice Cameron is taking over from former Justice Albie Sachs without whom – as was often noted in interviews, particularly by members of the Art Committee and artists – the art collection would likely not exist.[5] Both Cameron and Sachs

[5] Artist 6; Artist 8; Artist 13; Art committee member 4; Artist 2; Curator 4; Artist 29; Artist 14; Artist 9; Curator 2; Art committee member 5; Curator 3; Judge 6; Art committee member 3; Curator 1.

are important judicial personalities in South Africa. Cameron is well known for his HIV/AIDS advocacy and gay rights advocacy, while Sachs is well known for his role in writing South Africa's Constitution and activism against the apartheid regime. Their personal prominence lends the collection a share of recognition it might not have otherwise attained. The recognition of personality within the artworks sits alongside the recognition of judicial personality brought to the artworks.

Second, the campaign draws attention to the political economy of the art collection. The art collection is rooted in a deeply national and internally focused story, but it is supported by external donors. Since the Court's funding policy prevents it from accepting domestic backing, its reliance on international philanthropy positions the art collection as a type of foreign aid that is common in many post-conflict settings. The art collection becomes a meeting point of national and international interests, especially considering that the range of organisations which fund the collection – the Ford Foundation, Tides, the Flora Family Foundation, the Shelley and Donald Rubin Foundation – all have a liberal international agenda. That is, these organisations fund initiatives which are aimed at strengthening democratic values, advancing human rights, and enhancing international cooperation. In so doing they share a vision of the world based on their liberal underpinnings. This means that the art collection is recognised by these organisations as a way to support democracy-building in South Africa.[6] However, if this perception were to change, future funding for the collection could be at risk.[7] While the Court is acting with integrity over seeking funds from outside of South Africa, this has the consequence of embedding it within a specific international agenda that complicates the Court's national identity in the art collection. It is a South African Court, but it is also an institution circumscribed by the liberal agenda of global human rights discourse (discussed in Chapter 6). The language and practice of global human rights (articulated in the Constitution and reflected in the art collection) arguably have the effect of strengthening the work of the Court through appeals to international legitimacy and universality, while the economy of global human rights (captured in the funding of the art collection) has the effect of thinning the Court's appearance as a state institution. The Court was mandated by the state, but it is embedded beyond the state. This is an important dual focus captured in (and created by) the artworks.

This external–internal dynamic is also reflected in the collection where many of the artworks – especially major pieces in the public section – were

[6] For analysis of the Court's ability to consolidate democracy in unanticipated ways, see Theunis Roux, 'Constitutional Courts as Democratic Consolidators: Insights from South Africa after 20 Years', *Journal of Southern African Studies*, vol. 42, no. 1 (2016): 5–18.

[7] For example, perceptions could change if new judicial appointments were to be perceived as political.

Figure 5.2 View of open-air courtyard inside the Constitutional Court of South Africa. (Left) Willem Boshoff, *Prison Sentences* (2003), Zimbabwe black granite, eight panels, each 134 x 100 x 2 cm. (Right) Wilma Cruise, *Right to Life* (1994), stainless steel on concrete.
Photography by Akona Kenqu, 2014

donated by South African artists living abroad, including Marlene Dumas (lives in the Netherlands), Victor Gordon (Australia), and Paul Stopforth (United States). The South African diaspora is represented in the artworks. The collection provides an opportunity for artists abroad to continue their contribution to the transitional narrative of the nation while maintaining recognition in their nation of origin: '[P]recisely because of the ambivalence of their status, the Diasporic artists' voices resonate forcefully in transitional settings.'[8]

Near Miller's painting, in the open-air courtyard, are two artworks which make further reference to Mandela. The first is Willem Boshoff's *Prison Sentences* (Fig. 5.2), which consists of eight slabs of black granite, each marked with days tallied, representing the prison sentences of the eight Rivonia trialists: Nelson Mandela (9,377 days), Walter Sisulu (9,269 days), Govan Mbeki (8,548 days), Eliaz Motsoaledi (9,269 days), Andrew Mlangeni (9,269 days), Denis Goldberg (7,568 days), Raymond Mhlaba (9,269 days), and Ahmed Kathrada (9,269 days).[9] The sentencing of these eight leaders of the ANC in 1964 on charges of sabotage became a 'constitutive historical event that catapulted South Africa's struggle for freedom and justice onto the

[8] Bahun, 'Transitional Justice and the Arts', 159.
[9] Law-Viljoen and Law-Viljoen, *Art and Justice*, 130.

international stage, redefining and reinvigorating subversive activities'.[10] By engraving the thousands of days of each sentence onto the hard stone surface, Boshoff imbues the passage of time with a sense of permanence, commemorating – in the style of war memorials – the time served by each of the trialists. The austerity of each carved line is striking against the immense time and injustice it represents.

During the Rivonia Trial, Mandela – who was facing the death penalty – said from the dock:

> I have cherished the ideal of a democratic and free society in which all persons live together in harmony and with equal opportunities. *It is an ideal which I hope to live for and achieve. But if needs be it is an ideal for which I am prepared to die.*[11]

The second and third lines of this statement (in italics) form the other artwork in the courtyard space; the *Right to Life* by Wilma Cruise. *Right to Life* takes on heightened significance in the context of the Constitutional Court, as its first case centred on the unconstitutionality of the death penalty.[12] Together, Boshoff's and Cruise's artworks create a hallowed space where Mandela – the central icon of anti-apartheid struggles – is commemorated. Several people at the Court noted that flowers were left by visitors in this courtyard when Mandela died at the end of 2013.[13] The Court's art collection becomes a site of memorial where past figures involved in struggles for justice impel and embolden judges and legal practitioners in their own role of upholding justice.

The narrative of heroic anti-apartheid political figures is dominated largely by men; however, two artworks in the collection recognise the role of women. The first is Mason's *The Man Who Sang and the Woman Who Kept Silent* (*The Blue Dress* referred to earlier) (Fig. 5.3). This installation hangs prominently in the public art gallery of the Court, en route to the open courtyard – Mandela's memorial. *The Blue Dress* commemorates the deaths of Phila Ndwandwe and Harold Sefola. Sefola, along with his two colleagues, Andrew Makupe and Jackson Maake, was tortured and killed in 1987 by members of the security branch of the South African Police.[14] Reports on the decision by the TRC to grant the perpetrators amnesty describe how Sefola 'requested to be given permission to sing Nkosi Sikelel' iAfrica [God Bless Africa, now the national anthem]'[15] before he was killed. Sefola was the man who sang.

10 Awol Allo, in *The Courtroom as a Space of Resistance: Reflections on the Legacy of the Rivonia Trial*, ed. Awol Allo (Surrey: Ashgate, 2015), 2.

11 Nelson Mandela, 'Statement from the dock at the opening of the defence case in the Rivonia Trial' (Pretoria Supreme Court, 1964). Emphasis added.

12 Constitutional Court of South Africa, 'The State v T Makwanyane and M Mchunu'.

13 Curator 3; Curator 1.

14 The five applicants for amnesty in the murder of Harold Sefola were Hendrik Jack Cronje, Jacques Hechter, Wouter Mentz, Roelof Venter, and Paul van Vuuren.

15 H Mall et al., 'AC/99/0030: Amnesty Committee: Application in terms of Section 18 of the Promotion of National Unity and Reconciliation Act, No. 34 of 1995. Jacques Hechter

Figure 5.3 Installation view of Judith Mason, *The Man Who Sang and the Woman Who Kept Silent I-III (The Blue Dress)* (1998), triptych.
Photograph courtesy of the Constitutional Court Trust

Ndwandwe was a member of *uMkonte weSizwe* (spear of the nation), the armed wing of the ANC, who disappeared in 1988. At the time of her disappearance rumours circulated that she had become an *askari* (police informant).[16] Her family gave a statement to the TRC, which resulted in an investigation into her disappearance. This uncovered evidence against seven security branch officers, who subsequently applied for and were granted amnesty for Ndwandwe's abduction, detention, and murder.[17] The TRC report states that Ndwandwe 'was not prepared to co-operate with the police . . . they [the perpetrators] did not have admissible evidence to prosecute her and that they could not release her, so they killed her'.[18] Ndwandwe was the woman who kept silent.

Applicant (AM 2776/96)', 1999, Truth and Reconciliation Commission, www.justice.gov.za/trc/decisions%5C1999/99_hechter.html.

16 See Jacob Dlamini, *Askari: A Story of Collaboration and Betrayal in the Anti-Apartheid Struggle* (Auckland Park: Jacana, 2014); Rosemarie Buikema, 'Monumental Dresses. Coming to Terms with Racial Repression', in *Teaching Race with a Gendered Edge*, ed. Brigitte Hipfl and Kristín Loftsdóttir (Budapest: Central European University Press, 2012).

17 The seven applicants for amnesty in the murder of Phila Ndwandwe were Hendrik Johannes Petrus Botha, Salmon Johannes Gerhardus du Preez, Johannes Albertus Steyn, Andy Taylor, Roelof Brand Visagie, Jacobus Adriaan Vorster, and Lawrence Gerald Wasserman.

18 Truth and Reconciliation Commission, 'Truth and Reconciliation Commission of South Africa Report: Volume Two', 545. Dlamini unsettles the narrative of Ndwandwe's silence. He argues

The final report of the TRC mentions Ndwandwe's case repeatedly, in contrast to the stories of other MK operatives. Each time Ndwandwe is mentioned, emphasis is placed on the plastic bag found with her body:

> She was held in a small concrete chamber on the edge of the small forest in which she was buried. According to information from those that killed her, she was held naked and interrogated in this chamber, for some time before her death. When we exhumed her, she was on her back in a foetal position, because the grave had not been dug long enough, and had a single bullet wound to the top of her head, indicating that she had been kneeling or squatting when she was killed. Her pelvis was clothed in a plastic packet, fashioned into a pair of panties indicating an attempt to protect her modesty.[19]
>
> When she was exhumed, her pelvic bones were covered with a plastic supermarket packet with which she had tried to protect the dignity of her naked body.[20]

The focus is drawn to Ndwandwe's pelvis and the makeshift clothing which covered it. The plastic bag becomes implicated in a gendered narrative of feminine vulnerability, whereby the official report emphasizes modesty, dignity, and nakedness over and above Ndwandwe's political agency and her resistance to torture.[21]

The absence of any mention of sexual violence in the TRC report in relation to Ndwandwe highlights its failure to address the experiences of many women and to recognise the politics of sexual violence.[22] In this context, the form of the dress and the way in which it gestures to the role of women in anti-apartheid struggles are critical. *The Blue Dress* points towards the suspected sexual violence experienced by Ndwandwe; violence represented in the artwork by the imagery of the hyena tearing the dress in the dirt, compounded by the way in which the plastic dress has been ripped apart, surrendering to the effects of being on display for many years.[23] Other discussions of Ndwandwe's case make the sexual violence explicit: '[A]fter being sexually violated and

that she told 'her captors some of what they needed to know . . . She collaborated but refused to become a collaborator'; Dlamini, *Askari*, 225–228.

19 Commissioner Richard Lyster, quoted in Truth and Reconciliation Commission, 'Truth and Reconciliation Commission Report' (1998). The same excerpt is highlighted in the Truth and Reconciliation Commission, 'TRC Final Report – Summary and Guide to Contents' (1998).

20 Truth and Reconciliation Commission, 'Truth and Reconciliation Commission of South Africa Report: Volume Five' (1998).

21 Barbara Russell, 'The Woman Who Kept Silent: Remembering and Reconciliation in South Africa', in *Violent Depictions: Representing Violence Across Cultures*, ed. Susanna Scarparo and Sarah McDonald (Newcastle: Cambridge Scholars Publishing, 2009), 180.

22 See Andrea Durbach and Lucy Geddes, '"To Shape Our Own Lives and Our Own World": Exploring Women's Hearings as Reparative Mechanisms for Victims of Sexual Violence Post-Conflict', *The International Journal of Human Rights*, vol. 21, no. 9 (2017): 1261–1280; Hayner, *Unspeakable Truths*, 87–88; Russell, 'Violent Depictions'.

23 See Stacey L. Vorster, 'Storytelling and Fraught Histories: Phila Ndwandwe's Blue Dress', *Safundi*, vol. 19, no. 2 (2018): 164–189.

raped and left in the veldt, [she] found scatterings of blue plastic that she used to cover herself'.[24] *The Blue Dress* alludes to the sexual violence experienced by Ndwandwe which the official TRC record failed to acknowledge. In doing so, the dress comes to symbolise the many victims of sexual violence whose experiences remain absent from the official record.

Mason recalls hearing public broadcasts of the testimonies by the perpetrators of Ndwandwe's death and weeping when she learned that Ndwandwe had been shot after being kept naked for weeks in an attempt to make her inform on her comrades.[25] In response, Mason wrote an epitaph to Ndwandwe on the hem of the dress:

> Sister, a plastic bag may not be the whole armour of God, but you were wrestling with flesh and blood, and against powers, against the rulers of darkness, against spiritual wickedness in sordid places. Your weapons were your silence and a piece of rubbish. Finding that bag and wearing it until you were disinterred is such a frugal, commonsensical, house-wifely thing to do, an ordinary act . . . At some level you shamed your captors, and they did not compound their abuse of you by stripping you a second time. Yet they killed you. We only know your story because a sniggering man remembered how brave you were. Memorials to your courage are everywhere; they blow about in the streets and drift on the tide and cling to thorn-bushes. This dress is made from some of them. *Hambe kahle. Umkhonto* [Go well, Spear of the Nation].[26]

This epitaph commemorates Ndwandwe's struggle in two contrasting ways. On the one hand, her struggle against apartheid is extraordinary: she wrestles 'against the rulers of darkness' with the weapon of silence. On the other hand, Ndwandwe's act of resistance is ordinary: she shames her abusers through the 'frugal, commonsensical, house-wifely' way in which she makes clothing out of a plastic bag.

The contrast between grand and ordinary is also evident in the materiality of the artwork. *The Blue Dress* is 'monumental'[27] – a large, three-part installation. Yet, *The Blue Dress* is made from plastic bags, ubiquitous utilitarian items which pervade the South African landscape. The contrast between the extraordinary and the ordinary, the grand and the humble, embeds Ndwandwe's story in the heroic accounts of freedom fighters, at the same time that her mode of resistance speaks to the ways in which ordinary people battled apartheid brutality in everyday ways. In doing so, *The Blue Dress* 'calls

[24] Karin van Marle, Isolde De Villiers, and Eunette Beukes, 'Memory, Space and Gender: Reimagining the Law', *Southern African Public Law,* vol. 27, no. 2 (2012): 561. Also see Pumla Gobodo-Madikizela, Jennifer Fish, and Tamara Shefer, 'Gendered Violence: Continuities and Transformation in the Aftermath of Conflict in Africa', *Signs,* vol. 40, no. 1 (2014): 81–99.

[25] Judith Mason, 'The Man Who Sang and the Woman Who Kept Silent (Triptych) 1998', 2013, www.judithmason.com/assemblage/5_text.html.

[26] This epitaph is also recorded on a plaque which accompanies the installed artwork at the Court.

[27] Buikema, 'Monumental Dresses'.

for an engagement with survivors and victims that goes beyond the spectacular and looks for resistance in everyday acts instead'.[28]

The Blue Dress becomes a symbolic reparation. 'Symbolic reparations seek to recognise the wrongdoings and harm suffered by victims of human rights abuses.'[29] The bodiless dress is a haunting recognition of Ndwandwe's absence – of the harm she experienced, of her death. It is an attempt to restore the clothing Ndwandwe was previously deprived, a literal and symbolic redress.[30] Mason uses plastic bags to emphasize Ndwandwe's resistance to the violation of her bodily autonomy, and ultimately her life. In contrast to their material fragility, plastic bags become markers of Ndwandwe's defiance, of her courage, and of her strength. They are transformed from refuse into powerful sacred objects which not only commemorate Ndwandwe's struggle but symbolically restore her forced nakedness.

After hearing Ndwandwe's story, Mason describes feeling an 'abiding sense of shame' due to her identity as a white South African woman who benefitted from apartheid, but also because of her guilt at not doing more to help those who suffered under apartheid.[31] *The Blue Dress* is Mason's response to her shame – a way for the artist to acknowledge her role in the harm suffered by Ndwandwe. The reparative salience of the artwork is twofold: *The Blue Dress* recognises the abuse suffered by Ndwandwe; it is also Mason's acknowledgement of her involvement in that abuse – becoming a call for other beneficiaries of the apartheid system to do the same.

The full installation of *The Blue Dress* exists as a result of judicial intervention. *The Blue Dress* originally consisted of the dress and one painting in which a hyena appears to be tearing at the remains of the dress buried in the dirt. The second painting – in which a hyena is contained behind the fence, while candle-like objects glow in the foreground – was added at the behest of Justice Albie Sachs who felt the first two pieces would 'make people deeply depressed and distressed, and people come to the Court for succour, for a sense of relief, for protection'.[32] Consequently the second painting – dominated by the warm glow of flames – is intended to convey a 'sense of reconciliation, of coming to terms with the terrible pain of the past. The predator trapped in the fence, keeping it at bay, the dress soaring.'[33] The way in which the installation was created with direct judicial involvement highlights the normative position that

28 Nontsasa Nako, 'The Memory Market: Black Women's Stories and the Legacy of the South African TRC', in *Excavating Memory: Sites of Remembering and Forgetting*, ed. Maria Theresia Starzmann and John R. Roby (Gainesville: University of Florida Press, 2015), 284.

29 Simić and Volcic, 'In the Land of Wartime Rape: Bosnia, Cinema and Reparation,' 385.

30 See Kent Lindiwe Williams, 'Dress as a Site of Multiple Selves: Address and Redress in Judith Mason's *The Man Who Sang and the Woman Who Kept* Silent and Wanja Kimani's *You Have Not Changed*', *Image & Text*, vol. 29 (2017).

31 Mason in Albie Sachs, *The Strange Alchemy of Life and Law* (Oxford: Oxford University Press, 2009), viii.

32 Sachs in Mason, 'The Man Who Sang and the Woman Who Kept Silent (Triptych) 1998'.

33 Sachs in ibid.

a particular kind of uplifting and transformative art should be exhibited at the Court; at the same time, it raises questions about the power of members of the judicial and political elite to curate national imagination. This position implies that the art collection is being shaped by the Court in order to foster a transitional justice narrative where the pain of the past is transformed into the hope for a different future.

Although the artwork is intended to commemorate both Ndwandwe's and Sefola's deaths, the striking and repeated imagery of the blue dress makes Ndwandwe's story dominant. Unless viewers are familiar with the back-story of the installation or are informed by a guide when viewing the artwork, it is not necessarily clear that Sefola's story is represented in the paintings, beyond the artwork's title. This is reflected in how people at the Court – both visitors and staff – talk about the artwork, whereby the majority reference Ndwandwe but not Sefola. Of the twenty-two people who spoke about *The Blue Dress* during interviews, none mentioned Sefola's story.

The Blue Dress draws attention to Ndwandwe's story, keeping her acts of resistance alive in the space of the Court. Ndwandwe's story is a discursive memory for the people who work at the Court, but also for the people visiting it: 'The Blue Dress . . . I remember it struck such a chord when I did hear what happened and I have not forgotten about that.'[34] Several judges (four out of the six interviewed) spoke about *The Blue Dress* epitomising human dignity and the type of injustices the Court is trying to protect against – an artwork living in the 'judicial consciousness'[35] of the Court. This idea is particularly pertinent when considering *The Blue Dress* as a kind of visual jurisprudence (discussed in Chapter 6). The artwork lives in judicial consciousness as a reminder of things which must be prevented – Ndwandwe's rape and murder should never be repeated. It also contributes to a vision of human dignity – resistance against tyranny – which should be sustained. These two aspects instantiate an 'ethics of responsibility'[36] – that is, the responsibility to remember past violations of human dignity in order to prevent future ones and the responsibility to recognise past triumphs of human dignity in order to support future ones. In this way, the artwork embodies an entanglement where human dignity was violated on one level and achieved on another. Most importantly, the artwork calls for human dignity to be achieved again.

The second artwork which stands out as recognising the role of women is Sue Williamson's series of six prints, entitled *A Few South Africans* (Fig. 5.4). Part of a series of seventeen portraits – of which there are twenty editions in various major collections worldwide (including in the Tate Modern and the

[34] Visitor 5, lawyer from South Africa.

[35] 'Judicial consciousness' was a recurring phrase used by judges during interviews.

[36] Le roux makes the point that *The Blue Dress* institutes an ethics of responsibility by introducing a moment of alterity in constitutional jurisprudence, in Wessel Le Roux, 'Directory Provisions, Section 39 (2) of the Constitution and the Ontology of Statutory Law', *SA Publiekreg (SA Public Law),* vol. 21, no. 2 (2006): 400.

Figure 5.4 Sue Williamson, *A Few South Africans* (1984–1985), photo etching/silkscreen on paper, 121 x 97 cm, edition 6/95 (details).
Images courtesy of the artist and Goodman Gallery

Victoria and Albert Museum). These six prints depict images of Jeanette Curtis, Helen Joseph, Charlotte Maxeke, Virginia Mngoma, Caroline Motsoaledi, and Mamphela Ramphele. Each of these women were involved in different ways in the struggle against apartheid – as was Williamson. Curtis was involved in the black trade union movement; Joseph lead anti-apartheid protests; Maxeke was the first black South African woman to gain a university degree; Mngoma was an active member of the ANC; Motsoaledi was married to Rivonia Trialist Elias Motsoaledi who raised their seven children while he spent twenty-six years in prison; and Ramphele was one of the founders of the Black Consciousness Movement.[37]

For the artist, the series is 'about recognising people and giving people value as human beings'.[38] The series was intended 'to make visible the history of women involved in the struggle for freedom . . . At that time, the faces of these women almost never appeared in the popular press, and in white South Africa, little was known about them.'[39] Recognition plays a key role in the series. The prints portray an image and a face, so that people can be recognised, quite literally. The series is also about circulating these images. In addition to the

[37] For detailed descriptions, see Sue Williamson, 'A Few South Africans', www.sue-williamson.com/#!a-few-south-africans/cl06.

[38] Statement made in an interview with the author, attributed here with the consent of Sue Williamson, Artist.

[39] 'Sue Williamson', www.goodman-gallery.com/artists/suewilliamson.

fine-art editions of the prints, the portraits were printed as postcards, then disseminated both in South Africa and internationally. This was done during the 1980s, by way of circumventing the apartheid censorship of images of people involved in anti-apartheid activities.[40] The postcards functioned as 'little images of home', being a visual link for South Africans living in exile.[41] At the time of circulation, these postcards also gave the struggle a recognisable – and female – face: 'The feeling of the women is that I've [Williamson] taken their history out of the closet and put it on the walls for everyone to see.'[42] The prints continue to serve as a reminder of the roles of the women involved. However, like *The Blue Dress,* they raise important ethical questions about who has the ability to share people's stories, especially in the context of the South Africa; who benefits and who is empowered when these stories are shared in different forms?[43]

Recognition of personality is threefold in *A Few South Africans*. First, the prints are underpinned by a concern to insert missing images of women into South Africa's political history. They fill a representational void and interrogate the dominant narratives – or absent narratives – about the role of women in the struggle for freedom. They become an archive of heroines. Second, there is an element of didacticism in the prints which draws attention to the role that these women played, educating viewers in the process. Third, the prints celebrate the women: the boldly coloured and highly patterned backgrounds frame the women as icons; they are not monotone portraits which are easy to pass by. Williamson describes the backgrounds as referring 'to the way people in the squatter camps and townships elevated family snapshots to small artworks by framing these images with coloured paper cut with zig zag scissors'.[44] The rectangular positioning of the images which are topped by a semi-circle shape are also reminiscent of depictions of religious icons in the Christian tradition and of brightly painted *nichos*.

A Few South Africans occupies a central place outside the chambers of the Chief Justice, in the private area of the Court. This positioning is significant because it places the images of these women (both literally and metaphorically) at the heart of the Court's leadership – a curatorial reminder of their key significance. Despite the prints being unlabelled (they are not accompanied by explanatory notes), the women are recognisable figures to people who work at the Court. For one of Chief Justice Mogoeng's law clerks, Alexandra Fitzgerald, this is also deeply personal:

40 Other postcard series by Williamson were banned by the South African government in the 1980s; see Betty LaDuke, 'Sue Williamson: The Artist's Struggle toward Freedom in South Africa', *Journal of Social Theory in Art Education,* vol. 7 (1987): 41.

41 Statement made in an interview with the author, attributed here with the consent of Sue Williamson, Artist.

42 Williamson quoted in LaDuke, 'Sue Williamson,' 43.

43 Nako, 'The Memory Market', 284.

44 'Sue Williamson'.

> On my first day I realised when we went into the Chief Justice's office that outside his office is a collage print and it is Jenny Curtis and also her daughter. I was instantly like 'oh my goodness' because I have been starring at that picture nearly all my life ... she was my godfather's wife, she was unfortunately assassinated before I was born.[45]

It is noteworthy that these images are hung away from public view. In a sense, this perpetuates a degree of absenteeism of these women from the anti-apartheid narrative of heroism, working against Williamson's intention to make visible the history of women involved in the struggle.

Notably absent from the art collection are paintings of current or former judges. Portraits of judges are limited to black-and-white photographs – approximately 20 × 30 cm in size – which hang innocuously in a tight grid near the entrance to the main chamber, obscured by several columns. These portraits function more as administrative images or as proof of identity – they are accompanied by nametags – and are somewhat disconnected and only an adjunct to the art collection. This visual downplaying of judicial personality was a deliberate action by the first generation of judges who decided that having formally painted portraits of judges – a common sight in most courts – worked against the Court's role in challenging conventional notions of power and hierarchy.

The recognition of personality – particular historical figures – is captured mainly in artworks; however, several artists interviewed also spoke about having their voices recognised by being in the collection. Having an artwork in the collection was seen as a way of participating in South Africa's new democracy:

> I had to find a way to contribute without me being on a podium to deliver a speech because I might not have that chance [as an artist], so I had to come up with creative ways to let people know what I think of democracy and how we can achieve [it], by making sure that we follow the popular means of discussions, spreading of the word.[46]
>
> I was a product of the iniquitous system of Apartheid, a privileged white. It took many years of personal struggle to become politically conscientised and then to navigate a pathway to attempt an adequate response to my circumstance. Once one becomes aware of important social issues particularly where exploitation is apparent, it is then socially negligent not to respond on a humanist level and, in my case as an artist, with appropriate work.[47]

On the one hand, artistic participation in the Court is a way for artists to be involved in the democratic process. This view connects with the emphasis

[45] Statement made in an interview with the author, attributed here with the consent of Alexandra Fitzgerald, Law Clerk.

[46] Artist 5.

[47] Artist 6.

placed on civic participation as a means of realising equality in the space of the Court (discussed previously in Chapter 4). On the other hand, artistic participation is a way for some artists to respond to their complicity in the apartheid system. This view was shared by several artists in the collection and is particularly relevant to artworks which function as symbolic reparations, such as Mason's *The Blue Dress* or even Williamson's portraits. It may also explain in part why the public art gallery at the Court has many artworks that explicitly address the apartheid past, which are by artists who would have been beneficiaries of the apartheid system.

Several people interviewed (none of them artists) also suggested that for less well-known artists being represented in the collection was a boost to their reputation:

> Albie's attitude to a large extent was 'isn't that kind of them [artists] to donate to us? We would be rude to say no.' But you know they [the artists] are getting more out of this than we are getting out of it . . . some of these artists should not be in this collection.[48]

While having an artwork in the collection is understood by artists and the majority of interviewees as a way to contribute to the project of justice and a way of being politically responsive, it is also perceived by a small number of people as being motivated by self-interest. Artists exhibited in the collection become recognised through their artworks, both for their participation and for their reputational capital.

The recognition of personality within artworks and across the collection plays an important role in shaping the transitional justice narrative of the Court: one which both memorialises and reinscribes important figures in the anti-apartheid struggles, while simultaneously fostering new forms of political participation.

Recognising Community

Outside the judges' meeting room hangs Kim Lieberman's *Constellations* (2008), depicting small silhouettes of people who have moved through the space of the Court, connected by silk thread. Some of the silhouettes are recognisable as familiar figures involved in the Court (such as former judges) while other silhouettes (not necessarily as instantly recognisable) are given equal prominence in the artwork. Below each figure is a faint label in pencil, recording their name and title. *Constellations* is a visual representation of the Court community, a literal web of human connections, which reflects (serendipitously) a passage written by Justice Sachs describing the Court: '[R]elationships on the Court are so intricate that each individual profoundly

[48] Curator 4.

affects the total dynamic . . . ideas emerge like strands of silk from the bodies and minds and personalities of each one of us.'[49]

The recognition of community is a dominant theme in the art collection. It emerges both through the recognition of defined communities – segments of society – as well as through an implied universal community – humanity, such as Ndlovu's *Humanity* mentioned in Chapter 3. For instance, *Body Map* (Fig. 5.5) is a series of fourteen limited-edition fine-art prints created by the Bambanani Women's Group in Khayelitsha township, Cape Town; each body map is a self-portrait created by a woman who is HIV positive. The maps are accompanied by detailed first-person statements which describe what the different elements within each image represent: 'One day I went to my boyfriend to sleep with him and my stepfather hit me and stabbed me with a screwdriver. He stabbed me here on my left wrist you can see on my body map.'[50]

Body mapping is a form of art therapy intended as a communication tool to express painful and traumatic experiences. It is also often used as an advocacy tool to bring attention to the issue of HIV/AIDS, particularly in South Africa. Emerging from one workshop within a project called Long Life, stories of women (participating in a *Medécins Sans Frontières* pilot antiretroviral programme) were recorded as body maps, intended to help women come to terms with their diagnosis.[51] At the time of the workshop in 2002, antiretroviral drugs were not available through public health centres – a position the Court sought to change when it ruled on access to HIV/AIDS treatment and the right to health care, requiring the government to provide access to health services for pregnant women to combat the transmission of HIV from mother to child.[52]

Unlike other artworks by professional artists which bear witness to events, these artworks by non-professional artists provide testimony about injustice.[53] The *Body Map* series portrays a defined community of women who were HIV positive and all living in the same geographical location. In the context of the Court, these works draw attention to both the practice and subject of justice.

[49] Albie Sachs and Vanessa September, *The Free Diary of Albie Sachs* (Johannesburg: Random House, 2004), 176–177. Although the artwork was created four years after this passage was published, Lieberman did not discover the passage until she read the book in 2013; Kim Lieberman, e-mail communication to the author, 18 September 2014.

[50] Thomaza Ndevu, 'Body Maps', 2002, https://ccac.org.za/thozama-ndevu-body-maps-2009-0037/.

[51] Bambanani Women's Group, 'Background History of the Bambanani Women's Group', www.memorybox.co.za/index.php?option=com_content&task=view&id=12&Itemid=53.

[52] See Constitutional Court of South Africa, 'Minister of Health and Others v Treatment Action Campaign and Other', in *Case No. CCT 8/02* (2002).

[53] Milton distinguishes between the role of professional and non-professional artists in relation to injustice in Cynthia E. Milton, 'Images of Truth: Rescuing Memories of Peru's Internal War through Testimonial Art', in *Art from a Fractured Past: Memory and Truth-Telling in Post-Shining Path Peru,* ed. Cynthia E. Milton (Duke University Press: Durham, 2014), 37–74.

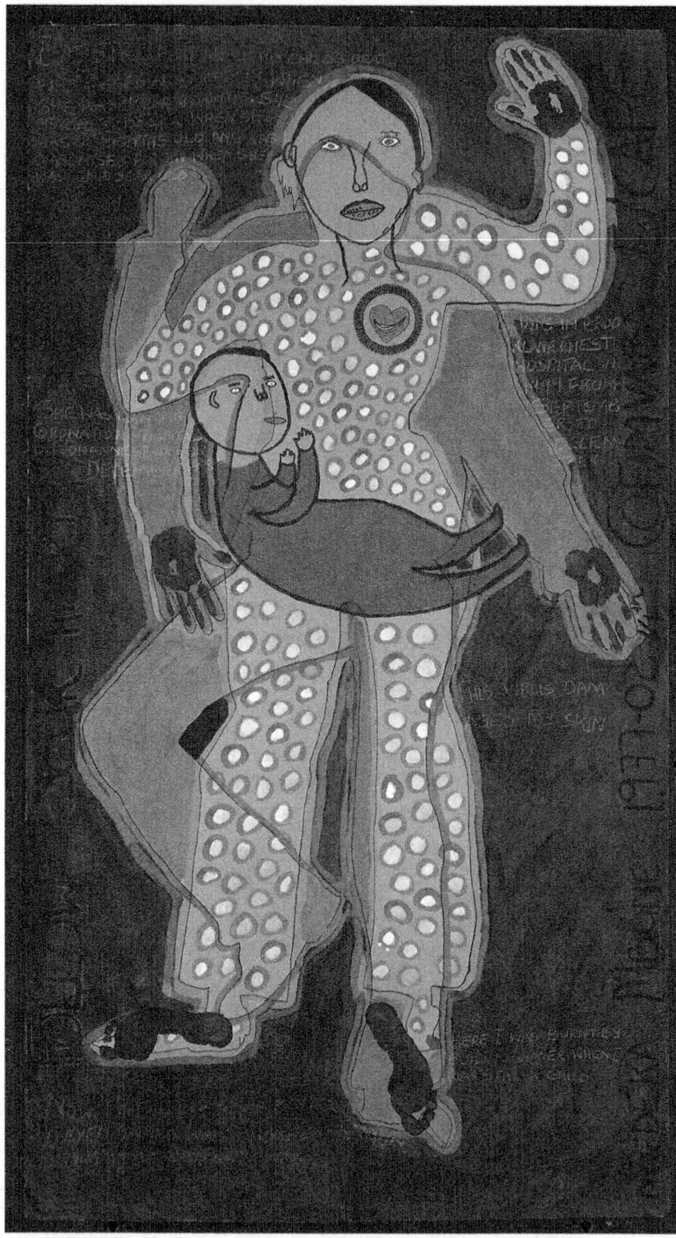

Figure 5.5 Ncedeka Mbune, *Body Maps* (2002), digital print on paper, 74 × 41 cm.
Image courtesy of the Bambanani Women's Group, South Africa

The series is hung in the public art gallery, and nearby is a billboard created by the Court to describe five landmark cases – one of which concerns the right to health care and HIV/AIDS treatment. There is a direct visual connection between the practice of justice enacted by the Court and the *Body Map* series which envisages the subject of that justice. The recognition of this defined

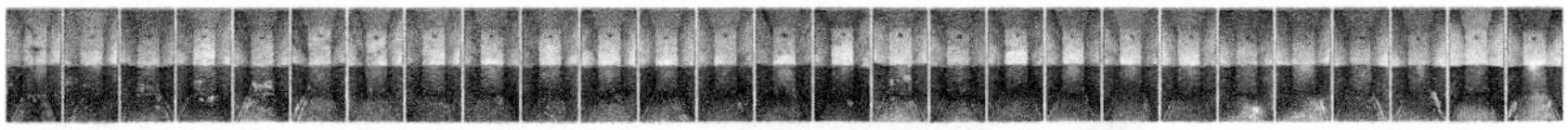

Figure 5.6 David Goldblatt, *Twenty-Six Punishment Cells and Lavatory. Number Four, Hillbrow, Johannesburg. 31 December 1999* (1999), photographic print on cotton paper, 25 × 350 cm. Photograph by David Goldblatt, supplied by Goodman Gallery

community gives a human face to the Court's decisions – portraying who is the subject of judgment and the purpose served.

Another artwork that stands out in regard to defined communities is David Goldblatt's *Twenty-Six Punishment Cells and Lavatory. Number Four, Hillbrow, Johannesburg. 31 December 1999* (Fig. 5.6), which depicts photographs of the isolation cells at Number Four prison (adjacent to the Court). The images are bleak, monotone, and empty. The repeated images of cells are sandwiched together to form one long and almost abstracted image. The complete work is over three metres in length – which is longer than the longest wall of a single isolation cell.

The cells represent a defined community – that of prisoners, specifically prisoners once incarcerated at Number Four and, at a more general level, prisoners subjected to solitary confinement. The representation of these cells in the Court is particularly significant considering that the original cells are approximately 50 m from where the artwork hangs. Goldblatt's photographs project the former prison directly into the Court. This projection takes on heightened significance given the location of the artwork; *Twenty-Six Punishment Cells* hangs in the corridor the judges and law clerks use to enter the court chamber. Each time a person traverses this corridor, they are confronted by the cells as a reminder of the injustices of the past penal system but also a warning against the failings of the present system. Importantly, this defined community is not necessarily a remote subject of justice. Some of the judges who have served on the bench of the Constitutional Court have at one time themselves been incarcerated as political prisoners, with some placed in isolation cells. Former Deputy Chief Justice Dikgang Moseneke was imprisoned for ten years on Robben Island at the same time as Mandela; former Justice Albie Sachs was held in isolation cells on multiple occasions.[54] This defined community is also a direct subject of justice; in 1999, the Court held that prisoners maintained the right to vote while incarcerated.[55]

As a touchstone of South Africa's new constitutional democracy, human dignity is emphasised in Goldblatt's work by its antithesis. By documenting the desolate inhumanity of the isolation cells, Goldblatt's photographs

[54] The curator on tours of the art collection emphasises that some of the judges have been incarcerated. See also Albie Sachs, *Jail Diary of Albie Sachs* (London: Sphere Books, 1969).

[55] Constitutional Court of South Africa, 'August and Another v Electoral Commission and Others', in *Case No. CCT 8/99* (1999).

Figure 5.7 Dumile Feni, *History* (1987/2003), bronze, cast by Tallix. Photography by Akona Kenqu, 2014.

implicitly urge the viewer not to lose sight of human dignity. That this image is located at the private judicial entrance to the Court chamber serves as a well-crafted reminder of this touchstone for the people who protect it the most. The art collection shifts from judicial consciousness to judicial confrontation.

Through these images of defined communities, the art collection circumscribes the subject of justice at the Court. Other artworks within the collection speak to a wider universal community, a cosmopolitan view of humanity which underpins the Court and the Constitution. Outside the main entrance to the Court sits a large bronze sculpture made up of four figures. The largest of the figures rests on all fours like an animal with a bit between its teeth. The man is strapped to a cart, pulling the other figures along. On the cart crouches another figure, on which two other figures sit – a woman (indicated by her bare breasts) and a man (implied by a bowler hat). At first encounter this sculpture – entitled *History* by Dumile Feni (Fig. 5.7) – resonates 'with the history of servitude that marked the dehumanizing institution of apartheid'.[56] The sculpture appears as a visual metaphor for the subjugated majority whose labour supported the dominant minority: the man is yoked to the cart, dragging its occupants. *History* provokes questions about the relationships between the figures and the relationship of the sculpture to the Court – why does the Court have a sculpture that references oppression outside its main entrance?

[56] Cameron and Sachs, World Policy Blog.

The figures share similar abstracted and exaggerated features; they appear to be of the same 'racial' origin. This complicates the initial reading of the artwork as a slave–master dynamic, especially in the context of South Africa where oppression has historically been divided along racial lines. *History* – as it looms large in its current state outside the Court – was cast in 2003 from a small marquette that Feni originally made in 1987, before his death in 1991. According to Sachs – to whom Feni gave the marquette – the artist intended the sculpture to illustrate 'how throughout history some people had given their bodies and souls to pull others along'.[57] On tours the curator extends this explanation to provide an interpretation of the artwork as a characterisation of universal human relationships, a sentiment echoed by the Court:

> The man drawing the cart is the only figure who is large and strong enough to accomplish this task . . . the four figures carry each other in a way that reflects the dependence, the interconnectedness, and the tension that have always characterized human relationships.[58]

At its most obvious, *History* represents the history of oppression in South Africa. However, the sculpture can also be interpreted as representing the manner in which humans have carried one another throughout history. A third interpretation reveals how the sculpture communicates multiple ideas about human relationships. Human participation is a central concern of the artwork, but not one that can be identified unequivocally. *History* captures a certain complexity in human relationships. Each figure within the artwork plays a role through which their value is visually recognised. However, this value is complicated by the implications of power that underscore the image of subjugation and labour. The recognition of humanity – the common (as opposed to defined) community captured in the artwork – remains circumscribed by the inherent intricacies and dynamics of human relationships; individual and collective agencies are in tension.

The dark bronze form of *History*, installed outside the Court, also positions it as a kind of monument – simultaneously celebrating humanity while confronting viewers to think more deeply about the balances of power and structures of dominance that have underscored, and continue to underscore, human relationships (especially in South Africa where the dominance of the 'haves' over the 'have-nots' remains palpable). While *History* is a sign announcing the new Court, it also challenges the Court to uphold human dignity in the face of ongoing structural injustices that inhibit the equalising right to human dignity stipulated in the Constitution.[59]

[57] Law-Viljoen and Law-Viljoen, *Art and Justice*, 193.

[58] Cameron and Sachs, World Policy Blog.

[59] The Bill of Rights says, 'Everyone has inherent dignity and the right to have their dignity respected and protected' in Constitutional Assembly; 'The Constitution'.

Figure 5.8 Installation view of Marlene Dumas, *The Benefit of the Doubt* (2000) (detail), triptych, fibre, 198 × 107 cm, 198 × 107 cm, 198 × 742 cm.
Photography by Akona Kenqu, 2014

Inside the main foyer of the Court hangs Marlene Dumas's *The Benefit of the Doubt* (Fig. 5.8). A series of three large horizontal tapestries, this work depicts eight close-up human faces around a central figure who is intended to embody liberty.[60] Dumas unusually portrays liberty as a young girl who appears to be shrugging her shoulders, rather than the more conventional portrayal of liberty as a heroic woman leading the people, such as in Eugéne Delacroix's *Liberty Leading the People*. Through this portrayal, Dumas appears 'to temper "the sexual power that is so characteristic of women that personify abstractions" in societies which accord them no real power'.[61] At the same time, this youthful figure appears quite androgynous, implicating freedom in a less gendered story.

In the context of the Court – where the tapestries hang at ceiling height on opposite walls, rather than together in a continuous triptych as originally intended – the figure of liberty is subsumed against the dominance of the large and slightly abstracted faces which appear within the three tapestries. The faces present a spectrum of feeling in which, as the title suggests, doubt is implicated in a narrative of ambiguity about guilt and innocence. The facial expressions are a mixture between austere, resigned, and pensive; closed eyes, direct stares, and sidelong glances are disconcerting in their uncertainty: the faces 'evoke an immediate and powerful sense of responsibility towards

[60] Marlene Dumas and Emma Bedford, *Marlene Dumas: Intimate Relations*, ed. Standard Bank Art Gallery (Johannesburg: Roma Publications, 2007), 39.

[61] D. van der Boorgerd in ibid., 40.

these unknown strangers ... [but they are also] completely decontextualised and therefore provide no starting point from which any concrete legal or moral response can be formulated'.[62] Doubt emerges from the gap between the faces being represented and the law under which they are implied subjects.

The Benefit of the Doubt is particularly significant for the political relationship it embodies. While the imagery presents a wider and more universal view of humanity, the artwork itself is embedded in the political structures of Dutch colonial rule and their influence on successive South African governments. The tapestries are a duplicate set of those originally designed for, and installed in, The Palace of Justice in the Dutch town of Den Bosch. In 2001, the prime minister of the Netherlands, Wim Kok, gifted a duplicate set to the Constitutional Court. The tapestries loom large inside the Court: it is almost as if the Dutch government is – as the artwork's title suggests – asking for the benefit of the doubt. International relations seep into the Court through the Dumas artwork, implicating the deliverance of justice in South Africa to a wider political circle.

The emphasis on shared humanity within the art collection is driven by both internal narratives of reconciliation within South Africa – unity in diversity – and external acts of inclusion. This is reflected in how people associated with the Court talk about the collection:

> The art collection is a recognition of the importance of the human spirit ... I mean the Constitutional Court is about human rights and it's about recognising the human rights of all of us within the constitution of the country. And you know that all the different artworks at the Constitutional Court obviously come from [a] great many different kind of artists and people: women, men, races, upbringings ... that's a very important thing to have there.[63]
>
> I like to think of the visual aspect of the court – being the collection – as not something which is pinned to any particular phase in our history but to serve as a reminder more generally to the potential for evil that exists within [hu]man and therefore within society. But on the other hand, to also serve as a reminder of the aspirations and the ideals and the high hopes and the dreams of more noble and higher things, but not in a way that it is sort of almost isolated within a particular historical context.[64]

The recognition of community – both defined and common – combined with the recognition of personality, reveals a reoccurring shift in the art collection: the shift from the individual to the collective; what it means to recognise the personal and the universal; and the differences and the similarities. The oscillation between the two constitutes a vision of community, where existence is inseparable from coexistence; specific historic figures are embedded in wider human narratives, while individuals are connected to wider communities. Through the art collection, the Court expands its understanding of humanity

[62] Le Roux, 'Designs of the Times,' 64.
[63] Artist 21.
[64] Art committee member 2.

to those who were previously excluded. This oscillation is indicative of an ethic of *ubuntu* (humanness) at the Court; that is, an ethic of communal existence.[65] Many people interviewed used ubuntu interchangeably with humanity.

In the art collection the politics of difference meets the politics of cosmopolitanism so that collective justice is probed by individual expectations. This means that appeals to a shared humanity which risk 'closing down analysis of the structures that continue to reproduce inequalities' are mediated by recognition of differences, such as gender or ethnicity, 'on which mobilisations against injustice commonly depend'.[66] There is simultaneous recognition in the art collection of conceptions of justice on a universal level (for example, everyone is equal and belongs to the same humanity) and practices of justice on specific levels (in order to realise equality and everyone's humanity, prevailing inequalities need to be addressed). This recognition is important because it draws attention to how the impossibility of attaining universal justice is what drives justice practices and the enactment of human rights in particular contexts. Considering the discrepancies between the shared humanity projected by some artworks and the ongoing violence and exploitation outside the walls of the Court, this recognition is crucial.

Recognising Temporality

The third narrative about recognition which emerges from the art collection is about time. Unlike the previous narratives about personality and community, the recognition of temporality is not about the human, but rather about shifts and transformations: where the past is brought into the present to imagine a different future. Thus, the 'arts' reference backwards and forwards and to the present.[67]

Several artworks in the collection make this recognition explicit. Boshoff's *Prison Sentences* marks the fluid metric of years in solid granite; the passing of time is transformed into something more permanent. Sipho Ndlovu's *Images of South African History* (Fig. 5.9) uses cartoon-style imagery to chart four periods in South Africa's modern history, almost as if each panel summarises a

65 The word 'ubuntu' translates from the Nguni languages roughly as humanness. As a philosophy, ubuntu is an ethic of communal existence, which means, 'I realise my humanity only when I realise yours', or put another way, 'a person is a person through other people'; see Spencer Wolff, 'Human Dignity and Freedom of Speech in the Post Apartheid State', *Macquarie Law Journal,* vol. 13 (2014): 106; Thaddeus Metz, 'Ubuntu as a Moral Theory and Human Rights in South Africa', *African Human Rights Law Journal,* vol. 11, no. 2 (2011), 532–559. The Court 'regularly emphasise[s] the overlap between ubuntu, rights articulated in the Constitution, and emerging international legal norms'; Chuma Himonga, Max Taylor, and Anne Pope, 'Reflections on Judicial Views of Ubuntu', *PER: Potchefstroomse Elektroniese Regsblad,* vol. 16, no. 5 (2013): 7.

66 Anne Phillips, 'Global Justice: Just Another Modernisation Theory?', in *Empire, Race, and Global Justice,* ed. Duncan Bell (Cambridge: Cambridge University Press, 2019), 5.

67 Artist 4.

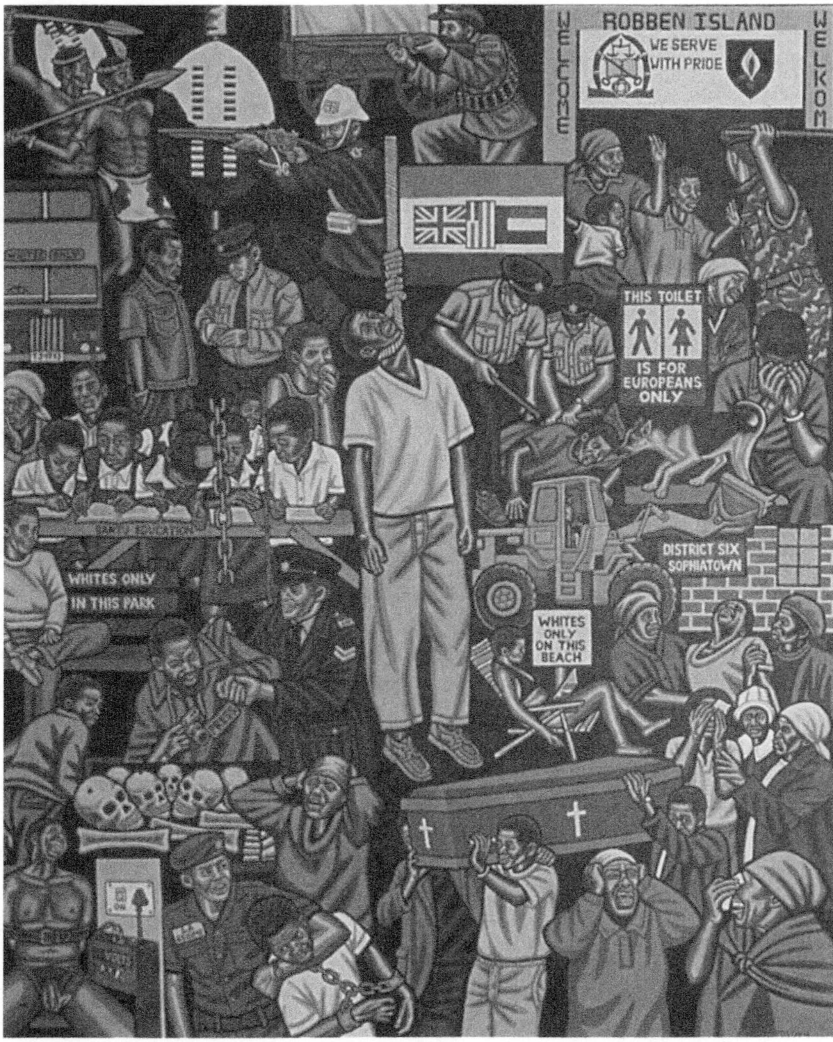

Figure 5.9 Sipho Ndlovu, *Images of South African History* (1998), four panels, acrylic on canvas, each 152 × 121 cm (detail). Image courtesy of the artist and the Constitutional Court Trust.

history lesson. The panels move from the graphic content of torture, death, violence, and protests to dancing, democratic elections, and sporting achievements, together charting the shifts between the colonial, the apartheid, and the post-apartheid eras. Ndlovu overtly combines a sense of the political with the temporal: time is marked by political acts, and over time, these acts are themselves politicised. These works hang outside the entrance to the Court's internal archive, as if they are signs of what is inside.

Figure 5.10 Remaining portion of the Awaiting Trial Block staircase inside the foyer of the Constitutional Court of South Africa, featuring (left) Georgia Papageorge, *Through the Barrier - 1956 Treason Trial Freeze and Ladder* (2003), mixed media, (wood, bone, metal, photographs, oil paint); (right) Thomas Mulcaire, *A luta continua* (2007), neon tubing, 40 × 400 cm. Photograph courtesy of the Constitutional Court Trust.

The temporal is also evoked in more subtle ways. Georgia Papageorge's *Through the Barrier – 1956 Treason Trial Freeze and Ladder* and Thomas Mulcaire's *A luta continua* (Fig. 5.10) together dominate the Court's entrance foyer. Installed against the remaining part of the Awaiting Trial Block, the artworks appear as new addition on an old wall – where the original prison graffiti contrasts with the polished art.

The red neon lights of *A luta continua* spell out the words of the title, reminiscent of the glow of a red-light district, or in the South African context, of a fish-and-chip shop.[68] It introduces an unusual set of visual references within the site. *A luta continua* translates from Portuguese as 'the struggle continues', a phrase widely used by the Mozambique Liberation Front (FRELIMO) in the 1960s and 1970s as the nation struggled for independence. This phrase continues to be used in anti-oppression campaigns across Southern Africa.

For Mulcaire, the artwork references the direct support of people from Mozambique in the struggle against apartheid 'on the ground in South Africa; in the trade union movements'.[69] At the same time, the artist intends *A luta continua* to be a kind of resistance to the contemporary xenophobia 'prevalent in the early 2000s where Mozambicans were being killed for taking work of

[68] On tours of the art collection the curator pointed out the fish-and-chip shop reference.

[69] Statement made in an interview with the author, attributed here with the consent of Thomas Mulcaire, Artist.

South Africans supposedly'.[70] *A luta continua* retains this past connection with the liberation history of neighbouring Mozambique, but it also implicates South Africa's own freedom struggles as incomplete and ongoing; casting a glow over an unsettling trajectory, where once welcomed internal support has shifted to an unwelcomed external interference. As in many of the other artworks in the collection (and throughout this book), there is an internal–external narrative at work. *A luta continua* makes reference to the past in order to calibrate the present: a kind of pulsing between what was and what is in order to recognise what should and should not be.

At the entrance to the Court chamber the artwork has the more immediate effect of signposting the deliberative space of justice inside:

> One of the ideals for our Constitution is that it's a working project . . . that's why we have the Constitutional Court, so that they could, if necessary, amend the Constitution. And the idea of putting up the struggle slogan [*A luta continua*] into the very entrance of the Constitutional Court . . . it's quite a representation of the values of the Constitution, but on another hand it's quite tongue in cheek because the fact that it's in neon lights gives me the sense that it's almost sarcastic . . . it is quite ostentatious, and that speaks to the way we think about the country and the early years of democracy it was like, 'rainbow nation, come to South Africa, we've worked it all out, we're over apartheid', but not really, the struggle does indeed continue.[71]
>
> It never actually ends because justice is something that always has to be upheld . . . the artwork speaks of that because . . . it's admitting that we're not there yet. It's not going this is the solution, it's saying that this Court is like a mode to keep going or a vehicle.[72]

This unresolved question speaks to the very heart of South Africa's transition, an acknowledgement that the process is problematic and ongoing.

Next to *A luta continua* stands Georgia Papageorge's *Through the Barrier – 1956 Treason Trial Freeze and Ladder*. While the title of the artwork relates directly to the 1956 Treason Trial (in which 156 people were accused of treason), the sculpture – specifically the ladder, rather than the accompanying freezes which are hidden at its base – presents symbolic associations about the journey to democracy: climbing over barriers. As the giant ladder ascends upwards, the rungs move from hurdles to hopes – from barbed wire, bars, and chains which symbolise oppression to an elephant bone and a chevron pattern which symbolise memory and infinity, respectively.[73] The ladder evokes a sense of movement, a narrative journey – an idea reinforced by the Christian metaphor of climbing towards the heavens.

70 Statement made in an interview with the author, attributed here with the consent of Thomas Mulcaire, Artist.

71 Curator 3.

72 Visitor 8, university student from South Africa.

73 Symbolism of the rungs is outlined in the artist's statement in the Court archive.

These artworks mark transitional time – 'a time which incorporates the paradoxical condition of being something that has both been already, but that is not anymore, and not been yet, but still to come'.[74] That is, the artworks recognise a *past* past (one that has happened) and a *future* past (one that is yet to happen). By doing so, they not only bring the past into the present in order to imagine the future, but they also bring the future into the present in order to imagine the past. In other words, the prospect of what is still to come is circumscribed by what went before, and what went before is calibrated by the prospect of something else to come.

The three narratives about recognition which emerge out of the art collection shape the appearance of justice at the Court, drawing attention to the actors of justice (recognition of personality), subjects of justice (recognition of communities), and the purpose of justice (recognition of temporality). They posit a vision of justice as something that arises out of the past and must be worked on continuously towards the future. The artworks serve as reminders of past violations and injustices underscored by a norm of non-repetition: 'It is only because and as long as we acknowledge the permanent fact of our responsibility to the victims of the past that our search for an appropriate constitutional response can have any ethical value.'[75] Through recognition and acknowledgement, the art collection positions justice as an ongoing process which sits in contrast with the static nature of the site of the Court, where its spatial transformation constitutes an intentional realisation of justice in time and space – a utopian charge discussed in the next chapter. This tension is important in understanding and calibrating what justice means and what it brings with it to the transitioning human rights discourse in South Africa.

[74] Claudio Corradetti, 'Transitional Times, Reflective Judgement and the "Hōs mē" Condition', in *Theorizing Transitional Justice*, ed. Claudio Corradetti, Nir Eisikovits, and Jack Volpe Rotondi (Oxford: Routledge, 2015), 188.

[75] Le Roux, 'War Memorials', 82.

6

The Visual Jurisprudence of Transition

> The more you know about art, philosophy, religions of the world, and psychology, the better you are as a lawyer.[1]

> The artworks do something in relation to the work of the Court, of the Constitution. When you read them in that context, they have value and they have meaning that relates back to the Constitution.[2]

> Art and justice perform different functions which often strive towards similar goals, especially when the goal is healing or transformation.[3]

> Art is also ingrained in the thinking of the Court ... it wasn't just hanging a picture on the wall about justice.[4]

> What the artworks do is – for me – they delineate our Court, they give it a character, they give it a kind of direction wittingly or unwittingly, and they influence the judgements which we give.[5]

The material interventions discussed in Chapter 4 – relating to accessibility, equality, dignity, freedom of expression, and justice under a tree – reflect the content of justice under consideration at the Constitutional Court: namely, the principles of moral agency embedded within the institutionalisation of a global human rights culture in a vernacular of South African national identity. The narratives about recognition – recognising personality, community, and temporality – in Chapter 5 draw attention to the subjects of justice; to whom or to what does justice apply. These are political and moral identities, circumscribed by narratives of transition. This chapter concerns the *how* of justice at the Court: the ways in which justice is located and expressed. I extend the physical location of justice (already discussed through the transformation of the site of the Court in Chapter 3) by explicitly locating justice in the art collection as a kind of visual jurisprudence.

[1] Judge 6.
[2] Curator 3.
[3] Law clerk 2 from the United States.
[4] Visitor 8, university student from South Africa.
[5] Judge 4.

Jurisprudence derives from the Latin phrase *juris prudentia,* meaning the knowledge, study, or science of law. While jurisprudence is broadly understood as the theory or philosophy of law, it is also often used to refer to a body of law, such as the constitutional jurisprudence of a particular country; a branch of law, such as human rights jurisprudence; and the decisions of courts, such as the Constitutional Court's jurisprudence. All of these uses go into shaping jurisprudence as a term which encompasses both the *values and principles* behind law, as well as the *practices and applications* of law. In considering visual jurisprudence, both these aspects are important.

Areas of legal scholarship which examine the visual most often take one of two approaches.[6] Either, first exploring problems associated with legal visuality: that is, how some images encourage belief through an appearance of being authentic.[7] For example, an eyewitness account 'may assert that the photograph corresponds to her memory without realizing that, even as she speaks, her memory is being sculpted by the photograph'.[8] Or second, by examining images of and about law: that is, how images represent the law and can be used to understand the law. For example, images of capital punishment in colonial Australia served to represent and communicate a principle of law at the time – that the crime of murder would be punished by death. From a historical perspective, these images can also be used to explore how this principle was applied differently due to racial discrimination.[9]

In post-apartheid South Africa, constitutional scholarship has undergone an aesthetic turn which expands the second approach to the visual in law: using aesthetic examples to not only represent but also to interrogate the law, to recast 'rights discourse in a critical light and to expose its fundamental assumptions'.[10] This scholarship explores individual artworks and literary works as illustrations and analogies of the law, and also uses them to enliven debate and comment on the law's shortcomings. For example, Mason's *The Blue Dress* has been discussed as a symbol of the new constitutional order; a symbol of how memory instantiates responsibility.[11] *The Blue Dress* has also

[6] For an overview of visual legal scholarship, see Costas Douzinas and Lynda Nead, *Law and the Image: The Authority of Art and the Aesthetics of Law* (Chicago: University of Chicago Press, 1999); Leif Dahlberg, ed. *Visualizing Law and Authority: Essays on Legal Aesthetics, Law and Literature* (Berlin: De Gruyter, 2012); Anne Wagner and Richard K Sherwin, eds., *Law, Culture and Visual Studies* (Dordrecht: Springer, 2014).

[7] See, for instance, Katherine Biber, *Captive Images: Race, Crime, Photography* (Cavendish: Routledge, 2007).

[8] Neal Feigenson, 'The Visual in Law: Some Problems for Legal Theory', *Law, Culture and the Humanities,* vol. 10, no. 1 (2014): 2.

[9] Desmond Manderson, 'The Law of the Image and the Image of the Law: Colonial Representations of the Rule of Law', *New York Law School Law Review,* vol. 57 (2012).

[10] Wessel Le Roux, 'The Aesthetic Turn in the Post-Apartheid Constitutional Rights Discourse', *Journal of South African Law* (2006): 108.

[11] Le Roux, 'Directory Provisions,' 400.

been used as an example through which to question and critique the formalism of this constitutional order.[12]

Both approaches to the visual in law – encouraging belief and representing and interrogating what the law means – share the idea that visuality has the potential to engender understanding either when used as evidence to support an argument and prove responsibility or when used to communicate the nature of law. Understanding, then, is created by the probity of visuals in some contexts (such as evidence in the courtroom) and by the application of visuals to other contexts (such as metaphors to elucidate legal arguments).

However, these burgeoning areas of legal scholarship make little to no reference to the concept of visual jurisprudence. The phrase 'visual jurisprudence' is a relatively recent one, conceived of as the 'array of visual evidence and visual argument'[13] used *inside* the courtroom. The concept is used to examine the proliferation of visual media – particularly screen imagery – in the law, exploring what it means for visuals to be seen as credible. This connects back to the problem of legal visuality (the first approach to visuals in law discussed above). Scholarship on visual jurisprudence also advocates visual-literacy training for lawyers, judges, and jurors so that visuals are better understood and utilised in procedures of law.[14] This conception of visual jurisprudence is largely a pragmatic response to an increasingly optic age, arising from the premise that visuals are more widely becoming part of legal decision-making processes, and therefore people involved in those processes need to be visually literate.

The idea of visual jurisprudence that I propose differs in two distinct ways from the purely visual as evidence or argument. First, I take as my starting point – as I do throughout the book – the inherent subjectivity of the world of visual art, which embodies a dynamic complexity and potential. In the context of the Court, the presence of the art collection, and the integration of art into the fabric of the building, is a unique instance of a large body of artworks being closely connected to, and blended with, the value and practice of justice (two tenets of jurisprudence mentioned above). This is a clear departure from the aesthetic turn in post-apartheid constitutional scholarship which uses single artworks to represent or illustrate claims about the law. In this scholarship artworks still remain on the periphery of justice as examples through which to understand the law, rather than as constituent parts of its value and practice. The art collection of the Court is central in forming the bodies of aesthetic knowledge that shape (a) how justice is understood (value) and (b) the

12 van Marle, De Villiers, and Beukes, 'Memory, Space and Gender.'

13 Richard K. Sherwin, 'Visual Jurisprudence', *New York Law School Law Review*, vol. 57, no. 11 (2012): 12. Other areas use the term 'visual law'; see, for example, Colette R Brunschwig, 'On Visual Law: Visual Legal Communication Practices and Their Scholarly Exploration', in *Zeichen und Zauber des Rechts: Festschrift für Friedrich Lachmayer*, ed. Erich Schweihofer et al. (Bern: Editions Weblaw, 2014).

14 Sherwin, 'Visual Jurisprudence'; Richard K Sherwin, *Visualizing Law in the Age of the Digital Baroque: Arabesques and Entanglements* (Oxford: Routledge, 2011).

appearance of justice in South Africa (practice). Chapter 4 about the transformation of symbolic intentions through material interventions and Chapter 5 on narratives about recognition addressed these claims, respectively.

Taking the Court's art as the specific starting point leads me to the second distinction, that visual jurisprudence is not restricted to what happens – or what is seen – inside the courtroom. My argument is that visual jurisprudence is as much about a way of conceiving justice as it is about its procedural provision. In other words, visual jurisprudence revolves around how visuality affects the thinking of law not only by engendering belief and understanding inside the courtroom or in legal scholarship but also by engaging the moral imagination, 'the capacity to imagine something rooted in the challenges of the real world' *outside* the courtroom.[15] This is not only bound to legal space but is also an orientation towards a philosophy of the visual in law, an orientation which began through the physical and symbolic transformation of the site of justice outlined in Chapter 3 and is continued below via two substantive claims about the instruction and affect of art which arose at the Court.

This idea of engaging the moral imagination through art intersects with the debate in human rights scholarship over whether moral discourse or sentimental education is more effective in promoting respect for human rights. The moral discourse of human rights reasons that all humans are the same, and therefore human rights should apply to everyone. This is a universalist premise – shared humanity is the basis for a moral obligation to respect the rights of all humans.[16] In contrast, sentimental education 'acquaints people of different kinds with one another so that they are less tempted to think of those different from themselves as only quasi-human'.[17] This is a culturally relativist premise: human rights are not instantiated by sharing a humanity; rather they are the result of circumstance and the capacity to imagine ourselves in another person's shoes.[18]

Sentimental education works by expanding our conception of who counts as 'our kind of people' and 'people like us'. This happens by increasing our ability to 'see the similarities between ourselves and people very unlike us as outweighing the differences'.[19] This involves seeing similarities, such as loving one's children or parents, and imagining similar experiences, such as the pain and suffering of the oppressed. The education results from long, sad, sentimental story-telling, like the kind imparted by novels or journalist reports.[20]

15 Lederach, *The Moral Imagination*, 29.
16 See Jack Donnelly, *Universal Human Rights in Theory and Practice* (Ithaca: Cornell University Press, 2013).
17 Richard Rorty, 'Human Rights, Rationality, and Sentimentality', in *Wronging Rights?: Philosophical Challenges for Human Rights*, ed. Aakash Singh Rathore and Alex Cistelecan (New Delhi: Routledge, 1993), 122.
18 Christopher J Voparil, 'General Introduction', in *The Rorty Reader*, ed. Christopher J Voparil and Richard J Bernstein (Chichester: Wiley, 2010), 44.
19 Rorty, 'Human Rights, Rationality, and Sentimentality', 123 and 129.
20 Ibid., 133.

In other words, sentimental education occurs when narratives evoke solidarity and sympathy between different people.

The goal of sentimental education is to strengthen moral identities. Becoming more just means forging wider loyalties between different groups, such as between religious or ethnic groups in particular places. 'The hope is to sew such groups together with a thousand little stitches – to invoke a thousand commonalities between their members, rather than specify one great big one, their common humanity.'[21] By doing so, the rights of other people become intrinsically envisaged as our own.

The moral discourse of human rights appeals to reason, whereas the sentimental education of human rights appeals to imagination. Both are criticised by the other side for being weak appeals to human rights. The former is criticised for being ahistorical and essentialist, and the latter for being contingent and conditional.[22] The divide between the two highlights an interesting tension at the Court: the simultaneous appeal to a universal norm of humanity and the sentimental engagement of moral identities.

The sentimental education being enacted in the art collection feeds into a universal moral discourse, and vice versa. Through the artworks the universalism of human rights becomes anchored by the 'particular commitment to a specially important group of people whose cause is close to one's heart'.[23] That is, by sharing stories about particular instances of suffering – such as Ndwandwe's story captured in *The Blue Dress* (see Fig. 5.1) – some artworks call forth the power to imagine ourselves in the place of the person suffering: 'the *Blue Dress* offered … an opportunity to understand the experience of trauma, to gain some insight into the subjectivity of the other that my privilege prevents me from knowing.'[24] This expands the shared recognition between people. At the same time, other artworks appeal to the universalist premise of a shared humanity – such as Ndlovu's *Humanity*. This reinforces the moral discourse of global human rights (which is also reflected in the Constitution).

By recognising the art collection as a unique kind of visual jurisprudence, it is possible to excavate how the claims to universality and to particularity frame justice at the Court, and what kind of impulses about human rights emerge in relation to South Africa's transition. The artworks are perceived to both instruct the moral imagination and affect the moral imagination – the two claims discussed later in this chapter. The visual jurisprudence of the art

21 Richard Rorty in Voparil, 'General Introduction', 44.

22 Sentimental education is also criticised for having the potential to breed intolerance to difference and failing to explain why some shared experiences are more important than others; see, for example, the critique by Bhikhu Parekh, 'Non-Ethnocentric Universalism', in *Human Rights in Global Politics*, ed. Tim Dunne and Nicholas J Wheeler (Cambridge: Cambridge University Press, 1999), 141.

23 Michael Ignatieff, *Human Rights as Politics, Human Rights as Idolatry*, The Tanner Lectures on Human Values (Princeton University, 2000).

24 Vorster, 'Storytelling and Fraught Histories,' 184.

collection both engenders belief in and understanding of foundational human rights, at the same time as it engages the moral imagination in the pursuit of these rights. This means that the divide between moral and sentimental appeals to human rights is thinned in the art collection because (as many people stated in interviews) the artworks connect personal stories and experiences to a 'bigger picture',[25] that of humanity.

Understanding the artworks at the Court as visual jurisprudence complicates the typical approach to the art collection as an exercise in memory mapping. Although little analysis exists purely on the art collection, scholarship that touches upon the artworks tends to subsume them under the same banner of memorialising as the architectural transformation of the site.[26] Thinking about the artworks solely in terms of their memorial capacity fails to take into account how the collection functions in relation to the ongoing provision of justice. While the artworks may arise out of memory and indeed play an important role in mapping memory and working alongside a memorial constitutionalism (discussed in Chapter 3), they also reflect and intervene in the thinking and understanding of justice at the Court. This is visual jurisprudence.

To be clear however, I am not suggesting that the art collection has a causal impact on justice at the Court – to consider it in these terms misses the point:

> An artwork functions at that subliminal level as much as literally, it actually can play a very significant role in locating the work that the judges do; it's not a guarantee that justice will be strongly rooted; it's not a guarantee that justice will be accepted by the broad population . . . It's not guaranteed that we judges will be wise and fair and come out with appropriate judgments, but art contributes towards – it goes into the mix – achieving those outcomes.[27]

The art collection cannot determine the outcome of justice, but it contributes to the provision of justice and what is considered just. The claims about the role of the art collection are about the thinking, the understanding, and the imagining of justice; a pulsing of justice; reverberations in the mix.

The Instruction of Art to Justice

> Justice will always be dictated by context, by art, by humanity, by human values.[28]

> Externalising and representing images that address unpleasant injustices are behaviourally instructive as visual reminders of what has been, and what ideally should not be.[29]

[25] Judge 6.
[26] See, for example, Stacy Douglas, 'Between Constitutional Mo(nu)ments: Memorialising Past, Present and Future at the District Six Museum and Constitution Hill', *Law and Critique*, vol. 22, no. 2 (2011); Le Roux, 'War Memorials'; Ashcroft, 'Constitution Hill.'
[27] Judge 2.
[28] Judge 4.
[29] Artist 26.

> It's the lawyers that need to be trained in art and that's about transitional justice; it's about understanding how to make your mind shift from the static idea of what is just or what is the law.[30]

> The art still speaks; to me it speaks of what happened in the past.[31]

Several judges, law clerks, artists, court staff, and visitors shared the view that the Court's art collection is normatively instructive. That is, the art collection 'is facilitative, is catalytic, it reminds us [the judges] of our duty'.[32] The idea of duty is seen through the artworks firstly as a normative awareness of the value of people in *deciding* justice:

> One would not sit and think in a judgment, like now, about the interpretation of the National Credit Act, and how interest must be calculated, and which credit providers must be registered, and which credit agreements must be exempt from registration. You'd think it would be hard for me to find inspiration in the artworks for that. However, generally it [the art collection] creates an atmosphere ... an awareness that we work with people; and for that matter then, even the National Credit Act I suppose.[33]

> The venue [the Constitutional Court] suits these [art] works perfectly because courts are places where most of us are tried for various incidences, so art would help any person who wishes to take decisions on our behalf to ensure that these standards are met, and that people need to be made aware of them.[34]

This normative awareness about the value of people in judicial decisions connects to the emphasis on humanity discussed in Chapter 5, and it also reaffirms the universal reasoning which underscores global human rights discourse: people are both the subjects of, and the reason for, justice.

Secondly, duty is understood as a normative responsibility for addressing wounds of the past in *pursuing* justice:

> It [the art collection] is hugely important, especially with a court like this one which is trying to not just issue judgements but, in some way, sees its role as being transformative in terms of this democratic and constitutional project that South Africa has had for 20 years. Art also functions in a very similar way; art has a lot to say about transformation in a society that is dealing with difficulties and a really hard past. So in the same way that the judgements are really trying not just to set down the real principles but they are also trying to take individual stories and make them accessible to people, and use those stories to heal wounds of the past ... you can say the same about a lot of the art pieces in the collection.[35]

30 Artist 2.
31 Visitor 9, businessperson from South Africa.
32 Judge 1.
33 Judge 6.
34 Artist 5.
35 Law clerk 2 from the United States.

> The *Right to Life* [artwork by Wilma Cruise], it's in our Constitution, it's like everyone has a right to live, so it's like a transition from there [the apartheid era] to here but it's actually being told in the art, by artists.[36]

This normative responsibility to the past connects to the emphasis on temporality discussed in Chapter 5. It also highlights the continuing memorial narrative which pervades not only the site of the Court but the way in which it conceptualises a responsibility to the shaping of a post-apartheid future. Responsibility arises from the past and is enacted through the recognition of people's stories and the sentimental education which results from making these stories accessible to other people.

These two aspects of duty – awareness of and responsibility to both people and the past – position the visual jurisprudence created by the art collection in terms of justice being about civic service; the law serving the universal (global human rights) and serving the particular (the citizens of South Africa). Understood in these terms, the Court's visual jurisprudence points towards the mobilisation of a global human rights discourse through the development of local – context-specific – stories.

The claims about the normative instruction of the art collection reveal a largely progressive conception of its ability and purpose to strengthen the work of the Court. The collection is designed to support the Court, and it does so through sharing the same normatively instructive goals as the Court. However, this progressive conception is not necessarily straightforward. Several artists suggested that the artworks bring about a questioning, a debate:

> It's most probably optimistic to think that particular [art]works in the Court try to bring about a restitution and reconciliation, but they keep that questioning and that debate on the table. And they do it when they work well through the very unresolved nature of the riddles they pose.[37]

This idea of keeping questioning on the table is implicitly productive in serving justice: 'outside the Court the art can play a bigger function . . . art can interrogate constitutional issues a lot more.'[38] The instruction of art lies not only in the duty it evokes but also in the unsettling it provokes. This unsettling is important because it prevents the art collection from being an instrument of the Court. The debate initiated by certain artworks – despite their selection with curatorial intent – means that the art collection resists becoming Court propaganda. Even though the collection is circumscribed by a strong sense of self-censorship by the Court (discussed in Chapter 4) about what types of art should be displayed, this does not prevent the artworks which *are* displayed from posing unresolved riddles. The riddles posed are deliberately directed towards the work of the Court, where civic duty and

[36] Court staff member 4.
[37] Artist 6.
[38] Artist 8.

responsibility to humanity are key topics under consideration. Even when they are solved, they need to be solved again.

The judges stressed that the normative instruction of the art collection does not have a direct influence on judicial decision-making: 'I don't think it [the art collection] would actively intervene to help us reach the right jurisprudential answer,'[39] implying that if the collection did this, it would indicate some sort of bias or intellectual fallibility. Rather, the art collection contributes to a general orientation towards normative thinking, towards a moral imagination: '[I]f you put a picture on the wall, the view and dimension of the room changes. The thinking is inspired, and in some cases, examples are made in reference to the pictures at hand.'[40] The presence of the art contributes to a judicial consciousness that is sensitised to normative instruction about civic duty and challenged by uncertainty, creating a visual jurisprudence grounded in human rights discourse and the commitment to dissensus which underscores a pluralist democracy.

The *Affect* of Art on Justice

> As to your question of whether it affects the delivery of justice, I can't truly say. Except that to live and work in a humane, liberating, aesthetically profound environment must affect all of us; it affects me.[41]

> You really are allowed to enter into someone else's life . . . that is what [the] art allows you to do and when you do that in the law. . . it can have drastic and profound affect [sic] on judgement.[42]

> The artwork is an emotional response to a legal idea.[43]

These three statements reflect how justice at the Court is circumscribed by feeling. The first statement made by a judge indicates that the Court's artworks create an affective space: justice is affected by the environment in which it occurs. The second statement made by a law clerk indicates that the Court's artworks facilitate empathy: justice is affected by the emotion captured in artworks. The third statement made by a curator indicates that the Court's art is affected by justice: justice affects art. The first two statements highlight what art does to justice, while the third statement draws attention to what justice does to art. When combined, these statements underscore the relationship between the affect of art and justice – a point which connects back to the argument in Chapter 2 about transitional justice acknowledging 'itself as a process inseparable from feelings of justice'.[44]

39 Judge 1.
40 Artist 5.
41 Judge 5.
42 Law clerk 2 from the United States.
43 Curator 2.
44 McNamee, 'Fields of Opportunity', 22.

Three main ideas arose about the affect of art on justice at the Court. First, the Court's art collection connects abstract ideas with felt experiences:

> The most powerful pieces in the collection are the ones that really allow you into those moments of empathy where suddenly you have this connection with something which may have seemed abstract to you before or maybe just overwhelming. For people who did not live under apartheid, it is quite abstract and for people who did, it is almost so all-encompassing that sometimes it is hard to access, you develop walls against the past ... art really seeps through those cracks.[45]
>
> ... standing there like, oh okay, wow; it's like you're responding in your heart [to the artwork].[46]

Artworks at the Court are perceived to make abstract ideas relatable or memories tangible for different viewers. They enable difficult thoughts and difficult conversations triggered by the emotions in art.

Second, the art collection fosters an understanding of a bigger picture. This was a recurring claim among judges and law clerks at the Court. On the one hand, the art collection is perceived as connecting the technical and meticulous practice of law with the much broader concept of what it is to be human:

> The work of lawyers is incredibly technical and it is our responsibility to get seeped in the detail ... we are talking commas in a judgement ... the role of art in the administration of justice is to remind us of the big picture and to keep us human when we do our work, because it is only through those emotive reactions to stories that we remember the deep importance of the difference between a semi colon and a colon.[47]

From this perspective, then, the artworks help to humanise the people who practice law; a direct reflection on their own experience of enacting law. This is done through story-telling which triggers emotion and presents as specific instances of sentimental education.

On the other hand, the artworks are perceived to situate the law within a greater human context:

> Judging is about human beings and it is about the human condition ... essentially to be a good judge – because you are judging human beings – my view is that you have to understand humanity, you have to understand human beings, you need to understand and empathise with human suffering, and you need to know that you are dealing with a human condition ... that is where art comes in, because art helps one understand the healing conditions better than law does, better sometimes even than science does – most often I suppose – and that is the relevance. The relevance of art to justice at the first level is the ability of all kinds

45 Law clerk 2 from the United States.
46 Court staff member 4.
47 Law clerk 1 from South Africa.

> of art to facilitate a deeper and a more empathetic understanding of humanity and the human condition.[48]
>
> I do like to see things in the bigger context of human existence and human questions – right and wrong, and suffering and power, and those kind of things – that is what it [the art collection] means for me. But not that I would look at a specific painting and say well, now that I've looked at that I think I will decide this on this case. It's just a constant way for me – more consciously – to be in touch with the broader picture of the bigger questions of human existence, and the contrast between people and oppression and human dignity especially, which is a lot what the Court is about.[49]

This understanding of a bigger picture links directly to the recurring focus on humanity at the Court; embedding the art collection within a reasoned appeal to a universal humanness, a cosmopolitan world view which underpins the 'larger visual rhetoric of the Court'.[50] Here the affect of art is about its ability to create understanding; this understanding arises from a fostering of empathy and an ability of artworks to appeal to an interconnected human existence. The bigger picture fostered by the art collection has two major dimensions: it reminds the people who practice law of their own humanity and it situates the practice of law within humanity. In this sense, then, the artworks help the people who practice law to understand the purpose of the law. This understanding emerges from the ability of artworks to share individual and collective stories which foster human connectedness through empathy.

Third, the art collection generates a 'certain coherence of vision, of mentality, of empathy, of feeling'[51] among people in contact with the Court:

> The artworks at the Court have an impact on judges, when judges look at the works of art, feelings run through you and most of the works of art at the Court send through all kinds of amazingly different feelings and understanding and so on, which makes me in a sense softer, more human, and able to understand human beings a lot better. Whereas if there was no work of art at the Court, I would imagine that that would not happen. What the works of art do creates an atmosphere . . . they create a kind of milieu in which everyone works, so the Court gets affected, the clerks get affected, the members of staff get affected, the judges, secretaries get affected, and everyone who comes to the Court gets affected.[52]
>
> [W]hen you enter into the space you start to feel a different mood, when you look into the [art] pieces you start to reflect, the combination of art and also the architecture enabled a mirror of seeing us in the court as a nation.[53]

[48] Judge 4.
[49] Judge 6.
[50] Art committee member 6.
[51] Judge 2.
[52] Judge 4.
[53] Court staff member 2.

The first statement (made by a judge) is particularly significant for the claim that without the artworks, the judges' own humanity and ability to understand humanity would be weakened, and so too would the humanity of people who come into contact with the Court. The art collection is seen to root the work of the Court in a common experience. Despite artworks being open to different interpretations, they provide a shared experience at and of the Court: an aesthetic environment which affects – in the influencing sense of the word – the mindset and the feelings of people at the Court.

The art collection establishes that justice at the Court is not reduced simply to reason and logic or science. Rather, the art collection positions feeling and empathy – affect – as important elements of justice. Reason and feeling are not antithetical, but both effect the provision of justice at the Court. Art draws attention to 'the importance of texture, colour, rhythm, vibrancy in the very character of court decisions . . . an expressivity and an acknowledgment that decisions have voice, they don't just have determining implications'.[54] This is reflective of the aesthetic turn in post-apartheid jurisprudence which seeks to revive critical legal thought by considering emotional and imaginative approaches to the law.[55] While some artworks are seen to facilitate someone to 'walk in another person's shoes', others are about seeing a common universe through the perspective of another. This dual understanding about the affect of art establishes the work of the Court in a narrative of justice that not only reflects glocal human rights – universality through locality – but also reflects long-standing debates in legal scholarship over how to approach the law: whether through reason or feeling.

The visual jurisprudence at and of the Court is embedded within these two claims about the instructive and affective role of the art collection. Building on the symbolic intentions and material interventions which shape how justice is understood (Chapter 4), and the narratives about recognition which shape the appearance of justice (Chapter 5), it is possible to see how the art collection at the Court is a unique instance of visual jurisprudence – where the philosophy of the visual in law is not only about engendering belief, but it is about engaging the moral imagination in the provision of justice, towards the normative instruction of civic duty and the emotional understanding of humanity.

The visual jurisprudence of the art collection contains an important utopian charge. As justice becomes realised by the spatial transformation of the site of the Court, it paradoxically remains in the art collection as something that must be strived for continuously, beyond the limits of the Court. The physical existence of the court building is a realisation of South Africa's transition; this is the *site of justice*. In the art collection, the moral imagination inspires towards justice, but the very nature of this inspiration means that it remains

[54] Judge 2.
[55] See Le Roux, 'The Aesthetic Turn'.

ongoing, and even when justice is achieved, it still needs to be achieved again. This is the *sight of justice*. In this way, the Court is simultaneously a utopian good place (a site constituting justice) and a utopian no place, a prospect yet to be realised (a sight of justice in the making).

This utopian charge is indicative of the Court being 'both activist and evangelical'.[56] It also intersects with the idea of human rights having a 'visionary capacity', in expressing both the normative and the aspirational.[57] Most importantly, the utopian charge is important in calibrating the visual jurisprudence of the Court as working towards duty and understanding social interconnectedness, especially in the face of ever-increasing social disparity in South Africa. The utopian charge of the collection is a reminder to the state that justice still needs to be strived for even when it is achieved. Justice remains in transition.

[56] Gevisser and Nuttall, 'From the Ruins', 511.

[57] Mark Goodale, 'Locating Rights, Envisioning Law between the Global and the Local', in *The Practice of Human Rights: Tracking Law between the Global and the Local*, ed. Mark Goodale and Sally Engle Merry (Cambridge: Cambridge University Press, 2007), 15.

Part II

Representing Transitional Justice on the Global Stage

The South Africa Pavilion at the Venice Biennale

7

From Banned to Embraced

> Historically South Africa managed to use Venice as a platform to promote the ordinary struggles of people back at home. 'Come back Africa' was first shown at the Venice film festival in 1959 and it was mainly because of that film that the world began to embrace and support ordinary people who were waging the struggles against apartheid . . . So Venice for us means that.[1]

> For a country that has been culturally isolated during the years of the cultural boycott to begin to take its place on the world stage is crucial. And to be able to take that place on the world stage on the same terms as every other player. That is, you come, you compete, you are the best, you present the best. Not that we come as the token country from Africa or we come via the assistance of development agencies. We come on the same terms. This is crucial.[2]

Venice regularly floods. During high tide it floods with the distinct murky green, slightly odorous water from the surrounding lagoon. During low tide it floods with tourists, shuffling shoulder-to-shoulder between attractions, chasing little coloured flags on sticks held by guides who disappear into waves of crowds. During *La Biennale di Venezia* (the Biennale of Venice, hereafter the Biennale) it floods with art, artists, arts professionals, arts ministers, art critics, art teachers, art students, art investors, and art lovers. Every other year, this contemporary art world descends for six months on the patchwork group of 118 islands which make up Venice. The Biennale consists of pavilions from around eighty-five nations and draws in heads of state, ambassadors, ministers, and diplomats who want to participate in and assure the quality of their state's representation on the global stage. It is a 'goliath exhibition'[3] that aims to take the pulse of contemporary art and a nation's identity, as well as to capture a global artistic moment and a global political opportunity. Smaller biennales for cinema, dance, film, music, and theatre run alongside the art biennale, and in alternate years Venice also plays host to a biennale for architecture. In this book, the Biennale refers specifically to the art biennale;

[1] Exhibition management 7.
[2] Exhibition management 3.
[3] Sarah Thornton, *Seven Days in the Art World* (London: Granta Books, 2012), 225.

arguably the most well known and by far the oldest of all biennales, worldwide. The city has been playing host to this 'world cup of art'[4] since 1895.

Under the guise of contemporary art, the Biennale is a highly networked exercise in cultural diplomacy. Venice lays claim to being the only city in the world where the cultural departments of external governments have their own buildings; these take the form of national pavilions.[5] National pavilions map out historic alliances and contemporary struggles. Long-standing member states of the Biennale have permanent pavilions in the *Giardini* (gardens) while more recent member states rent temporary pavilions in the *Arsenale* (arsenal). Other states 'whose independent Governments are acknowledged by the Italian Government'[6] find short-term exhibition spaces around the city. The national pavilions distinguish Venice's biennale model from other biennials which have emerged largely in the second half of the twentieth century. These other biennials predominantly organise participation around artists rather than nations, even though the nationalities of artists are always emphasised.[7]

The set-up of the Biennale resembles that of other international institutions with large memberships. Membership is highly political, dependent on recognition by the Italian government and other member states. In the first instance states compete to be invited to stage an exhibition in Venice; and in the second instance, they compete against each other to be awarded the Golden Lion for the best national pavilion – judged by a jury comprised of international curators. Each state appoints an ambassador (called a commissioner) whose job it is to liaise between the Biennale and the respective governments, as well as between participating states.

All of this happens at the behest of the Biennale administration, an organisation that is as deeply embedded in politics as its membership. The management of the Biennale has undergone many iterations, from being run by the Venice City Council, to being run by the Italian government under Mussolini, to its current form as a foundation run by a president nominated by the Italian Minister for Cultural Affairs.[8] The president serves a term of four years and is supported by a board of directors comprised of the mayor of Venice and three people nominated respectively by the Regione Veneto (the Veneto Region),

[4] Artist 1.

[5] Thornton, *Seven Days in the Art World*, 238.

[6] Visual Arts and Architecture Department La Biennale, 'Procedure for National Participations' (2015).

[7] See Charles Rick Green and Anthony Gardner, *Biennials, Triennials, and Documenta: The Exhibitions That Created Contemporary Art* (Chichester: Wiley, 2016); Chin-Tao Wu, 'Biennials without Borders', *New Left Review*, vol. 57 (2009).

[8] For an overview of early changes to the structure of the Biennale, see Lawrence Alloway, *The Venice Biennale, 1895–1968: From Salon to Goldfish Bowl* (Greenwich: New York Graphic Society, 1968).

the Consiglio Provinciale di Venezia (the Provincial Council of Venice), and private backers.[9] The identity of these private backers remains unspecified.

Art at the Biennale consists of three elements: the national pavilions, a central pavilion curated by a different guest curator each year, and collateral events. The collateral events are dominated by exhibitions by states not officially participating as national pavilions. This means the governments of these states either did not apply or were not invited by the Biennale to stage a national pavilion. Rather, the collateral exhibitions are organised by independent groups. For instance, at the 2013 Biennale, the collateral event entitled *Otherwise Occupied* featured the work of two Palestinian artists, Bashir Makhoul and Aissa Deebi. Organised by a non-profit organisation called the Palestinian Art Court al Hoash and sponsored by The University of Southampton UK and the American University in Cairo, the exhibition intended to draw attention to the simultaneous existence of 'no Palestinian state and many Palestinian states', using art to imagine the nation 'outside and beyond the conflict'.[10] Visitors still referred to and perceived the exhibition as the Palestine Pavilion.[11] The positioning of *Otherwise Occupied* as a collateral event rather than a national pavilion indicated that at the time of the Biennale in 2013, Italy did not formally recognise the state of Palestine – in 2015, the Italian government voted in favour of a symbolic recognition of the Palestinian state.[12] Some collateral events also proclaim themselves to be national pavilions despite the Biennale's contrary categorisation. For example, in 2003, the Taiwan Pavilion was changed by the Biennale from being an official national participant to being a collateral event, corresponding to Taiwan's ambiguous international and diplomatic situation.[13] Despite this change, Taiwain still refers to its exhibition as a national pavilion.

The management of and participation in the Biennale is delineated politics and intensely circumscribed by diplomacy and international relations. The Biennale serves as a meeting place where states come to exhibit their art and to share themselves with the international community. This international community is complex, being historically orientated around an imperial world order, privileging the states of the global north and demarcated by privilege – only people able to afford to visit Venice can attend and only states able to

9 'From the '70s to the Reforms of 1998', www.labiennale.org/en/biennale/history/vb3.html?back=true.

10 Bruce Ferguson and Rawan Sharaf, 'Otherwise Occupied', 2013, www.palestineatvenice.com/curatorialstatement.html; Bruce Ferguson and Rawan Sharaf, 'Otherwise Occupied (exhibition handout)', ed. La Biennale di Venezia (2013).

11 For example, Biennale staff member 3 and Visitor 0 from Australia called it the Palestinian Pavilion.

12 Ammar Awad, 'Italian Lawmakers Urge Recognition of Palestinian State', 2015, *Reuters*, www.reuters.com/article/us-italy-palestinians-vote-idUSKBN0LV1FY20150227. However, Palestine did not have an official national pavilion in the 2015 Biennale.

13 Chu-Chiun Wei, 'From National Art to Critical Globalism: The Politics and Curatorial Strategies of the Taiwan Pavilion at the Venice Biennale', *Third Text*, vol. 27, no. 4 (2013): 475.

afford to exhibit abroad can participate. States are complicit in supporting the diplomatic and political structures of the Biennale, structures which confer prestige and re-orient art in a globalised world along firm national lines. This is despite the Biennale's 'decolonising and democratic claims'.[14]

How a state displays itself at the Biennale can affect how that state is perceived on the world stage. Unlike art fairs which are primarily concerned with the art market, biennales 'function to create new sequences, new histories and genealogies, responding to the contemporary and materializing relationships between art and the outside world'.[15] At the Biennale in Venice, these relationships materialise in the form of cultural diplomacy: 'the exchange of ideas, information, art and other aspects of culture among nations and their peoples to foster mutual understanding'.[16] While cultural diplomacy provides much of the content of public diplomacy – 'which basically comprises all that a nation does to explain itself to the world' – it is not as aligned with policies or focused on generating support for particular policies, nor is it as reactive to trouble-shooting immediate problems.[17] Unlike other areas of diplomacy, cultural diplomacy is complicated by the fact that states require the support of nongovernmental actors, such as artists.[18] This complexity plays out at the Biennale where states present a cultural face through the work of artists – artists who often challenge the state.

The Biennale is often described by analogy to big sporting events. At the opening of the 2013 South Africa Pavilion, the Minister of Arts and Culture, Paul Mashatile, described the Biennale as the 'Olympics of art'.[19] During interviews, the Biennale was regularly referred to as the 'world cup of art'.[20] Members of the curatorial team for South Africa's 2013 exhibition, entitled *Imaginary Fact*, described that 'if art were to get the kind of support that sport does, it does have the potential to pull together a group of people that otherwise are not being pulled together to support something'; 'Lots and lots of money has been put into sport because people have thought sport is an arena where we can reconcile . . . But the arts are far more potent, plus they

[14] Wu, 'Biennials without Borders.'

[15] Bennett, *Practical Aesthetics*, 18–19.

[16] Cynthia P Schneider, 'Cultural Diplomacy: The Humanizing Factor', in *International Cultural Policies and Power*, ed. J. P. Singh (London: Palgrave Macmillan, 2010), 101.

[17] Cynthia P Schneider, 'Culture Communicates: US Diplomacy That Works', in *The New Public Diplomacy*, ed. Jan Melissen (Hampshire: Springer, 2005), 147 and 157.

[18] Jessica C E Gienow-Hecht, 'What Are We Searching For? Culture, Diplomacy, Agents, and the State', in *Searching for a Cultural Diplomacy*, ed. Jessica C. E. Gienow-Hecht and Mark C. Donfried (New York: Berghahn, 2010), 10.

[19] Paul Mashatile, 'Speech on Occasion of the Opening of South African Pavilion at the 55th Venice Biennale', 2013, www.dac.gov.za/content/speech-paul-mashatile-occasion-opening-south-african-pavilion-55th-venice-biennale. For a discussion of sport and cultural diplomacy, see Sifiso Mxolisi Ndlovu, 'Sports as Cultural Diplomacy: The 2010 FIFA World Cup in South Africa's Foreign Policy', *Soccer and Society*, vol. 11, no. 1–2 (2010).

[20] Artist 28; Exhibition management 1; Artist 1; Exhibition management 4; Biennale staff member 3; visitor 10.

offer the opportunity for a kind of reconciliation which is therapeutic.'[21] By comparing the two – art and sport – the Biennale can be seen as an event that is identifiable in language as important, big, world-class, competitive, international, and long-running. Art and sport share the ability to generate communities around shared interests.

Equally, like sport, art has the ability to divide. During apartheid, South Africa was expelled from the international community. Between 1946 and 1981, the United Nations General Assembly passed sixty-four resolutions condemning apartheid and urging the international community to boycott South Africa – to break diplomatic relations and cease trade – in an effort to isolate the state and pressure political change. Some states upheld this boycott more than others.[22] Boycotting South Africa was a way of severing the lifelines of the regime.

In 1956, anti-apartheid activist Ahmed Kathrada – who was tried alongside Nelson Mandela in the Rivonia trial and subsequently spent twenty-six years in prison – said:

> [T]he perpetrators of racialism in this country [South Africa] derive strength and courage from the closeness that they (the racialists) feel to the outer world; indeed from the almost tacit consent and recognition that they receive from particularly the Western countries in the form of cultural and sports contact, economic and military association.[23]

Cultural contact is emphasised in this statement as being complicit in supporting apartheid. In 1968, United Nations (UN) resolution 2396 requested 'all states and organizations to suspend cultural, educational, sporting, and other exchanges with the racist regime'.[24] This was the first resolution of many which specifically targeted a cultural boycott of South Africa. It galvanised the cultural boycott by many international institutions and artists.

Banned from the Biennale

In the same year as the cultural boycott began, student protestors in Venice led the boycott-the-Biennale movement. They campaigned against the Biennale as an establishment that turned culture into a commodity, primarily through the sale of artworks.[25] At this time the Biennale was heavily geared towards the art

[21] Curatorial team member 3; Curatorial team member 2.

[22] See Michael C. Beaubien, 'The Cultural Boycott of South Africa', *Africa Today*, vol. 29, no. 4 (1982). For a timeline of the resolutions, see Enuga S. Reddy, 'The United Nations: Partner in the Struggle against Apartheid', www.un.org/en/events/mandeladay/apartheid.shtml.

[23] Ahmed Kathrada in Ben White, 'Apartheid and Cultural Boycott', 2015, www.middleeastmonitor.com/resources/reports-and-publications/20863-apartheid-a-cultural-boycott-then-and-now.

[24] General Assembly United Nations, 'The Policies of Apartheid of the Government of South Africa', in *Resolution 2396* (1968).

[25] See Chiara Di Stefano, 'The 1968 Biennale: Boycotting the Exhibition', in *Starting from Venice*, ed. Clarissa Ricci (Milan: EtAl, 2010).

market, with an official desk that managed the sales of artists' work and received commissions from these sales on behalf of the Biennale.[26] The protestors also campaigned for the reform of the Biennale's charter, which was considered a reflection of 'an imperialistic conception of culture as a bastion of its principle of authority'.[27] Re-written during the Fascist era, the charter gave full control of the event to the Italian government in order to ensure the Biennale's loyalty to the government.[28] Amid these campaigns in 1968 and in reaction to the heavily armed police presence they attracted to the Biennale, several exhibitions were not opened and many artists withdrew their works from display, refusing to reinstate them until the police departed and the Biennale committed to reform.[29]

At a time when anti-capitalist, anti-imperialist, and anti-racist protests were sweeping the globe, the Biennale was targeted as an institution that breached all three of these goals. The boycott manifesto declared the Biennale to be 'the instrument of the bourgeoisie to codify a policy of racism and cultural underdevelopment through the commercialisation of ideas'.[30] The specific mention of a policy of racism was a reference to the anti-apartheid demonstrations which became an important part of the protests in Venice.

South Africa had been exhibiting at the Biennale since 1950. In 1968, for only the second time, South Africa exhibited artworks by black artists in the Biennale – works by Lucas Sithole, E. Mdluli, P. Majozi, and E. Mkhizi. The organisers claimed that the exhibition 'was built up out of the creations of people belonging to different races and different social backgrounds, working in different artistic styles, but connected by their common purpose'.[31] However, the exhibition catalogue betrays the pervasive racist ideology of apartheid, contrasting figurative artwork by 'Bantu artists' with the more abstract artwork by 'their colleagues of white extraction' – drawing upon burgeoning debates over the hierarchies of artistic styles to portray teleological narratives about progress and racial superiority.[32]

This was further compounded by the privileging of man's art over women's craft in the exhibition catalogue. For instance, the tapestries by Mdluli, Majozi, and Mkhizi – all female artists – were listed under 'African Weaving', rather

[26] Georgina Adam, 'Trading Places', *Financial Times*, 6 June 2009.

[27] 'Manifesto degli student, operai e intellettuali rivoluzionari per il boicottaggio della Biennale', 1968, ASAC. Original in Italian, translation by the author.

[28] Nancy Jachec, *Politics and Paintings at the Venice Biennale 1948–64: Italy and the 'Idea of Europe'* (Manchester: Manchester University Press, 2007), 36. Also see Maria Stone, 'Challenging Cultural Categories: The Transformation of the Venice Biennale under Fascism', *Journal of Modern Italian Studies*, vol. 4, no. 2 (1999): 185.

[29] Stefano, 'The 1968 Biennale'.

[30] 'Manifesto degli student', 1968, ASAC.

[31] Mattys Bokhorst, *South Africa: Venice Biennale 1968* (Cape Town: Disa Printers, 1968), Exhibition catalogue, in foreword. Bokhurst was director of the National Gallery of South Africa at this time.

[32] Ibid.

than under the artists' names.[33] By contrast, the four male artists were listed under their name. The catalogue also attributed these tapestries to the Evangelical Lutheran Church Art and Craft Centre at Rorke's Drift rather than providing any background information on the artists themselves. This was in contrast to the curriculum summary of each male artist in the catalogue. Furthermore, no first names were provided in the catalogue for the female artists; only their initials and marital status (Mrs E., Mrs P. and Miss E.) were recorded.

Of the twenty-nine artworks in the exhibition, twenty-two were available for purchase. Of these, only three by Sithole were listed for sale. The inventory list indicates his remaining three artworks and the three artworks by Mdluli, Majozi, and Mkhizi as held in private collections.[34] The lack of opportunity for the sale of artworks by black artists at the Biennale is significant. It reiterates the tension in the exhibition over the South African government showing work by black artists while undermining the opportunity for these artists to participate fully in the Biennale, which at that time was heavily focused on commerce (as highlighted in the 1968 protests). The inclusion of black artists was intended to show how they 'could thrive under apartheid and thus "put a feather in the cap of the South African Government"'.[35] However, this intention was unsuccessful; there were anti-apartheid protests and South Africa was subsequently excluded from participating in future Biennales.[36]

Until this exclusion, the South African government had been trying to secure a permanent exhibition space at the Biennale; its exhibitions between 1950 and 1968 were in temporary spaces assigned by the Biennale. Correspondence between the Biennale and South Africa throughout the 1960s indicates tensions over the lack of a decision about a permanent exhibition space for the state, and the delays in confirming even the availability of temporary exhibition spaces.[37]

Firstly, South Africa was not permitted to participate in the Biennales of 1960 and 1962 because of a lack of exhibition space: 'The country was obliged to cancel its planned entries for the years 1960 and 1962 owing to the pressure

33 Ibid.

34 'SA Entry to Venice Biennale 1968', ASAC.

35 Philippa Hobbs and Elizabeth Rankin, *Rorke's Drift: Empowering Prints* (Cape Town: Juta, 2003), 56.

36 For an overview of South Africa's relationship to the student protests of 1968, see John Daniel and Peter Vale, 'South Africa: Where Were We Looking in 1968', in *1968: Memories and Legacies of a Global Revolt*, ed. Philipp Gassert and Martin Klimke (Washington, DC: German Historical Institute, 2009).

37 See letters between the Secretary General of the Biennale, G A Dell'Acqua, and the Organising Secretary of the South African Association of Arts Cape Town, L. A. Sanderson, and letters between South African Ambassador to Italy, G F Marais, and the President of the Biennale, between 1963 and 1966, ASAC.

upon guest space.'[38] However, this explanation came at a time when international anti-apartheid sentiment – particularly in Venice – was growing. In 1959, the film *Come back, Africa* was first shown at the Venice film festival, where it won the Italian Critics' Award.[39] Detailing the struggle of one man and his family to survive in a township in Johannesburg, *Come back, Africa* exposed the cruelty and injustice of the apartheid regime. The film's international debut in Venice helped to galvanise support for those fighting against apartheid.[40] Given this, South Africa's absence from the Biennale for the following four years took on a heightened significance.

Secondly, while South Africa did have an opportunity to participate in the Biennales of 1964 and 1966, the offer was at short notice – three months and three weeks, respectively.[41] In early 1966, Secretary General of the Biennale, Gian Alberto Dell'Acqua, replied to multiple inquiries about exhibition space from the Organising Secretary of the South African Association of Arts Cape Town, L A Sanderson:

> I am aware of your wish of receiving, as soon as possible, a final reply [regarding exhibition space], in a positive or negative sense; but, unfortunately, I must defer again for some time the same reply, though I make no secret of the fact that, for the present, the reasons of difficulty seem to prevail.[42]

Dell'Acqua's reference to the 'reasons of difficulty' remained somewhat ambiguous in the letter; he explained that detailed reasons were provided by the president of the Biennale who 'has written to the South African Embassy in Rome, to explain the situation and to point out the difficulties that are interfering'.[43] While this detail of diplomatic correspondence is unknown, the reasoning provided is in relation to other states' 'requests accumulated from several months' and the 'inadequacy of an available space'.[44] Similar reasons recur in letters to South Africa throughout the 1960s, placing South Africa in a position which was disempowered and reactive. For example, a few weeks before the opening of the 1966 Biennale, South Africa was offered a temporary exhibition space for that year.[45] South Africa responded by sending artworks by air, instead of by sea, so they would arrive in Venice in time to be

38 Letter from Organising Secretary of the South African Association of Arts Cape Town, L A Sanderson, to Secretary General of the Biennale, G A Dell'Acqua, 13 June 1963, ASAC.

39 'Come Back Africa', https://comebackafrica.com/about/.

40 See Litheko Modisane, 'From Africa to America, and Back Again: Come back, Africa (1959)', in *South Africa's Renegade Reels: The Making and Public Lives of Black-Centered Films* (New York: Palgrave Macmillan, 2013).

41 Letter from Mario Marcazzan to L A Sanderson, 7 February 1964, ASAC; Letter from Secretary General of the Biennale, G A Dell'Acqua, to Organising Secretary of the South African Association of Arts Cape Town, L A Sanderson, 28 April 1966, ASAC.

42 Letter from G A Dell'Acqua to L A Sanderson, 10 February 1966, ASAC.

43 Ibid.

44 Ibid.

45 Letter from G A Dell'Acqua to L A Sanderson, 28 April 1966, ASAC; Letter from L A Sanderson to G A Dell'Acqua, 3 May 1966, ASAC.

hung – demonstrating the state's eagerness to participate, aware that at this time the Biennale was one of the last international institutions open to it.[46]

Thirdly, there were also reported delays in settling the monies owed to South Africa after the sale of artworks at the Biennale during the 1960s, especially after the cultural boycott began.[47]

The Biennale stated that the delays over the confirmation of exhibition space for South Africa and the settling of the sale of artworks were a product of genuine difficulties encountered in arranging a sizeable art exposition and accommodating competing requests for space made by multiple states. However, when the three points of analysis above are taken together, the correspondence over several years suggests a deeper level of reservation – or at least reprioritisation – by the Biennale to include South Africa in the exposition. It appears the logistical concerns over space were accompanied by a deliberate effort to deter South Africa's participation in the exposition and to prevent it from becoming a permanent member of the Biennale at a time when the apartheid regime was becoming increasingly shunned by the international community – on the back of several UN resolutions. The Biennale faced increased scrutiny about how it was run and which states were permitted to exhibit – as reflected by the 1968 protests. The Biennale was not only heavily influenced by the politics of this period but also deeply involved in them.

The 1968 protests at the Biennale sparked institutional change on two fronts: business and politics. First, commercial activity, including the sale of artworks, was banned, shifting the emphasis of the exhibition away from the art market. This was also reflected in the style of the main Biennale catalogues which were produced to accompany the guest-curated central pavilion and to act as a directory of national participants. Prior to the early-1970s, these catalogues were filled with advertisements for luxury goods, art fairs, and art galleries. Since the mid-1970s, they became free from advertising, other than the inclusion of sponsors' logos. Also since this time, they have been released in English as well as Italian, signalling a change in how the Biennale views itself and its position in the international community.

However, the ban on commercial activity at the Biennale has not deterred the commodification of culture. In the current art market, the de-commercialised space of the Biennale accrues symbolic capital. An artist gains reputational importance from exhibiting at the Biennale, which often translates into an increase in the prices of their artworks – for some artists this translates into exhibitions of their work being sold out before the Biennale even opens.[48]

[46] Letter from G A Dell'Acqua to L A Sanderson, 12 May 1966, ASAC; Letter from L A Sanderson to G A Dell'Acqua, 10 August 1966, ASAC.

[47] Letter from L A Sanderson to the Director of Sales at the Biennale, 8 February 1965, ASAC; Letter from K Gunther to G A Dell'Acqua, 7 February 1969, ASAC.

[48] Adam, 'Trading Places'.

Many of the artists who exhibited in South Africa's 2013 Pavilion were of the opinion that exhibiting at the Biennale brought market advantages: 'However you look at it, participating in something like the Venice Biennale is kind of a feather in your cap in terms of your exposure'[49]; 'I mean I'll just be brutally honest, it's a good thing to have on your CV [curriculum vitae]'[50]; 'For South Africa to get space there, it's good for local artists to be recognised internationally . . . it's good for art and good for business as an artist.'[51] Similarly, the Chief Executive Officer of the National Arts Festival (NAF) – the organisation responsible for the 2013 Pavilion – has spoken openly about the market benefits of the Biennale: 'It is also a step toward establishing their [the artists'] names and reputations in the global arts market and getting due recognition and reward for their talent.'[52] The economic benefits of exhibiting in the Biennale are also a persistent theme in the South African government's reasons for participating in the event (discussed later in the chapter).

The Biennale still plays a vital role in the art market, even if it claims to have divorced itself from commerce. In fact, by professing its separateness from the market, the Biennale now trades on the perception that it is untainted by money. Paradoxically, this increases the value – both financially and symbolically – of artworks which are exhibited in this 'pure' environment.[53]

Second, South Africa was explicitly banned from participating in the Biennale. At a time when the Biennale was still run by the Italian government – the charter did not change until 1973 when the Biennale became led by a board – the banning of South Africa aligned with the cultural boycott spearheaded by UN and the boycotting practices of other major cultural institutions.[54] The specific banning of South Africa from exhibiting at the Biennale signalled an important exclusion by the international community – an exclusion which reinforces the connections between art and politics at the Biennale, and the sphere of influence wielded by this event.[55]

[49] Artist 25.

[50] Artist 15.

[51] Exhibition management 1.

[52] Artsmart, 'NAF Curators of SA Pavilion', 2013, http://news.artsmart.co.za/2013/02/naf-curators-of-sa-pavillion.html.

[53] Point also made by Jeannine Tang, 'Biennalization and Its Discontents', in *Negotiating Values in the Creative Industries: Fairs, Festivals and Competitive Events*, ed. Brian Moeran and Jesper Strandgaard Pedersen (Cambridge: Cambridge University Press, 2011), 78; Nikos Papastergiadis and Meredith Martin, 'Art Biennales and Cities as Platforms for Global Dialogue', in *Festivals and the Cultural Public Sphere*, ed. Gerard Delanty, Liana Giorgi, and Monica Sassatelli (London: Routledge, 2011), 49.

[54] For a timeline of selective changes to the Biennale's charter, see La Biennale, 'From the Post-War Period to the Reforms of 1973', www.labiennale.org/en/biennale/history/vb2.html?back=true.

[55] Information about this ban is conspicuously absent from the Biennale ASAC archives – the archives contain correspondence mainly about logistical, commercial, and curatorial information around 1968. This absence may be reflective of the Biennale being run by the government at the time of the ban – since the decision was a diplomatic one, it is a record of foreign policy. However, the Cultural Department of the Italian government was also not able to provide any further information.

The severing of artistic ties between South Africa and the Biennale was a ruling against the apartheid regime – one that continues to reverberate in the thinking around South Africa's participation, particularly by the exhibition organisers of the 2013 Pavilion:

> It's important that we were banned [historically from the Biennale]. I mean it was right. I still get shocked when people play . . . cricket matches in Zimbabwe and you have teams going to Zimbabwe, and you think Christ there's this disgusting dictatorship. I don't know if the art [in the 2013 South Africa pavilion] would have been any different if we had or hadn't been banned. Maybe it would have been different.[56]
>
> It [the boycott] was necessary in the broader context of what was going on in South Africa at the time and it was an effective way of helping us, of isolating South Africa, which was necessary in order to achieve the change we needed to as a country. That is not to say that it did not do any harm, it did do harm but the end justified the means. What appealed to me in terms of the project [the 2013 Biennale] was that here is an opportunity for us to really stand out and one thing that we try to introduce to the business is this greater sense of internationalism and where we are as a country.[57]

As these quotes imply, and as I suggest in Chapter 9, the form of *Imaginary Fact* would likely have been different had the exhibition not been generated in part by the preoccupation to show a survey of artworks to make up for previous absences.

The Biennale continues to serve as a site of political protest. In 2015, the *Gulf Labor Coalition and the Global Ultra Luxury Faction* (known as G.U.L.F.) occupied the Israel Pavilion and staged a series of protests to 'raise awareness about the labour conditions of migrants in the Gulf nations, and the situation faced by Palestinian workers in the West Bank'.[58] In the same year the Ukraine art collective, called *On Vacation*, asked visitors to don military camouflage and take photographs of themselves inside the pavilion of an 'occupying power' of their choice.[59] The collective also staged an occupation of the Russia Pavilion, protesting the Russian occupation of Ukraine.[60] In 2013, protestors at the Biennale, operating under the banner of Occupy Gezi, campaigned against the excessive force being used by the

[56] Exhibition management 5.
[57] Exhibition management 6.
[58] ArtReview, 'Gulf Labor Occupies Israeli Pavilion and Calls for Cultural Boycott', 2015, http://artreview.com/news/news_4_aug_2015_gulf_labor_occupies_israel_pavilion/. For a description of the protest, see Gulf Labor Artist Colalition, 'An Intervention at the Biennale: G.U.L.F and Gulf Labor at Venice', 2015, http://gulflabor.org/2015/an-intervention-at-the-biennale-g-u-l-f-and-gulf-labor-at-venice/#more-2068.
[59] 'On Vacation', 2015, http://on-vacation.info/.
[60] Sarah Cascone, 'Ukrainian Guerrilla Art Group Protests Occupation with a Vacation', 2015, https://news.artnet.com/art-world/on-vacation-ukraine-protest-contest-306633.

police against protestors in Turkey.[61] Political protests remain commonplace at the Biennale, where national pavilions become proxies for the nations they represent and the actions of states can be confronted and contested under the spotlight of the art world.

Biennale Embraces South Africa

South Africa was invited to return to the Biennale in 1993 – the same year that UN passed resolution 48/1, requesting states to restore relationships with South Africa.[62] Through this invitation, South Africa was being rewarded for political change – an invitation to exhibit at the Biennale once again was an invitation to re-join the ranks of 'elite' artistic nations, a sign that the international community was willing to re-engage the nation.

The timeline that follows outlines South Africa's participation in the Biennale since 1993, assembling key information about exhibitions – the theme, the artists involved, the reception – as well as the mode in which the state came to exhibit at the Biennale. The implication is that an invitation to exhibit at the Biennale is a form of diplomatic recognition by the international community, whereas an application to exhibit at the Biennale is recognition by the applicant state of the importance of being included in this diplomatic zone. The timeline provides a recent history of South Africa's involvement in the Biennale – a compilation which does not exist elsewhere – in order to contextualise the analysis of the 2013 Pavilion, in light of the twenty years since the end of the boycott which preceded it. Importantly, it reveals the national and international politics and diplomatic negotiations involved in becoming and remaining a member state of the Biennale.

1993 After a twenty-five-year absence, South Africa was invited back to the Biennale by its director, Achille Bonito Oliva. This invitation was issued as an acknowledgement of the demise of apartheid and the prospect of a change to democracy:

> I invited South Africa . . . in recognition of the elimination of apartheid that has brought the country within the scope of democracy and respect for civil rights. Recognition also of the cultural climate, and the search for artists who with their own language have fought for freedom. A demonstration of how creation represents an act of resistance against every colonial anachronism.[63]

[61] Hrag Vartanian, 'Resistance to Turkey's Protest Violence Reaches the Venice Biennale', 2013, http://hyperallergic.com/72413/resistance-to-turkeys-bloody-protests-reach-the-venice-biennale/. Global Project, 'Occupied Turkish Pavilion at the Venice Biennale (flyer)', (2013).

[62] General Assembly United Nations, 'Lifting of sanctions against South Africa', in *Resolution 48/1* (1993).

[63] Achille Bonito Oliva, e-mail to the author, 8 January 2016. Original e-mail in Italian, translation by the author. Also see Glenn Babb's statement in *Incroci del Sud: Affinities* (Venice: Palazzo Giustinian Lolin, 1993), 7.

Bonito Oliva's emphasis on artistic and creative agency in fighting for freedom and resisting oppression embedded South Africa's participation in relation to politics, explicitly linking the state's presence at the Biennale to its liberalising transition.

Without the prospect of this transition, South Africa would not have been welcomed back into this international community. This view is supported by correspondence in the early 1990s from the South African Association of Arts (the organisation responsible for the state's Biennale exhibitions in the 1960s) and the South African Embassy in Rome, to the Biennale which outline new 'non-racial' approaches to the selection of artists for international exhibitions, as well as to the teaching of art in South Africa.[64] Prior to Bonito Oliva's invitation, South Africa was trying to prove to the Biennale that its transition was genuine and lobbied for its return.

The 1993 exhibition, entitled *Incroci del Sud: Affinities* (Southern Crossings: Affinities), consisted of artworks by twenty-seven South African artists.[65] *Incroci del Sud* was technically a collateral event under the patronage of the Biennale and not a national pavilion. This distinction was important because it indicated that while South Africa was being welcomed by the Biennale, it was not yet a fully fledged member of the institution. The state's 'seat at the table' was provisional, dependent on the direction of its political transition.

The large number of artists in *Incroci del Sud* were selected 'to illuminate the diversity and extraordinary variety which is characteristic of contemporary South African art'.[66] This reflected a concern to show a range of work from South Africa, to compensate for its long absence from the Biennale – a concern also at the heart of the 2013 Pavilion. The exhibition intended to show how 'South Africa is poised on the verge of a new era and the art of this country mirrors the accompanying search for individual and collective identity'.[67] Information sent to the Biennale by the South African Embassy in Rome draws attention to the different approaches artists and the South African government were taking to this new era and search.

64 Letter from National President of the South African Association of Arts, Louis Jansen van Vuuren to Director of the Visual Arts at the Biennale, Giovanni Carandente, 14 January 1991; documents sent to the Biennale include, 'Declaration of Intent of the South African Association of Arts', 8 August 1991; Sally Arnold-Seibert, 'Prerequisites for the Selection and Presentation of an International Exhibition of Contemporary South Africa Art', August 1992; 'Preamble: Mission of the Sub-Department of Fine Arts, University of South Africa', all in ASAC.

65 Federica Martini and Vittoria Martini, *Just Another Exhibition: storie e politiche delle biennali* (Milan: Post media books, 2011), 113; Sophie Perryer, *10 Years 100 Artists: Art in a Democratic South Africa* (Cape Town: Bell-Roberts, 2004), 430.

66 Louis Jansen van Vuuren, 'Affinities', in *Incroci del Sud*, 13. The exhibition also toured to Rome, Italy.

67 Oliva's statement in ibid., 8.

This information included an essay written by Sally Arnold, one of the exhibiting artists and commission members. In the essay, Arnold highlights the task facing South Africa as being one of 'bridge-building' and art having the capacity to facilitate this task.[68] However, in the fax sent to the Biennale this paragraph has been crossed out – presumably by someone at the South African Embassy – and replaced with handwritten text, describing South African art as coming into its own right 'under Venetian skies', despite being geographically 'peripheral'.[69] This change shifts the attention from art being seen to advance reconciliation, to art being used to reestablish South Africa as part of the art centre, as part of this international community. Excerpts of Arnold's essay were used in the exhibition's media release.[70]

The differing views highlighted by this handwritten change are also reflected in the catalogue for *Incroci del Sud*. Commissioner of the exhibition, Glenn Babb – who was then South Africa's ambassador to Italy and had been since 1978 – opened the catalogue with a statement about South Africa's 'long, involuntary silence'[71] from the Biennale but made no mention of apartheid or why this absence had occurred; a revealing omission by a government official. Instead, he states that '[d]iscussions on the growing significance in Europe of other cultures sparked ideas for an inclusion of the dynamic, exciting art from South Africa, so little known elsewhere.'[72] This implies South Africa's entry to the Biennale occurred because Europe was now interested in the state, rather than because the state had been deliberately shunned by Europe in the years prior.

The official narrative of the South African government – offered by Babb – glosses over the reasons for South Africa's absence from the Biennale, indicative of the fact that the exhibition occurred when the apartheid government was still in office, before the democratic elections of 1994. Instead, the official narrative focuses on South Africa taking its place 'at one of the most prestigious of the art world's events'[73] – a narrative about reestablishing position and about measuring the state's self-importance by being included in the Biennale.

However, other catalogue essays by artists and organisers make reference to 'the sour fruits of apartheid'[74] and the hope that the exhibition 'will help to create realistic and practical openings that will

[68] Fax from Media and Arts Advisor at the South African Embassy Rome Clara Woerner to Exhibition Activities at the Venice Biennale Roberto Rosalen, 6 May 1993, ASAC.

[69] Ibid.

[70] 'South African Art in Italy', ASAC.

[71] Glenn RW Babb, 'Introduzione', in *Incroci del Sud*, 7.

[72] Glenn RW Babb, 'Introduzione', in ibid.

[73] Glenn RW Babb, 'Introduzione', in ibid.

[74] Es'kia Mphahlele, 'Art as Language' in ibid., 15.

be useful for social change'.[75] The non-governmental narrative offered by artists and organisers draws upon the potential of art to help the transition from apartheid. It is a narrative about self-reflection and using art to heal the nation.

The official narrative of the South African government at later Biennales, particularly in 2013, takes the opposite approach to that of 1993, by explicitly acknowledging the reasons the state was absent for so long from the Biennale (discussed further below). This change in official narratives reflects the shift in national governments from one seeking to avoid blame to one seeking to apportion it. It is also evidence of the fact that national politics plays out in the international sphere of the Biennale.

Incroci del Sud was staged across three venues. Artworks by three 'principal artists'[76] appeared in the main Biennale venues, the Giardini and the Arsenale, while the remaining twenty-four artists were staged in the Palazzo Giustinian. These venues are significant because it meant South Africa's re-reentry into the Biennale was not confined to the periphery.[77] This is despite pressure from the Rockefeller Foundation for South Africa not to show in the central pavilion in the Giardini, alongside their exhibition of art from the Cote d'Ivoire and Senegal. Correspondence from the Rockefeller Foundation to the Biennale outlines the considerable consequences – the Rockefeller Foundation would be 'forced to reconsider its support' for the Biennale – and the 'significant international embarrassment' which would ensue if South Africa was to exhibit alongside the part of the exhibition funded and arranged by the Rockefeller Foundation in the central pavilion.[78]

It appears that the Rockefeller Foundation did not want their exhibition of 'artists of black Africa'[79] – artwork from Senegal and Cote d'Ivoire – to be associated with South Africa. Despite this pressure, the work of Jackson Hlungwane – a black South African artist – was hung in the central pavilion as part of *Incroci del Sud* alongside the Rockefeller portion of the exhibition. In the catalogue Bonito Oliva emphasised the points of reference between 'the art of black South Africans' and those of 'other black artists working on the African continent'.[80]

[75] Mary Angela Schroth, 'Notes on Incroci del Sud', ibid., 17.

[76] Statement by Luis Jansen van Vuuren in ibid., 11.

[77] Letter from Director of the Biennale Achille Bonito Oliva to South African Ambassador to Italy Glenn Babb, 24 February 1993, ASAC. This letter includes the architectural plans of the exhibition space alongside Senegal and the Cote d'Ivoire in the central Italian Pavilion in the Giardini.

[78] Fax from the Director for Arts and Humanities of the Rockefeller Foundation, Alberta Arthurs, to the Curator-Visual Arts of the Venice Biennale, Achille Bonito Oliva, 29 March 1993, ASAC.

[79] Ibid.

[80] Oliva's statement in *Incroci del Sud*, 9.

At a time when South Africa was trying to move away from racial politics, it re-encountered the problematic divisions of 'black' and 'white' Africa in the space of the Biennale.

The Biennale says that exhibition space is assigned according to the needs of states[81]; however, it is evident from correspondence that greater politics were involved – as shown by South Africa's struggle to acquire exhibition space in the 1960s and 1990s. Not only do governments play a central role in the Biennale – after all, the Biennale exists in its current form because states continue to participate in it and are complicit in maintaining its structure – but other major organisations also exercise influence over how these states participate. The influence of the Rockefeller Foundation, an American organisation, takes on heightened significance in the context of the 1995 Biennale when the USA Pavilion – which is partly funded by the Rockefeller Foundation – denied South Africa's request to install an artwork nearby (discussed further below).

The politics of the relationships between states stand in contrast with how the Biennale portrays *itself* as the sole controller over the participation of member states. This image of the Biennale is evident in its 'Procedure for National Participants':

> Participating in the Exhibition will be those Countries officially invited by la Biennale to exhibit inside their own pavilions ... Participation in the Exhibition will also be extended to those Countries ... without a pavilion that have officially applied to participate in the Biennale, and for which la Biennale has confirmed the invitation, following the procedures.[82]

Even states with a long-standing relationship with the Biennale, which have their own pavilions built at their expense and which are run by the cultural departments of their governments, still need to be officially invited by the Biennale to exhibit inside their own pavilions, while other states without pavilions need to apply to be invited. This emphasis on officialdom and invitations portrays the Biennale as having the final word, whereas in reality its decision-making is heavily circumscribed by power, politics, and diplomacy.

Incroci del Sud was criticised for lacking curatorial intent, described 'as a salad of South African art under apartheid; though much of the art was of real quality, the exhibition as a whole lacked perspective'.[83] Twenty years later, in 2013, three of the artists who exhibited in *Incroci*

[81] Visual Arts and Architecture Department La Biennale, e-mail to the author, 3 December 2015.
[82] Visual Arts and Architecture Department La Biennale, 'Procedure for National Participations'.
[83] Ivor Powell, 'Venice: A Site of Memory', 1995, http://mg.co.za/article/1995-06-09-venice-a-site-of-memory.

del Sud – David Koloane, Penny Siopis, and Sue Williamson – reappeared at the Biennale in South Africa's group exhibition *Imaginary Fact.* This exhibition also intended to show the diversity of contemporary South African art and was also criticized, not for lacking perspective, but for including too many artists in a relatively small space (discussed in Chapter 9).

While the South African government saw *Incroci del Sud* as a re-engagement of the state by the international community, several South African artists resisted this view, expressing concern about representing South Africa, stating instead that they were representing themselves at the Biennale. This was due to the fact that the apartheid government had a role in facilitating the exhibition – as mentioned, Commissioner Babb had been South Africa's ambassador to Italy for fifteen years.[84] The tension between the artists and the South African government over representing the state draws attention to the difficulties of cultural diplomacy. Unlike other forms of diplomacy which can be directly controlled by the government, cultural diplomacy requires the support of nongovernmental actors – in this case, artists – who may contradict intended narratives or resist their work being used to say something with which they do not agree.[85]

South Africa Embraces the Biennale

1995 In the same year that the Truth and Reconciliation Commission was established, South Africa formally requested to participate in the Biennale.[86] The South African Department of Arts, Culture, Science and Technology selected Malcolm Payne – who had also exhibited work in *Incroci del Sud* – to present *Untitled (USA), Untitled (Holland), Untitled (United Kingdom)* at the Biennale.[87] With this came a shift in the management of South Africa's participation, directly to a government department – from the South African Association of Arts, which became an independent organisation in this year – signalling an important change in the state's approach to membership of the Biennale. Shifting responsibility to the government increased the political, public, and national sense of ownership.

[84] Alan Cowell, 'South African Artists on Show at the Biennale', 1993, *The New York Times*, www.nytimes.com/1993/06/26/arts/south-african-artists-on-show-at-the-biennale.html; *Incroci del Sud.*

[85] Gienow-Hecht, 'What Are We Searching For? Culture, Diplomacy, Agents, and the State', 10.

[86] 'Richeste partecipazione paesi senza padiglione', XLVI, ASAC. This document sorts states into categories, separating those which have 'formally requested and participated in the previous Biennale' from those which have 'formally requested and did not participate in the previous Biennale' from those who have 'asked to participate'.

[87] Malcolm Payne, 'Chronology', www.malcolmpayne.co.za/; Perryer, *10 years 100 artists*, 432.

It also arguably weakened an important part of cultural diplomacy, the 'arms-length' of government.[88]

Payne's *Untitled (USA), Untitled (Holland), Untitled (United Kingdom)* installation comprised three brick walls with inclusions: '[T]he urn-like inclusions presented the names of selected dead South African black artists who for obvious reasons were denied participation at events like the biennale.'[89] While the 1993 exhibition sought to celebrate South Africa's re-entry into the Biennale at a time when the state was poised on the edge of change, the 1995 exhibition was a commemoration; a somber recognition of previous absences at a time when South Africa was facing difficult truths about itself through the TRC, all the while cultivating the euphoria of the rainbow nation transformation.

Payne intended these commemorative walls to be built outside the pavilions of the United Kingdom, the United States, and Holland: 'three main coloniozing [sic] powers affecting our region'.[90] The Biennale granted Payne permission to build these walls; however, final permission was required from the commissioners of each of the respective pavilions.[91] In a diplomatic setback, all three commissioners denied South Africa and Payne's request to build these walls (3 metres high by 2.5 metres wide) outside their pavilions in a process of 'cultural reclamation'.[92] The South African Embassy was unsurprised by this response: '[W]ith regard to the replies of the Commissioners of the Netherlands, the United States and Britain, as expected, it was negative.'[93] The memorial walls proved too problematic – for both political and logistical reasons – to be installed in association with these pavilions. At a time when South Africa was undergoing an intense process of internal examination, it is significant that states implicated in the legacies of colonialism within South Africa – Holland and the United Kingdom – refused to partake in an external examination of their own role as conveyed in Payne's artwork.[94]

Staging a national pavilion in the form of Payne's outdoor installation meant that South Africa could be accommodated in the main venue, the Giardini. Earlier, in December 1994, the Biennale informed South Africa it would be unable to accommodate its exhibition in a

88 Isabelle Alice Zaugg and Emi Nishimura, 'Angola and Kenya Pavilions in the 2013 Venice Biennale: African Contemporary Art and Cultural Diplomacy in the "Olympics of Art"', *The Journal of Arts Management, Law, and Society,* vol. 45, no. 2 (2015): 145.

89 Malcolm Payne, e-mail to the author, 13 July 2013.

90 Ibid.

91 Letter from Malcolm Payne to the Pavilions of UK, USA and Holland, 28 April 1995, ASAC.

92 Ibid.; Fax from Advisor of Media and Information at the South African Embassy in Rome Kobus Ferreira to Dario Ventimiglia, 5 May 1995, ASAC.

93 Original quote in Italian in Ibid. Translation by the author.

94 In relation to these implications, see Tim Keegan, *Colonial South Africa: Origins Racial Order* (Charlottesville: University Press of Virginia, 1996).

space within the main exhibition venues at the 1995 Biennale and suggested South Africa find a space to exhibit elsewhere in the city.[95] Since the state's exhibition was not under the patronage of the Biennale as it was in 1993, but rather South Africa was seeking inclusion as a national pavilion, it was left to the government to find an exhibition space on the outskirts of the Biennale. However, after permission was denied for the walls to be built outside the pavilions of the United Kingdom, the United States, and Holland, South Africa requested permission for them to be built in the general area of the Giardini.[96] While this new proposal was at first denied by the Biennale, it was eventually accepted and the walls were built at the main entrance to the Giardini.[97] This result was significant because it not only meant South Africa was able to exhibit in the main venue, but it was also positioned at the entrance of the centre, which is pertinent to the geopolitics of the pavilions (discussed in Chapter 8). The form of the artwork thus facilitated South Africa's position on this world stage, at a time when the state was still sharply in the spotlight of world politics and critique.

In this same year, South Africa launched a Johannesburg biennale – the state was re-engaging the international community through art from abroad and from within: hosting 'a biennial puts you on the map, because today biennials *are* the map'.[98] The simultaneous development of the Johannesburg Biennale and South Africa's participation in the Venice Biennale highlighted an ongoing debate within the nation, over whether South Africa should look towards the 'centre' – criticised for being Eurocentric – or should play a role in de-centering; away from Europe and grounded in Africa.[99]

95 Letter from Gian Luigi Rondi, Biennale to South African Ambassador to Italy Glen Babb, 6 December 1994, ASAC.

96 Fax from Kobus Ferreira to Dario Ventimiglia, 5 May 1995, ASAC.

97 Letter from the President of the Biennale Gian Luigi Rondi to South African Ambassador to Italy Glenn Babb, 11 May 1995, ASAC; Letter from Dario Ventimiglia of the Biennale to the President of the Biennale Gian Luigi Rondi, 15 May 1995, ASAC.

98 Monica Sassatelli, 'The Biennalization of Art Worlds', in *Routledge International Handbook of the Sociology of Art and Culture*, ed. Laurie Hanquinet and Mike Savage (Oxford: Routledge, 2015), 281. For an analysis of how the two Johannesburg biennales shaped South Africa, see Sabine Marschall, 'The Impact of the Two Johannesburg Biennales (1995 and 1997) on the Formation of a "New South African Art", *Social Dynamics*, vol. 25, no. 2 (1999). Also see Okwui Enwezor, 'Mega-Exhibitions: The Antinomies of a Transnational Global Form', in *Other Cities, Other Worlds: Urban Imaginaries in a Globalizing Age*, ed. Andreas Huyssen (Durham: Duke University Press, 2008), 174–176.

99 For an example of this ongoing debate, see this pro-Biennale piece by Marilyn Martin, 'Death in Venice', *Artthrob*, no. 73 (2003). And this anti-Biennale response by Mario Pissarra, 'Death to Venice! A South African Perspective on the Irrelevance of Representation at the Venice Biennale', 2006, Africa South Art Initiative, http://asai.co.za/death-to-venice-a-south-african-perspective-on-the-irrelevance-of-representation-at-the-venice-biennale/.

2011 In this year, South Africa returned to the Biennale after another long absence – eleven years and seven art biennales. This time the absence did not result from international boycott, but rather South Africa did not apply to participate. South Africa had a clear focus on developing domestic art expositions, such as the Johannesburg Biennale, and participating in regional arts expositions, such as the Dakar Biennale in Senegal, during this time – a focus which is reflected in how the government sought to shape its regional leadership in the decade after apartheid, with an emphasis on pan-Africanist foreign policy in direct contrast to the previous apartheid regime which favoured cultural relations with Europe and North America.[100] While the work of individual artists from South Africa was included in various exhibitions at the Biennale during this period, the state did not officially appear as a national participant.[101] This was notwithstanding calls from high-profile members of the arts community for South Africa to participate in the Biennale.[102]

The return of South Africa to the Biennale coincided with a change in the state's Arts and Culture Minister, from Lulama Xingwana to Paul Mashatile, in October 2010. The commissioner of the 2011 South Africa Pavilion, Lethole Mokoena, describes that the return was due to his lobbying of the government, the new minister being more receptive to the Biennale than the former minister.[103] The Department of Arts and Culture's (DAC) *Strategic Plan 2011–2016* also stated that participating in the Biennale will 'strengthen and expand global bilateral partnerships', aligning with their focus on 'the importance of cultural diplomacy in our international relations and expand[ing] South Africa's network with the world'.[104] The emphasis on cultural diplomacy within DAC's new strategic plan clearly situates membership of the Biennale as an important site for South Africa to enhance relationships within the international community.

The 2011 national pavilion was entitled *Desire: Ideal Narratives in Contemporary South African Art* and featured the work of Siemon Allen, Lyndi Sales, and Mary Sibande, curated by Thembinkosi Goniwe. Housed just outside the main Biennale venues – in the Torre

100 This policy position and regional focus is reflected in the section on International Cultural Cooperation in Department of Arts Culture Science and Technology, 'White Paper on Arts, Culture and Heritage', 1996, www.dac.gov.za/content/white-paper-arts-culture-and-heritage-0#CHAP6.

101 For example, at the 2000 Biennale several artists from South Africa exhibited in the *Authentic/Ex-centric: Africa in and out of Africa*, see Perryer, *10 Years 100 Artists*, 441.

102 See, for example, Martin, 'Death in Venice.'

103 Lethole Mokoena, 'Radio Interview: South African Pavilion', 2011, www.spreaker.com/user/roma_radio_art_fair/south_african_pavilion_lethole_mokoena. See also, Sean O'Toole, 'The Venice Effect', 2011, www.timeslive.co.za/lifestyle/2011/05/27/the-venice-effect.

104 Department of Arts and Culture, 'Strategic Plan 2011–2016' (2011).

di Porta Nuova accessible only by boat – *Desire* intended to offer 'three approaches to re-thinking the ideals and experiences promised by democracy'[105]; consolidating that the artists' 'affirmative work is not simply passive but rather reflective'.[106] The organisers saw the Biennale as a platform for the three artists to 'share and engage with the gift their country has given them: the opportunity to make democratic ideals possible'[107] – re-connecting with the celebratory tone of the 1993 exhibition.

However, *Desire* generated controversy within South Africa about the way in which the exhibition was organised – with one artist, Zwelethu Mthethwa, withdrawing his participation on the basis of a lack of transparency about the way in which the Pavilion was being managed.[108]

DAC did not issue a call for proposals to stage the exhibition, and there was no public tender process. This is significant for two reasons. First, it remains unclear how DAC selected the commissioner of the Pavilion. Some sources state that it was because the commissioner approached the minister to participate in the Biennale in the first place, while others imply it was the result of nepotism.[109]

Adding to the uncertainty about the appointment of a commissioner was the conflict of interest which resulted from this appointment.

105 Victor Dlamini, 'Press Release, Desire' (South Africa Pavilion, 2013).

106 Thembinkosi Goniwe, 'DESIRE: Ideal Narratives in Contemporary South African Art South Africa's exhibition at the Venice Biennale, 4 June–27 November 2011', *African Identities,* vol. 9, no. 2 (2011): 247.

107 Dlamini, 'Press Release, Desire'.

108 See David Krut Projects, 'Zwelethu Mthethwa Pulls Out of South Africa's Venice Biennale Pavilion', 2011, http://davidkrut.bookslive.co.za/blog/2011/06/01/zwelethu-mthethwa-pulls-out-of-south-africas-venice-biennale-pavilion/.

109 Sources which state the former include O'Toole, 'The Venice effect'; Mokoena, 'Radio Interview'; ArtAfrica, 'DAC Provides Documentation on South African Pavilion at 2011 Venice Biennale', 2012, http://artsouthafrica.com/component/content/article/212-archived-featured-articles/1254-dac-provides-documentation-on-south-africa-pavilion-at-2011-venice-biennale.html. Sources which imply the later Matthew Blackman, 'Taxpayers Dish Out R10m for "Private" Exhibition', 2012, http://mg.co.za/article/2012-04-02-taxpayers-dish-up-for-private-initiative-exhibition; Matthew Blackman, 'Department Mum on Venice Biennale Exhibition', 2012, www.misa.org/media-and-children/item/328-department-mum-on-venice-biennale-exhibition; Matthew Blackman, 'Silence from South African Art World Following Venice Biennale Controversy', 2011, www.theartnewspaper.com/articles/Silence+from+South+African+art+world+following+Venice+Biennale+controversy/24634; Matthew Blackman, 'Department States It Has No Reason to Doubt Faked Invoices', 2013, http://artthrob.co.za/News/Department_states_it_has_no_reason_to_doubt_faked_invoices_by_M_Blackman_on_30_July.aspx; Matthew Blackman, 'Open Letter to the Minister of Arts and Culture Regarding the Venice Biennale 2011', *South African Art Times* 2012. For an overview, see Gabriel Clark-Brown, 'Cause for Alarm: The DAC Shady Dealings: Venice Biennale Debacle 2011', ibid; and the Visual Arts Network of South Africa, 'VANSA Statement on the Venice Biennale', 2011, http://vansa.co.za/voice/art-voice/copy_of_vansa-statement-on-the-venice-biennale.

Mokoena is the founder of a commercial gallery – Gallery MOMO. As commissioner, Mokoena appointed the curator, and in turn, the curator selected two of Gallery MOMO's artists to exhibit in *Desire*. Despite statements of curatorial independence, this decision meant that potentially, the Commissioner stood to benefit financially from any sales of the artists' work, as well as benefit from the reputational capital garnered by the artists' exposure at the Biennale.[110] This is not to suggest that the artists who exhibited in *Desire* were not qualified to be there – the contrary is true – but rather that the problems of the exhibition related to the way in which it was organised.

While the Biennale does not officially allow sales at the exhibition – a change prompted by the 1968 protests – it still functions as a conduit to the art market. Given that the role of commissioner is intended to be a diplomatic one, acting as the mediator between national governments and the Biennale, it is problematic that the commissioner was seen to have had a vested commercial interest in how South Africa represented itself at the Biennale. Most member states appoint high-profile diplomats or public figures from outside the art world to be commissioners, in order to avoid this conflict.[111]

Second, DAC allocated a significant budget – reported figures vary between 10 million and 14.1 million rand (approximately £460,000 to £645,000) – to stage the Pavilion.[112] The lack of a tender process for the expenditure of this public money, as well as the inconsistent reporting on how it was spent, resulted in a parliamentary debate, with the minister facing questions about the tender process and contractor selection from the Shadow Arts and Culture Minister, Niekie van den Berg.[113] DAC also reportedly failed to respond to a request for information about the Pavilion under the Promotion of Access to Information Act. However, information was later released – after an application was made to the Western Cape High Court – stating that the reason for the absence of a tender process was owing to time constraints.[114] The fact that debate about how South Africa participates in the Biennale reached Parliament and was the subject of legal proceedings portrays the significance of this event at the level of national politics.

110 David Krut Projects, 'Zwelethu Mthethwa Pulls Out of South Africa's Venice Biennale Pavilion'.

111 See an example of these appointment processes listed in Visual Arts Network of South Africa, 'VANSA Statement on the Venice Biennale'.

112 Blackman, 'Taxpayers Dish Out R10m for "Private" Exhibition'; Niekie van den Berg, 'Controversy Surrounds South Africa's Participation in the 2011 Venice Biennale', 2012, www.da.org.za/archive/controversy-surrounds-south-africas-participation-in-the-2011-venice-biennale/.

113 van den Berg, 'Controversy Surrounds'.

114 Blackman, 'Department Mum on Venice Biennale Exhibition'.

DAC underestimated the significance of national representation at the Biennale and consequently miscalculated how many of the decisions which go into staging a national pavilion are subject to greater scrutiny stemming from a sense of public ownership and accountability. The problems surrounding the 2011 Pavilion signal a misconception about the Biennale – perhaps understandable, given the state's long absence from the forum. The 2011 Pavilion appears to have been organised as if it was an art fair, where curatorial and financial decisions are subject to private business practices. DAC went as far as to describe the 2011 Pavilion as a 'private initiative',[115] missing the fact that being a member state of the Biennale is about cultivating national identity and representing the nation-state within the international community. In addition, since participation was funded by a substantial amount of taxpayer money, this inevitably incurs a heightened sense of public ownership, especially in a country gripped by severe poverty and the political legacy of oppressive private initiatives. Given the minister described the Biennale as the art Olympics (mentioned at the start of this chapter), it is difficult to imagine participation in the Olympics being similarly denigrated to being a private initiative.

In the 2010 consultation draft on the assessment of the visual arts in South Africa, DAC recognised a distinction between art fairs and biennales:

> Art Fairs have an overtly commercial character, functioning as trade shows for the visual arts which attract both domestic and international exhibitors. Biennales, by contrast, are curated exhibitions involving the participation of artists and curators from a variety of national contexts, usually in the context of national pavilions/exhibits. Though they are overtly more engaged in the construction of art-critical discourse than in selling, in so doing they also play an influencing role in the market in developing the reputations of particular artists and curators.[116]

While this definition acknowledges the differences between art fairs and biennales in the commercial sphere, it does not adequately capture the wider and more direct political implications of biennales – the Venice Biennale in particular – in which artists, curators, and commissioners are representing their state in the diplomatic sphere.[117] The political stakes are higher in representing the state at the Biennale than they are in representing artists in art fairs. Consequently, the decisions

[115] DAC spokesperson Percy Mthimkhulu in Clark-Brown, 'Cause for Alarm'. Also see ArtAfrica, 'DAC Provides Documentation on South African Pavilion at 2011 Venice Biennale'.

[116] The Human Sciences Research Council, 'An Assessment of the Visual Arts in South Africa' (2010).

[117] For an overview of the similarities and differences between biennials and art fairs, see Tang, 'Biennalization and Its Discontents'.

which go into staging a national pavilion at the Biennale are subject to more intense scrutiny.

Correspondence between the minister and the South African ambassador to Italy emphasises the economic potential of the Biennale over its diplomacy. In January 2011, the minister wrote to the ambassador informing her of the decision that DAC was going to take part in the Biennale that year: 'I have taken a decision that the Department of Arts and Culture participates at this year's Art Biennale' and stated 'we will be able to showcase South Africa's creative talent and expose our artists to the world markets'.[118] While this acknowledges the Biennale is about showcasing South Africa – representing the state through artists – the end goal of this showcase is explicitly linked to market expansion. This connection is also made by the curator who, in the exhibition catalogue, draws parallels between South Africa's participation at the Biennale and its joining of BRIC (Brazil, Russia, India, China) economies in the same year.[119] The narratives which refer to the Biennale as being part of South Africa's economic development overshadow the goals of cultural diplomacy – bilateral partnerships and mutual understanding – stated in DAC's *Strategic Plan 2011–2016;* a point which gains further traction in 2013.

2013 This year marked the first year in South Africa's twenty-year lease on an exhibition space in the Arsenale. DAC believed that securing this lease would abate price fluctuations, ensuring 'we don't have to negotiate prices on a yearly basis. We will instead focus on preparing our country's best ideas and products to compete at the highest level with their international counterparts.'[120] Such an arrangement ensured South Africa's place in the Biennale for the near future, reducing the uncertainty of membership and the burden of negotiating for space each year. Beyond price fluctuations, the arrangement is a contract between the Biennale and South Africa, signalling the state's formal embrace of, but also acceptance by, this international community as a semi-permanent Biennale member.

This time DAC issued a public call for proposals. A jury comprised of academics and curators appointed by DAC, selected NAF – an organisation responsible for an annual international arts festival in Grahamstown – to stage *Imaginary Fact: Contemporary South African Art and the Archive.*[121] The Consul-General of South Africa to Milan,

118 Letter from Paul Mashatile to Thenjiwe Mtintso, 5 January 2011, ASAC.

119 Thembinkosi Goniwe, *Desire: Ideal Narratives in Contemporary South African Art* (CulArt Productions, 2011), 7.

120 Lisa Combrinck, 'Press Release: Participation of South Africa at the 55th la Biennale di Venezia' (Department of Arts and Culture, 2013).

121 'South African Exhibition at the 55th International Art Exhibition – Venice Biennale 2013: Expression of Interest: Visual Arts Curators', *Newspaper advertisement*, 25 January 2013.

Saul Molobi, was appointed to the role of commissioner. The selection of a non-profit arts organisation subsequent to a tender process, and the appointment of a diplomat as commissioner, demonstrated efforts made by DAC to redress the problems of 2011:

> So this [2013] is, in fact, was the first time that it was done in – if I could put it – a transparent manner, where they [DAC] actually called for bids and it was adjudicated. And even though it happened quite late, at least there was a process that I believe was far more transparent and equitable.[122]

However, as mentioned in this statement, the process also occurred very late – the deadline for proposals to be submitted to DAC was the beginning of February 2013 and it was awarded to NAF at the end of that month, just three months before the Biennale was due to open.[123] This shortened time scale – a 'fatal tardiness'[124] – undermined South Africa's ability to compete against other states that had much longer to prepare (in some cases upwards of two years) along with greater institutional knowledge of the Biennale and the unique challenges of staging exhibitions in Venice, such as challenges posed by the volume of visitors, and greater financial backing.

The Biennale awards a Golden Lion to the best national pavilion as judged by a jury comprised of international curators and selected each year by the board of the Biennale Foundation. While participation in the Biennale already confers a sense of acceptance into this international community, these awards confer an added layer of prestige to the national pavilions, increasing the stakes of participation. The lack of adequate time to prepare for the Biennale undermined South Africa's chances to participate fully in this competition.[125] The government's failure to prepare for the Biennale reveals that while they may

The jury consisted of Stephen Inggs (Michaelis School of Art, University of Cape Town), Avitha Sooful (Vaal University of Technology), Nombeko Mpako (Chair of Department of Art History, Visual Arts and Musicology, University of South Africa), Andre le Roux (SAMRO Foundation), Ester le Roux (Director of Oliewenhuis Art Museum), Monica Newton (CEO of the National Arts Council), Melissa Goba (Independent curator), and Mmutle Kgokong (Tshwane Art Museum) in Combrinck, 'Press release'.

122 Curatorial team member 2.

123 Department of Arts and Culture, 'Participation of South Africa at the 55th la Biennale di Venezia', news release, 27 February 2013 2013, www.dac.gov.za/media_releases/2013/27-02-2013.html; 'South African Exhibition at the 55th International Art Exhibition'.

124 Sue Williamson, 'Sue Williamson's Diary: Venice and the World', 2015, *Artthrob*, http://artthrob.co.za/2015/03/30/sue-williamsons-diary-venice-and-the-world/.

125 The shortened timescales continue to effect South Africa's participation in the Biennale. For instance, in 2015, DAC announced the successful bidder from the tender process to stage the exhibition in Venice, only two months before the Biennale was due to open. See Stefanie Jason, 'Venice Biennale: SA Pavilion finally announces artists', 2015, http://mg.co.za/article/2015-04-16-venice-biennale-sa-pavilion-finally-announces-artists.

want the kudos for, and potential beneficial outcomes of, being a member of this international community, they are yet to facilitate an adequate process to realise these benefits.[126]

NAF 'wanted to make a fresh start for the country' by differentiating their exhibition and themselves from the controversy of the 2011 Pavilion.[127] To do this they staged a large group exhibition, consisting of work by seventeen artists, curated by Brenton Maart and a curatorial committee of four members.[128] The number of people involved reflects a concern to present an exhibition that was more inclusive and open than that of 2011. It was a deliberate move by NAF and DAC to present an image of South Africa which would abate criticism from a national audience – distancing from the problems of the 2011 Pavilion – and educate an international audience about the diversity of contemporary South African art while reinserting the nation's art history to compensate for its previous years of absence.

In his speech opening the South Africa Pavilion in May 2013, Arts and Culture Minister Mashatile raised three important points about the Biennale:

> We believe that South African art and artists can hold their own against the best in the world. Our presence at the Biennale is part of our overall commitment to give exposure to our artists; opening up opportunities for them to access new markets for their works. By strengthening trade in artistic goods and services; we ensure the sustainability of our sector and enhance its contribution to the national effort to create jobs and grow our economy . . . We have brought a total of 17 of our finest artists to this year's Venice Biennale . . . In you, we have worthy Ambassadors of South African visual arts. I have no doubt that you will continue to fly the South Africa flag high.[129]

First, the minister's words capture the reputation of the Biennale, where the best in the world compete. While these words reflect the government's outward orientation, towards this international community, they also draw attention to the political importance for the minister and DAC to lead this participation – something several previous generations of governments in South Africa had attempted but failed to achieve.

[126] Idea raised by Artist 21 and Artist 1.

[127] Exhibition management 6.

[128] The seventeen artists were: Joanne Bloch, Wim Botha, David Koloane, Donna Kukama, Gerhard Marx, Maja Marx, Philip Miller, Zanele Muholi, San Nhlengethwa, Johannes Phokela, Cameron Platter, Andrew Putter, Athi-Patra Ruga, Penny Siopis, James Webb, Sue Williamson and Nelisiwe Xaba. The curatorial team members were: Brett Bailey, Nomusa Makhuba, Jay Pather, and Dominic Thorburn.

[129] Mashatile, 'Speech on occasion of the opening of South African Pavilion at the 55th Venice Biennale'.

Second, it is significant that the government believed that exhibiting at the Biennale would strengthen trade, create jobs, and grow the economy. These are benefits which reach beyond the arts; benefits which the government uses to justify participating in the Biennale for a domestic audience and partly to abate criticism of the 10 million rand (approximately £460,000) budget the government designates per annum to stage the exhibition.[130] Even though the exhibition is in an international space and is intended for an international audience, the claims made by the minister recognise that the exhibition has political ramifications at home. On top of the Biennale being an exercise in cultural diplomacy for an external audience, it is circumscribed by national politics for an internal audience. The focus on trade acknowledges this dual role.

Furthermore, these comments about economic growth emphasise the continued focus by DAC on the commerce of the Biennale over and above its diplomacy – an issue which surfaced in 2011. However, it remains unclear if this emphasis on the Biennale as potentially creating jobs and growth is justified, since DAC's *Annual Report for 2013–2014* provides a very general figure of around 1,000 jobs having been created through the 'Touring Venture' platforms for that financial year.[131] As the Biennale was only one of twenty ventures, the implication was that, on average, approximately fifty jobs were created by the Biennale.[132] However, given that it is unclear how this job figure of 1,000 was determined (especially given that one venture on its own produced '250 projects' and was likely to have generated a greater number of jobs than any other venture), then fifty jobs attributable to the Biennale is perhaps an unlikely outcome.[133] Thus, justifying participation in the Biennale on the promise of growing the job market appears to be problematic, even if the economic benefits of South Africa's international art exposure remain difficult to determine in such quantifiable terms.

Third, calling the artists ambassadors emphasised the diplomatic role of exhibiting in the Biennale; the artists are interpolated as being agents of the state. This sentiment positions the pavilion as an extension of South Africa's diplomatic core (an idea analysed in Chapter 10). The repeated connections between diplomacy and economics – between the external and internal value – positions the Biennale as an important international institution, membership of which has significant ramifications for South Africa.

130 Blackman, 'Department Mum on Venice Biennale Exhibition'.
131 Department of Arts and Culture, 'Annual Report 2013–2014' (2013–2014).
132 ibid.
133 Ibid. The venture which is reported to have included 250 projects is the South African Season in France.

This timeline shows that changes to the Biennale overtime – spurred by the 1968 protests – mark a significant shift in emphasis from business to politics; sales were ostensibly replaced with diplomacy. South Africa was greatly affected by this shift. Being denied the opportunity to participate in the Biennale was punishment for the apartheid regime and led to South Africa becoming isolated from an important international platform. The ramifications of this ban continue to reverberate in South Africa's contemporary participation in the Biennale, both through the way in which the government engages with this institution (emphasising its economic benefits) and the substance of what is exhibited in the national pavilion – particularly in the case of *Imaginary Fact*. South Africa's history and evolving relationship with the Biennale demonstrate the political imperatives and diplomatic relations which underscore the participation in, and the membership of, this international institution.

8

Mapping Political Art-Scapes

> When you walk into the pavilions I find that it makes you feel as though you're walking through that country . . . it makes you think about the country and aware of what's going on in other parts of the world. So when I walked into the South African Pavilion, same as when I walked into Palestine's or Iraq's pavilions, it conjured up the same feeling of war torn countries which are seeking justice.[1]

> The orchestration of national pavilions in Venice is more accurate in mapping the current global political order than the countries' actual geographical positioning. Art in the context of the Venice Biennale does not imagine the world 'differently' but rather more accurately than it often presents itself.[2]

> [E]very biennial can be seen as a model of such a new world order because every biennial tries to negotiate between national and international, cultural identities and global trends, the economically successful and the politically relevant.[3]

The Biennale is an exercise in geo-political mapping. It transforms the local city space of Venice into a global art-scape: 'marked in its very architectural structure by the inequalities of the colonialist world order that has funded and continues to fund the art displayed'.[4] The globe of Venice has two cradles of influence and prominence. The Giardini and the Arsenale house the majority

[1] Visitor 0 from Australia.

[2] Jonas Staal, 'Ideological Guide to the Venice Biennale', 2013, http://venicebiennale2013.ideologicalguide.com/about/. The Ideological Guide to the Venice Biennale was an application for smart phones produced for the 2013 Biennale which provided information on the political, economic, and ideological frameworks of national pavilions, written by artists and philosophers. It offered users the ability to plan visits according to geopolitical alliances, such as members of the Northern Atlantic Treaty Organization, states which acknowledge the International Criminal Court, or members of the League of Arab States or Group of Eight.

[3] Boris Groys, 'From Medium to Message: The Art Exhibition as Model of a New World Order', *Open: The Art Biennial as a Global Phenomenon,* vol. 8, no. 16 (2009): 65.

[4] Yahya M. Madra, 'From Imperialism to Transnational Capitalism: The Venice Biennial as a "Transitional Conjuncture"', *Rethinking Marxism,* vol. 18, no. 4 (2006): 526. Appadurai uses the suffix 'scape' to refer to dimensions of 'global cultural flows' in Arjun Appadurai, *Modernity at Large: Cultural Dimensions of Globalization* (Minneapolis: University of Minnesota Press, 1996), 33–36.

of the national exhibitions. In the garden compound – the Giardini – twenty-nine permanent pavilions were built by states which are long-standing participants in the Biennale, that are laid out like art embassies. These are the colonial 'old money' of the Biennale. The walls and moats of the Giardini prominently delineate the borders that separate it from other exhibition venues: 'the border that separates the North from the South, the core from the periphery'.[5] The Arsenale houses semi-permanent rented spaces of states that are new to the Biennale – the *nouveau riche* who apply to exhibit – butted against each other in the long corridors of crumbling ex-naval warehouses. And the newer states – those on the margins of this art bonanza, the post-colonial dwellers – are dotted around the city, churches, palazzos, and courtyards becoming temporary exhibition spaces. States jostle for the best locations, knowing that although it will never be possible to join the imperial ranks of the Giardini – the garden is closed to new nations – the closer they are to the epicentre, the more visible, the more visited, and the more remembered the exhibitions will be.

In the Gardens of Good and Evil

Inside the Giardini are the geopolitical axes of the mid-twentieth century; a grouping that has its roots in post-war Europe. The first state to be invited to build a permanent pavilion here was Belgium in 1907; the last was South Korea in 1995. Over half the pavilions in the Giardini belong to European nations. Germany (built in 1909), Great Britain (1909), and France (1912) all inhabit similar neo-classical structures, although Great Britain did not build their own, but rather inherited the former teahouse[6] – fitting for an empire built partly on the tea trade. The former Czechoslovakia Pavilion (1926) is divided in two, to accommodate a dissolution: the Czech Republic on one side and Slovakia on the other. Sweden and Norway share the Nordic Countries Pavilion (1962). And finally, Hungary (1909), the Netherlands (1912), Spain (1922), Denmark (1932), Poland (1932), Romania (1932), Austria (1934), Greece (1934), Switzerland (1952), and Finland (1956) are housed in a mix of pavilions.[7]

The pavilions in the Giardini are in prime locations. Architecturally distinct, they resemble the individual embassies found in the diplomatic circles of nations' capitals (Fig. 8.1), while collectively they map out symbolic and historic political relationships. For example, '[t]he Romanian Pavilion is the

[5] Madra, 'From Imperialism to Transnational Capitalism,' 526.

[6] British Council, 'From the Outside In', 2013, http://venicebiennale.britishcouncil.org/media/album/item/from-the-outside-in-.

[7] For an overview of the history of individual pavilions, see Gabriele Basilico, ed. *Common Pavilions: The National Pavilions in the Giardini of the Venice Biennale in Essays and Photographs* (Zurich: Scheidegger and Spiess, 2013). The bracketed dates indicate in what year the national pavilion was built/opened in the Giardini.

Figure 8.1 National pavilions inside the Giardini. (Left to right) Belgium, France, Russia, sign to Australia.
Photography by author, 2013

last, at the end of the row. Which is to say, at the margin ... Likewise, Romania today is at the terminus of the European Union, a frontier of this agitated conglomerate'[8]; and 'Czechoslovakia acquired, through its pavilion, a position in the centre of events ... This position reflected precisely the Czechoslovak cultural elite's view of their place within Europe.'[9]

The other half of the Giardini is owned by non-European nations. The USA Pavilion (1930) is visible from almost every corner of the Giardini, fitting for a

[8] Bogdan Ghiu, 'The Myth of Place', 2013, http://commonpavilions.com/pavilion-romania.html.
[9] Henrieta Moravčíková, 'Sensing the Common Ground', 2013, http://commonpavilions.com/pavilion-czech-slovak-republic.html.

geopolitical hegemon. With its modernist edge and tightly controlled borders, Israel (1952) is in a snug spot next to USA. The 'colonies' of Australia (1987) and Canada (1958) are on the edges of the garden island, in line with Great Britain, which rises on its hill above. Australia in particular is in a location that is 'down under', sunken on the banks of the Giardini, behind Uruguay (1960); it requires concerted navigating to reach – a spatial remark on the country's geographic isolation. Then there is the Russia Pavilion (1914) whose monolithic walls, hiding in plain sight, dominate the low-lying structures of the pavilions at its borders, namely Venezuela (1954) and Japan (1956). On a small island located at the very back of the garden compound – 'in an area often missed by those who make insufficient use of their map'[10] – hidden among some smaller European nations, are Brazil (1964) and Serbia (1932). And finally, there is Egypt (1952), which is the only state from the African continent in the Giardini and the only Islamic nation.

Through these embassy-like pavilions the Giardini creates, reflects, and reinforces a microcosm of political hierarchies and boundaries: 'The position of the pavilions relative to each other reveals in a remarkably accurate way the history of transnational alliances by which states continue to promote their political, economic, and military interests.'[11]

Entering the Arsenal

The new world order in the Arsenale is more fluid than in the Giardini. Some states remain, others change year-in, year-out as applications and invitations to the international community are negotiated. At the 2013 Biennale, the Arsenale housed twenty-three national participants, including four states showing for the first time – Bahamas, Bahrain, Kosovo, and the Holy See.[12] The long corridors of former rope-making factories (Fig. 8.2) – the Arsenale was built in the twelfth century as a shipyard – were home to many 'developing' and post-conflict states, creating a sense that this venue housed national pavilions which were more politically sensitive than the ones in the Giardini:

> In the Giardini a lot is concentrated on imagination, sometimes it's a bit theosophical and spiritual, and [the Arsenale] brings it back to reality.[13]
>
> Developing countries where there's been some kind of political struggle tend to be more focused [in their exhibitions at the Biennale] on social issues than others . . . There is much more of a tendency in this country [South Africa] and other countries, like the South American countries.[14]

[10] Thornton, *Seven Days in the Art World*, 236.
[11] Staal, 'Ideological Guide to the Venice Biennale'.
[12] The twenty-three national participants were housed in sixteen national pavilions in the Arsenale; the Latin America Pavilion housed eight states not represented elsewhere as individual national participants.
[13] Visitor 19 from Belgium.
[14] Artist 24.

Figure 8.2 National pavilions inside the Arsenale. (Left) South Africa and UAE Pavilion; (middle) warehouse housing many pavilions; (right) long corridor entry to pavilions.
Photography by author, 2013

Under the protection – or watchful eye – of the active naval base adjacent, the national pavilions in the Arsenale become sites of political contestation.

The open warehouse spaces of the Arsenale mean that nations which do not usually sit side by side – either in geographic or political terms – are forced into a relationship with their exhibitions bleeding one into the other. In 2013, Akram Zaatari's film about an Israeli pilot who refused to bomb a school in Lebanon in the Lebanon Pavilion led to Chile, where an abyss of murky green water hid Alfredo Jaar's model of the Giardini that rose slowly and then sank again, drowning the dominance of the states within the compound; '[I]t manages to conjure the illusionism implicit in a world order [of the Giardini] that still believes in its own existence, when in fact it has sunk long ago and is only a phantom of itself.'[15] Chile deliberately staged an exhibition questioning its place within a world order perpetuated by hegemony, as well as the idea of national pavilions reflecting an 'essence' of a nation-state.[16] Yet the fact that this exhibition was still attributed as the Chile Pavilion and was staged by the Chilean National Council for Culture and the Arts complicates this critique of nationalism at the Biennale. The set-up of the Biennale reinforces national narratives, national borders, national identities, and 'imagined communities'.[17]

Continuing in sequence, Chile led to Kosovo, where the state's inaugural showing at the Biennale consisted of a shelter made from twigs in which visitors could catch glimpses of personal objects (such as a discarded suit) evoking the remnants of the nation's troubled history. Kosovo led to Turkey, where the stillness of the twig shelter was traded for violent video projections in which the human body was subjected to various practices of pain, related to

15 Chile's entry in Massimiliano Gioni, *Il Palazzo Enciclopedico*, vol. I and II (Venice: Fondazione La Bienale di Venezia, 2013), 34.

16 Adriana Valdes's statement in Madeleine Grynsztejn and Adriana Valdes, 'Pavilion of Chile: Alfredo Jaar Venezia, Venezia', ed. La Biennale di Venezia (National Council for Culture and the Arts, 2013).

17 The phrase 'imagined communities' is borrowed from Benedict Anderson, *Imagined Communities: Reflections on the Origin and Spread of Nationalism* (London: Verso, 2006).

surgery and sadomasochism. This exhibition – titled *Resistance* – became the site of several protests against the Turkish government.[18] Turkey led to the Kingdom of Bahrain; Bahrain led to the Republic of Indonesia; Indonesia led to Latvia; and Latvia led to the Latin America Pavilion in which sixteen artists from South America and three artists from Europe exhibited as part of an exhibition titled *El Atlas del Imperio* – *The Atlas of the Empire* – itself a metaphor for the Biennale. Each national pavilion frames the exhibition of the next, forcing surprising comparisons and unexpected relationships.

Unlike the Giardini, which brings together remarkably accurate groupings 'of transnational alliances by which states continue to promote their political, economic, and military interests', the Arsenale brings together groupings of states which posit unusual relationships.[19] Two of these groupings punctuated the former barracks at either end of the central corridor. At one end, Italy as host positioned itself to share the mammoth warehouse with 'the other' superpower of China – both exhibitions with equally grandiose scale and mass. China was flanked by the Georgia Pavilion housed in a temporary structure – called a *kamikaze loggia* – an extension, hanging (seemingly precariously) onto the existing architecture; a metaphor for Georgia's precarious fate under the shadow of Russia. Italy was flanked by the Bahamas, which showed an exhibition about polar ice; a reminder to some states about the effects of global warming on smaller island nations.

Across the small harbour and opposite the China Pavilion, outside the official Biennale venue and accessible only by boat, was *Voice of the Unseen* – a collateral event showing the work of 188 Chinese artists staged by the Guangdong Museum of Art as an alternative to the state-run China Pavilion. That the Biennale boat to reach *Voice of the Unseen* was only one way was an apt metaphor in itself; once visitors left the confines of the military arsenal, there was no return, especially if they went to visit the exhibition of art from China not staged by the Chinese government.

At the other end of the Arsenale, South Africa shared a space with the UAE above Argentina and the Holy See. This block of states provoked interesting comparisons. Argentina and South Africa – two countries plagued by legacies of political oppression – took very different approaches to addressing their pasts. Argentina explored the many sides of Eva Peron, mythologising her political journey and returning the nation to a time before the 'dirty war'. South Africa offered insights into how its troubled past is ever-present, ensuring the struggle against apartheid was firmly at the centre of the pavilion. The Holy See exhibited artworks telling the story of the first book of Genesis, while upstairs the UAE exhibited an immersive installation about being lost at sea – ironic considering the country's scarcity of water. The biblical reference of its title, *Walking on Water* (when translated from Arabic into English), took

18 Global Project, 'Occupied Turkish Pavilion at the Venice Biennale (flyer)'.
19 Quote by Staal, 'Ideological Guide to the Venice Biennale'.

on heightened meaning in this grouping. Despite claims that biennales – in general – contribute to the disintegration of borders and the growth of global culture, the spatial organisation of the Venice Biennale reifies political borders and national cultures while dispersing geographic ones.[20]

Border Crossings

Comparisons between states are forced upon them by virtue of exhibiting in the Biennale, especially in the Arsenale where pavilions lack the physical walls of separation which demarcate the embassy-like pavilions in the Giardini. The closeness of pavilions in the Arsenale presents a unique opportunity for border crossings. The grouping of South Africa and the UAE in the one open exhibition space provided marked contrasts between these nations. The contrasts were both visual and conceptual.

The UAE's exhibition was visually streamlined and direct. *Walking on Water*, by Mohammed Kazem, consisted of a dome structure which visitors entered to be immersed in a 360-degree film replicating the feeling of being on a boat in the middle of the sea, its vast waves undulating against an empty horizon. The installation was all encompassing and its effects immediate; the watery, dimly lit inner sanctum of the dome offered respite from the voluminous crowds of visitors and the stifling Venetian humidity.

In contrast, South Africa's exhibition was full and drawn out. Artworks by fourteen artists, as well as live performances by three artists (one which occurred on the streets of Venice and two staged inside the Pavilion), were exhibited in an almost equal-sized space to UAE's single installation. Visitors were led through the South Africa Pavilion, down corridors into specially constructed rooms and viewing corners. Each artwork crossed into the next, competing for sight and sound – three of the artworks included aural elements, which at times layered over one another. The density of artworks in the South Africa Pavilion mirrored the density of artworks on display at the Biennale. South Africa exhibited the work of more artists than the three national pavilions in its immediate vicinity combined, Argentina, the Holy See, and the UAE.

Conceptually, *Walking on Water* fitted in with established exhibition paradigms of national pavilions at the Biennale. National pavilions commonly exhibit the work of one artist or a small number of artists who represent the spirit of the nation at that moment in time. Some national pavilions exhibit a body of work by an established artist, where exhibiting at the Biennale is reward for a lifetime's achievement. Other pavilions commission new single artworks by up-and-coming artists, where the Biennale is a steppingstone to

[20] See Sassatelli, 'The Biennalization of Art Worlds'. Also see Charlotte Bydler, 'The Global Art World, Inc.: On the Globalization of Contemporary Art ', in *The Biennial Reader*, ed. Elena Filipovic, Marieke van Hal, and Solveig Øvstebø (Bergen: Hatje Cantz, 2010).

artistic greatness. Both styles of exhibition regularly take the form of interactive installations – site-specific works which are intended to shape perceptions of the space around them – in which the audience becomes immersed in the artworks. These conventions serve to make the impact of the art immediate and hopefully memorable, allowing visitors to quickly absorb each exhibition and move on to the next; an important consideration given that most tickets to the Biennale allowed only one entry to each of the main venues, resulting in visitors having limited time to see many national pavilions, as well as the central guest-curated exhibition, which in 2013 included work by 161 artists. However, choosing one artist to represent the nation can also be problematic, as it has the potential to reinforce fixed perspectives and ideas while silencing dissenting viewpoints. 'The conflict in Venice is, do you choose somebody to make history or do you confirm history'?[21]

By presenting a large group exhibition, the South Africa pavilion moved away from the conventional national pavilion model, making a deliberate choice to dispense with the authorial voice of national pavilions and 'to open it up to a kind of multiplicity of authors, to show that a group of people in an area is more than just one or two voices'.[22] The number of artists in *Imaginary Fact* was a deliberate move to present two ideas: spread and depth. The exhibition presented a range of artists who had produced work on the archive in South Africa over the last twenty years – the spread. The exhibition also showed different ways in which artists in South Africa work with archives – the depth. These ways included the multiple conceptual approaches artists took to archives, as well as the different mediums used: video, sound, collage, painting, photography, printing, sculpture, and performance. However, such a large group exhibition runs the overall risk that visitors might not be able to fully engage, owing to the extensive demands of viewing the Biennale.

The visual differences between the UAE and South Africa pavilions (a high-tech dome versus a variety of media from works on paper to screen works) as well as the conceptual differences in the nature and form of the exhibitions (a solo installation versus a group show) presented a stark contrast between the two nations. These contrasts take on heightened significance given the status of national pavilions, deliberately selected and staged by the governments of both nations – especially in the light of the different political systems of the UAE and South Africa.

The UAE pavilion presented an image of a state united. The seven distinct emirates – governed by absolute monarchs – are presented through one artist as a united front on the cutting edge of technology. The sci-fi-esque display sits between two worlds: the world of hyper-modernity and primordial sea forces – an apt metaphor for the state at a crossroads between technological transformation and cultural tradition. The sleek production of *Walking on Water* and

21 Thornton, *Seven Days in the Art World*, 239.
22 Curatorial team member 3.

the biblical reference in its title – at least when it is translated from Arabic into English – implies a kind of power.[23] This implication is ironic, since the work was inspired by the artist being lost at sea; a situation of powerlessness.[24] The polish of the installation masks the internal struggles of the labour involved in achieving this high-tech production. An analogy can be drawn to the UAE's luxury cities built by migrant workforces. Outwardly the UAE presented a glossy unified façade while internally the struggles run deeper.

Conversely, the South Africa pavilion presented an image of a state trying to accommodate the competing voices within its borders; an allegory of its transition to constitutional democracy. The density of artworks coupled with a group exhibition intended to show 'the very different and vibrant ways, [artists] draw on the archived record in order to make sense of our worlds today' directed attention to a range of ongoing challenges faced by the nation.[25] In contrast to the UAE, South Africa presented an image of an unsettled state, but like the UAE, internally the struggles run deeper.

The border-crossings between pavilions also manifest at personal levels. Walking through the streets of Venice I met a staff member from the Lebanon Pavilion, who was with a colleague whom I knew from the UAE Pavilion. This person mentioned being on his way to meet a member of staff from the Israel Pavilion, whom he had met earlier at the Lebanon Pavilion. Referring to being from Lebanon and connecting with someone from Israel, he said, 'that's what's nice about the Biennale, it brings people together that wouldn't normally talk.'[26] The same can be said for states; the Biennale offers a forum for states to interact, where they may not otherwise have strong diplomatic relationships.

States in the City

The many islands of Venice become home to almost as many national pavilions as are found in the main venues and even more collateral events. At the 2013 Biennale, thirty-five national pavilions and forty-seven collateral events were spread across the city – compared to the combined total of thirty-eight national pavilions in the Giardini and Arsenale.[27] Staged in palazzos,

23 The biblical reference being Jesus walking on water – an interesting reference to Christianity given the dominance of Islam in the UAE.

24 See Reem Fadda, ed. *Mohammed Kazem* (Bologna: Damiani, 2013).

25 Maart, *Imaginary Fact*, 10.

26 Field note, 8 October 2013.

27 The thirty-eight national *pavilions* in the main venues hosted fifty-one national *participants* because some pavilions, such as the Latin America Pavilion, incorporated several states. The total number of pavilions stated here, as well as the figures mentioned in the previous sections, is based on the listing of national pavilions on the official maps provided by the Biennale in 2013, rather than the figures provided by the Biennale in the exhibition media packs, which are calculated based on national *participants* as opposed to national *pavilions*. Basing the figures on participants inflates the appearance of official member states without acknowledging that some

churches, courtyards, gardens, and any space available to rent, these national pavilions and collateral events – many of which become unofficial national pavilions, such as the exhibition of Palestinian art – provide unexpected encounters with the Biennale. Art-goers get lost in winding alleyways as they hunt for pavilions, while tourists unaware of the Biennale stumble upon exhibitions, unexpectedly encountering international relations among Venice's well-known sites. The national pavilions outside the main venues transform the city, extending international relations into the streetscape.

In 2013, the Iraq Pavilion occupied the Ca'Dandolo, a palazzo on Venice's Grand Canal. Although this pavilion was far from the member states located in the Giardini and Arsenale, it was in the geographical centre of Venice, in a very visible spot along the main ferry transport route. Hanging on the façade of the building was a banner which read 'Welcome to Iraq'. For the duration of the Biennale, the exhibition in the Ca'Dandolo became Iraq. The central location and visibility of the Iraq Pavilion made it stand out, putting the state at the centre of the Biennale's geo-politics; an apt metaphor for the way in which Iraq has been at the centre of many political battles in recent history.

The pavilions located across the city highlight an interesting tension about access to the Biennale. On the one hand, there is a sense that being outside the main Biennale venues means these pavilions are on the periphery of the institution – not yet fully fledged member states, still awaiting access to the centre.[28] On the other hand, being outside the main Biennale venues means these pavilions attract a wider audience – the pavilions are free to enter (unlike the ticketed Giardini and Arsenale venues) and are frequented by both Biennale and non-Biennale audiences. However, being off the main route also means these pavilions may not be visited by time-poor Biennale audiences, especially if they are hidden in difficult-to-find venues.

The structure of the Biennale makes it an exercise in mapping art-scapes. Despite the weight of globalisation, national pavilions at the Biennale continue to chart and reify the shifting world orders of states, creating a geo-political map, both literally and figuratively. National pavilions reaffirm geo-political borders, but they also become points of engagement or 'spaces of encounter'[29] with these borders.

While many art scholars posit that the Biennale model has shifted 'away from the display of national visual cultures in an international frame toward a

participants choose to collectively exhibit as a single regional pavilion, effectively showing as one collective member.

28 For example, Berns makes the point that African art has historically been marginalized by being put in 'hard-to-find off-site locations'; Marla C Berns, 'Africa at the Venice Biennale', *African Arts,* vol. 36, no. 3 (2003): 1.

29 Enwezor uses the phrase 'spaces of encounter' to refer to 'a space in which knowledge systems, aesthetic systems and artistic systems converge, sometimes in harmony and sometimes in great disharmony'; Okwui Enwezor, 'A Space of Encounter: Interview with Victoria Lynn', *Art and Australia,* vol. 46, no. 2 (2008).

survey of current trends in art, providing an intimation of global culture',[30] the persistent organisation of the Biennale into national pavilions undercuts this claim by continually reinforcing which state inhabits which space, and which state displays which artworks. Any semblance of global culture is challenged by national possession. The viewing experience of the Biennale – diffused throughout the city – across multiple interactions and comparisons creates a discursive impression as visitors bear witness to the artworks and the different faces of nations they represent.

Pavilions become proxies through which states present an image of themselves to the international community. These images are both reinforced and undermined by the relationships and inherent competition which results from the spatial organisation of the Biennale. Although the artworks are not reducible to the states they represent, the set-up of the Biennale means that the artworks are automatically implicated and actively involved in creating an image of each state; the image perceived, however, may well not be what the state intends.

30 Papastergiadis and Martin, 'Art Biennales and Cities as Platforms for Global Dialogue', 48.

9

The Art of Representation

> For South Africa, it becomes odd to simply show pretty pictures when things are not so pretty.[1]

> People in the arts, they're more like the mirror of the nation; you wake up in the morning and you take a bath and you dress up, the mirror tells you 'come on, shift this, do this', so you must listen to the mirror and take criticism from the mirror.[2]

> I was very interested in seeing how these nations compete with each other or negotiate their identities within only art and culture, and how political it could be.[3]

The overall theme of the 2013 Biennale – *Il Palazzo Enciclopedico* (The Encyclopaedic Palace) – was based on an imaginary museum, a conceptual skyscraper, originally conceived by mid-twentieth-century Italian American artist Marino Auriti: 'to house all worldly knowledge, bringing together the greatest discoveries of the human race'.[4] The Encyclopaedic Palace – parts of which were in the central pavilion in the Giardini and others in the central corridor of the Arsenale – displayed artworks by contemporary artists alongside historical pieces, in what the curator intended as 'a meditation on the many ways in which images have been used to organize knowledge and shape our experience of the world'.[5] It was an attempt at curatorial order of artistic knowledge on an immense scale – showing the work of 161 artists. The sprawl across multiple venues and the volume of artworks on show made the exhibition overwhelming to the point of visually exhausting, the art world's equivalent of a hoarder's paradise.

As a theme, The Encyclopaedic Palace proffered two important invitations to the national pavilions. First, the theme encouraged an examination of knowledge, an encyclopaedic journey through history. This paved the way for exhibiting artworks that were not new. That is, not all the artworks were

[1] Curatorial team member 1.
[2] Artist 28.
[3] Biennale staff member 3.
[4] Gioni, *Il Palazzo Enciclopedico*, I and II, 23.
[5] Ibid.

contemporary pieces – somewhat unusual for the Biennale, in which the global artistic pulse of the moment is under scrutiny. Instead, this Biennale was about seeing old artworks anew: how knowledge is produced through the organisation of artworks and how artworks organise certain kinds of knowledge. Second, the theme implied monumentality and the assemblage of artworks on an encyclopaedic scale. Combined, these invitations were designed to guide the exhibitions in the national pavilions – some embraced the thematic invitations more than others.

In the South Africa Pavilion, *Imaginary Fact* drew on both invitations – to journey and to assemble. The spread of artworks in the exhibition presented a journey over twenty years, while the depth of artworks presented an assemblage of methods and mediums. The exhibition's title alluded to the creation of knowledge and the knowledge of creativity, playing on the idea that facts evolve from imaginative processes over time as well as from the gathering of these processes through archives. *Imaginary Fact* suggested it would impart facts and simultaneously invited reflection on these facts and their construction, the veracity of which were always in question through reference to imagination. This spectrum of display of artworks and artists presented in *Imaginary Fact* was both its political strength and its pragmatic weakness.

Pragmatic Weaknesses of *Imaginary Fact*

The most common feedback about the exhibition from visitors related to the volume of artworks in the exhibition space; that there were too many artworks displayed in a relatively confined venue.[6] This was perceived as a weakness for two reasons, largely pragmatic. First, the plethora of artworks meant that each work did not have enough space to be viewed without disruption, particularly considering the congestion caused by large numbers of visitors. On average, 3,087 visitors attended the main venues each day. By the last day of the Biennale, a total of 472,247 visitors and 7,110 journalists had attended during the six months of the exposition being open.[7]

Second, it was not possible to engage with all the artworks in the South Africa Pavilion given the visual fatigue caused by seeing so many pavilions at the Biennale – 'ticking off' the states visited was an apparent competition among many visitors. The South Africa Pavilion required an investment of time in order to engage with all the artworks on display, time which visitors did not have given the vastness of the Biennale. The majority of tickets to the Biennale allowed only one entry to the Arsenale and one entry to the Giardini. Accordingly, unless visitors purchased a multi-day pass, they only had one opportunity to visit each of the main venues, which housed a total of

[6] Over half of the seventy-six people interviewed mentioned there were too many artworks in the exhibition.

[7] La Biennale, 'Extraorindary success at the Biennale Arte 2013', news release, 2013.

38 national pavilions and works by 161 artists in the central exhibition. It is telling that many visitors were dressed in hiking-style clothing, the implication being that the Biennale is an arduous viewing experience, entailing physical endurance; art to be conquered.

The demands on viewers at the Biennale are significant and the reason why national pavilions often opt for biennale art. Biennale art is usually large in scale and has a temporal thrill factor; factors which make it memorable.[8] For instance, the 2013 Russia Pavilion exhibited an installation by Vadim Zakharov entitled *Danaë* where gold coins rained from a great height onto the umbrellas of female viewers below – only women were allowed to enter to collect coins, men had to watch from a mezzanine floor. Viewers were able to take away a gold coin as a physical reminder of the interactive installation. Whether viewers thought more deeply about the meaning of the installation afterwards – especially the implications about gender, tradition, and materialism – is a separate question, but at the very minimum the thrill of showering gold coin gifts in the pavilion was memorable.

Whereas the Russia Pavilion hosted an *installation*, the South Africa Pavilion hosted an *exhibition*: the former transforms public space, while the latter makes objects visible for public judgement.[9] The density of artworks on display in *Imaginary Fact* aligned with the curatorial vision to exhibit the multiple voices within contemporary South African art in a spatially competitive way; a microcosm of a larger scene. However, while this may have been conceptually intended, the internal competition of the exhibition – competition for space and attention – arguably detracted from prolonged engagement with the artworks. The density of the exhibition was problematic in practice because it resulted in some artworks eclipsing some of the other quieter or more interrogative pieces.

For instance, numerous people interviewed – including exhibition organisers, artists, and visitors – spoke about the dominance of Wim Botha's artworks in *Imaginary Fact*. Visitors found Botha's artworks distinctive and were especially curious as to how they are made. Created from books bolted together and then carved into human forms, Botha's sculptures functioned well in the context of the Biennale because their figurative style made them relatable, while their method of construction made them intriguing and memorable. For exhibition organisers and artists, the dominance of Botha's works – resulting from the space allocated to them compared to the space allocated to the work of other artists – was problematic because it gave the impression that NAF was 'promoting one artist at the expense of others'.[10]

[8] See Enwezor, 'Mega-Exhibitions', 157. Also see the discussion of the negative inferences of the term in Sassatelli, 'The Biennalization of Art Worlds', 284.

[9] Distinction made in Groys, 'From Medium to Message,' 58 and 60.

[10] Artist 17. Similar views were expressed by Curatorial team member 4; Artist 23; Curatorial team member 3; and Biennale staff member 5.

Botha's series of six portrait-style busts hung in the main exhibition corridor, leading to an installation entitled *Study for the Epic Mundane*, which consisted of two larger-than-life figures suspended from the double-height ceiling of the stone warehouse. *Study for the Epic Mundane* was the only artwork commissioned by NAF specifically for *Imaginary Fact*; the other artworks in the exhibition – with the exception of the three performance pieces – existed in the same form prior to being shown at the Biennale. The commissioning of *Study for the Epic Mundane* underscores the emphasis placed on Botha's artwork at the conceptual stage of the exhibition, which manifested in the physical execution of the exhibition.

The commission process also draws attention to the commerce of *Imaginary Fact*; the majority of the artworks were on loan from private collections for the period of the Biennale. For instance, Botha's works were on loan from several private collections located in South Africa and Europe.[11] Although the artworks in the exhibition were not for sale, the fact that they were being loaned by private collectors – indicated on the artwork labels – signalled their worth and their collectability. Similarly, the labels and exhibition catalogue indicated the commercial gallery responsible for representing the exhibiting artists. The convention of including gallery representation on labels means that viewers are directed to where they can inquire about purchasing artworks by these artists; this is essential information if participating in the Biennale is going to expand the markets for these artists and achieve the economic goals stipulated by DAC (discussed in Chapter 7).

The labelling of artworks also highlights an important issue about access and translation in the context of the Biennale. In the first days of the exhibition there was wall text which gave general context about South African art, but there was no text accompanying each artwork; individual explanatory labels were added after the opening week. Viewers were expected to read the exhibition catalogue if they wanted to know more about the artworks beyond what they could interpret upon sight.

Like the exhibition catalogue, the wall text was only in English. This restricted access to those who understand English, unlike many other national pavilions where exhibition text is published in English, Italian, and the official language of the state being represented. The gallery invigilators also became translators of the artworks, mediating the viewing experience when asked by visitors for further information. The four gallery invigilators who looked after the exhibition were fluent between them in five languages: Italian, English, Mandarin, Spanish, and German. Unlike most other national pavilions, the gallery invigilators were not from the state being represented, but were from the Venetian area; a significant absence of people-to-people links in regards to cultural diplomacy.

[11] The collections of Konrad Huettner, Xavier Huyberechts and Briget Grosskopff, Vincenzo Penta, Hans Porer, Micahel Roets, and Gordon Schachat.

For South Africa, which has eleven official languages and is accustomed – at least at official levels – to working across languages, the issue of translation and mediation is particularly important. While visual art can cut across language barriers and explanatory text is not always needed or even welcomed – as it can fix an interpretation of the artwork, preventing alternative ways of seeing – in the case of *Imaginary Fact*, information about the artworks was important to help time-poor and visually fatigued Biennale visitors to engage with, and understand, the large exhibition. The primacy of English reflects how South Africa engages with the international community. Of the eleven official South African languages, English is the primary language used by the government to participate in international relations.

Political Strengths of *Imaginary Fact*

The form of *Imaginary Fact* manifested the internal political situation of South Africa. A conscious trade-off was made when selecting multiple voices over a single authorial voice of the nation; a trade-off against the physical and visual comfort of visitors, and against Biennale conventions of single-artist installations. The diverse representation of artists reflects the political drive, concern, and pressure for more equal representation and inclusion within South Africa, resulting from the legacy of severe discrimination. This diversity in the exhibition is an important statement, and step, towards redressing three wounds.

The first and most important wound is the legacy of discrimination resulting from apartheid. By exhibiting artists who would have once been hidden from the international spotlight and silenced under the apartheid regime, *Imaginary Fact* was an attempt to rebalance past injustices of representation:

> We tried to find a grouping of artists that would be representative in terms of gender, in terms of race, in terms of representation of gallery and independent artists . . . because we have a complex society, we still have lots of political issues to grapple with, and it's not just the race issue but it's also the gender issues, and then class issues and the issue of privilege.[12]

This perception of representational balance was also questioned for being 'token' – there was a disproportionate emphasis on work by 'white artists', and all of the artists exhibited are established, being represented by major art galleries in South Africa.[13]

The way in which the participating artists were announced led to the perception that some artists were only included in the exhibition during later stages in order to fill a gap. NAF stated that the short period of time between

[12] Curatorial team member 1.
[13] Artist 3.

DAC selecting them to stage the South Africa Pavilion and the opening of the Biennale resulted in the exhibiting artists being announced in stages as each artist agreed to exhibit.[14] However, the staggered announcements of artists led to debates about representation and the inclusion of no black female artists.[15] In other words, there was a perception that the representation of artists in *Imaginary Fact* was forced for the sake of appearances: 'It was described as a rainbow nation show which was kind of an insult because it was sort of saying that it was too diverse and it was just trying to incorporate everybody'; 'It was characterized by a kind of one of everything approach – black, white, other, male, female, young, old, straight, gay, sculpture, painting, installation, video'.[16] This is a criticism which South African art exhibitions have faced over several decades.[17]

The amount of money spent by the South African government on sending certain artists to the Biennale and renting an exhibition space in the Arsenale was also perceived as imprudent: 'One needs to interrogate how much money it's costing and whether it's the same people who are showing overseas and what benefit does it bring back to the country.'[18] The economic benefits which DAC claimed exhibiting at the Biennale would bring to the whole nation are undermined by the perception that it is the same artists who are repeatedly representing South Africa in the international community, and thus any economic benefits are limited to specific individuals and galleries. Both these counter-arguments about the process and economics of representation are not unique to *Imaginary Fact*. Rather, they are indicative of broader debates which are ongoing within South Africa about what equality of representation means in practice.

The second wound is the years of isolation experienced by South African artists during the cultural boycott. Being banned from exhibiting at the Biennale for twenty-five years meant the state was largely unable to 'show off' its artists and cultural production to the international community. Showing a significant number of artists as well as a range of art production within the country is a way to reinsert the history of South Africa back into the Biennale: 'Because it's part of our reintroduction back into the Venice Biennale . . . what we needed to do was to show what South Africans have been up to over the past 10, 15 years.'[19] *Imaginary Fact* was making up for lost

14 Brent Meersman, 'An Imperfect Past and Its Impact on the Present', *Mail and Guardian*, 2013.

15 See ibid. The announcements of artists exhibiting in the 2015 South Africa Pavilion faced the same criticisms; see Jason, 'Venice Biennale'.

16 Artist 15; Williamson, 'Sue Williamson's Diary'.

17 See, for example, the debates over selection processes in Marschall, 'The Impact of the Two Johannesburg Biennales (1995 and 1997) on the Formation of a "New South African Art",' 126–127.

18 Exhibition management 2.

19 Maart in Theresa Smith, 'SA Art Back in Global Showcase', 2013, www.iol.co.za/tonight/what-s-on/western-cape/sa-art-back-in-global-showcase-1.1515423#.UouNJ2S4GLE.

time – the number of artists was a way to show the world what they had been missing: 'If you're going to Venice as a country it's a strategic move and you want to show . . . the world what we're made of . . . that's the reason why we had so many artists . . . also we have not been in Venice for so many years.'[20]

The exhibition was also intended to capture a new movement in contemporary South African art, focused on how the past impacts the present: 'Because these new social movements in South Africa are grounded in advocacy and because advocacy is grounded in human rights and because human rights are grounded in history, what you have now is an attempt [by artists] to be able to redress history in the contemporary by looking at how we got to where we are today.'[21] This new movement draws a distinct break with two art movements in South Africa from the recent past: art focused on political resistance to fight against apartheid; and art focused on identity formation in the immediate wake of apartheid.[22] *Imaginary Fact* therefore was both rebuilding South African identity into the Biennale's memory while at the same time exploring how history affects that living memory. South Africa's urge to *inform* the international community about their art follows a similar pattern to other nations which have also been absent from the Biennale.[23]

The third wound is the controversy of the 2011 South Africa Pavilion (discussed in Chapter 7) in which the work of only three artists was exhibited, two of whom were represented by the same commercial art gallery: 'I can understand with the history – especially with South Africa's past participation at the Biennale – the extended history and the sort of micro history of all the controversy with the last Pavilion that [the curatorial team] had to put together something that was slightly jam-packed.'[24] The NAF was selected by DAC to stage the 2013 Pavilion in part because of its non-profit status; it was perceived as lacking the interests of a commercial art gallery in exhibiting particular artists at the Biennale as well as being perceived as having the credentials to run events which are accountable to the public.[25] In other words, NAF was intentionally selected, and *Imaginary Fact* was deliberately staged, to act as a counterpoint to the 2011 Pavilion, to correct previous mistakes. Even the exhibition's website emphasised this point: 'The National Arts Festival has a proven track record of independent curation . . . not beholden to specific galleries or commercial imperatives.'[26]

20 Artist 1.

21 Curatorial team member 3.

22 Maart, *Imaginary Fact*, 10. All of the thirteen artists interviewed spoke about these shifts in art movements in South Africa.

23 For example, when Taiwan first started exhibiting in the Biennale, it positioned itself and 'its artists on the premise that the outside world was uninformed about Taiwan'; Wei, 'From National Art to Critical Globalism,' 476.

24 Artist 25.

25 Exhibition management 3 and 6.

26 'Imaginary Fact', 2013, www.imaginaryfact.co.za.

The form of *Imaginary* Fact – as a group exhibition – was also seen as a necessity. It was a necessity for South Africa in the context of its fraught history of discrimination to negotiate its transition away from the past, through active representation of different artists. The range of artists and artworks represented in *Imaginary Fact* was perceived as continuing the state's 'mania for inclusiveness', 'wanting to be overly democratic in terms of a selection and show a diversity of artists'.[27] This inclusivity was also described as a process of 'over-democratisation',[28] symptomatic of the state's self-consciousness in wanting so badly to achieve democracy in some areas yet being restrained by severe economic, social, and political impediments in others.

Imaginary Fact was also perceived as laying the groundwork for South Africa to stage different kinds of exhibitions at future Biennales; a first step in Pavilion evolution. As one artist put it, 'the time for that kind of show is over. Hopefully god please, that [the curator's] show was the one that put an end to it, that will allow us to move on.'[29] *Imaginary Fact* harkened back to an earlier exhibition style of the late 1990s: it 're-echoes [the group shows] that happened in the earlier days of immediate post-apartheid exhibitions. A lot of those exhibitions were identity politics type exhibitions ... there would be questions of representation. How many black artists were on show, how many white artists, how many women, how many men; these sorts of questions came up then.'[30] *Imaginary Fact* referenced an exhibition vernacular particular to the post-apartheid moment. One visitor from Sweden remarked on the similarities between *Imaginary Fact* and past South African exhibitions: 'We've seen a lot of exhibitions in South Africa and this one reminds me a lot of them.'[31] Ironically, the curatorial intent of the exhibition was to explore a new movement in South African art in reference to what has come before: how 'the past continues to live with us, and haunt us, in everything we do'.[32] Arguably, then, the exhibition embodied the subject matter it sought to explore; it was an echo to the past of the past. This echo suggests that the trajectory of South African art exhibitions at the international level is following a similar pattern to the evolution of art exhibitions within the country. While art exhibitions within South Africa may have moved beyond certain approaches to identity politics, the state's participation in the Biennale remains embedded in the remaking of the nation, carving out its identity within this international community.

27 Artist 24; Exhibition management 2.
28 Artist 15.
29 Artist 19.
30 Artist 3.
31 Visitor 6 from Sweden.
32 Maart, *Imaginary Fact*, 33.

Agency of Artists and Archives

As its title indicates, *Imaginary Fact: Contemporary South African Art and the Archive* was concerned with the creation of history, particularly through the various ways in which artists work with different types of archives, broadly interpreted. Not restricted to annals of historical repositories, the exhibition positioned archives as sources of knowledge being made and imagined. Archives are not neutral; rather, they are constructed, circumscribed by politics and discourses of authenticity and legitimacy. The types of archives referenced in artworks were varied, including conventional archives such as historical files, government documents, museum collections, and personal records, as well as more unusual archives such as remembered events, lived experiences, musical compositions, and embodied movements. The broad interpretation of archives meant that the exhibition was able to incorporate a large range of artworks and issues: 'It was useful within the theme, one could cover many bases.'[33]

The curator described the exhibition as presenting different ways in which artists use archives to understand the present:

> South Africa's key practitioners who, in very different and vibrant ways, draw on the archived record in order to make sense of our worlds today . . . The agency of archives has been demonstrated by their ability to both construct and destroy ideologies. Working with archives, in a creative way, therefore allows the artist to create work with the potential to change the course of our contemporary world.[34]

Two points stand out from this description. First, the artists exhibited within *Imaginary Fact* are seen as key practitioners of South Africa; a title which confers not only artistic status but also national importance and aligns with the sentiments of the South African government (discussed in Chapter 10), calling the artists ambassadors. The potential agency of these artists to create and shift meaning is given prominence – a point which underscores the importance of the role of artists in this international event.

Second, archives are afforded a special place in the construction of contemporary perceptions and ideologies, a statement which connects to the archival movement within contemporary South African art. An archival movement – concerned with access to information and the ramifications and effects of this information – which is timely given the process of decentralisation of state archives in South Africa and ongoing concern and debate throughout 2013 over the Protection of State Information Bill (the 'secrecy bill'[35]). In creating a system for classification of state-held information in the interests of

[33] Curatorial team member 2.

[34] Maart, *Imaginary Fact,* 10.

[35] Curatorial team member 3. However, the exhibition theme also faced criticism for not being 'urgent enough' in the context of South Africa's problems, in Anonymous author of the South African section in Staal, 'Ideological Guide to the Venice Biennale'.

national security, this bill threatens to restrict freedom of expression, freedom of information, and democratic accountability.[36] In the lead-up to the Biennale, and throughout the exhibition, several iterations of this bill were approved by Parliament, although the final version is still waiting to be signed into law by the president. Importantly, the bill was openly criticised by several member states of the United Nations, who urged South Africa to ensure all legislation complies with international human rights law; a call which is particularly pertinent given the legacy of apartheid era laws which actively concealed state information and in doing so cultivated a climate of secrecy.[37]

Within this context of national and international scrutiny over access to information and archival processes, the theme of *Imaginary Fact* took on greater political importance, reflecting on what happened to information under apartheid and suggesting what could happen again. Without access to information, facts may have to be imagined. Although the South African government openly supported the exhibition as 'using the arts to question and challenge our reading of the past, to reach a new understanding of it and to craft a new and inclusive narrative for our country',[38] there was a simultaneous – albeit subtle – critique emerging from the exhibition, concerning the government's own approach to archives. Not only did *Imaginary Fact* reflect on the past – predominantly on apartheid and colonial oppression – and how this past affects South Africa today, but the exhibition was circumscribed by debates over the current government repeating the mistakes of the past. Ostensibly, the exhibition inhabited a tension in which the South African government uses artists as ambassadors to interrogate the nation's past, while at the same time the artists were interrogating the nation's present and the practices of the current government. These opposing forces highlight how the cultural diplomacy of *Imaginary Fact* is complicated by the fact that art cannot easily be co-opted for political purposes (discussed in Chapter 10).

Together these two points on the agency of artists and archives emphasise a focus on representation: representation *of* artists *by* the state at the Biennale and representation *of* the state *by* artists at the Biennale. In this context, representation is the process by which artists and states participate in politics

[36] Human Rights Watch, 'South Africa', in *World Report* (2014). For an overview of the bill, see South African government, 'Govt's Q&A advertorial on the POSIB', 2011, www.politicsweb.co.za/news-and-analysis/govts-qa-advertorial-on-the-posib. For an overview of reactions to the bill, see David Smith, 'ANC's Secrecy Bill Seen as Assault on South African Press Freedom', 2012, www.theguardian.com/world/2012/jun/06/south-africa-secrecy-bill-press-freedom; Right to Know, 'What's STILL Wrong with the Secrecy Bill?', 2014, www.r2k.org.za/2014/09/11/whats-still-wrong-with-the-secrecy-bill.

[37] David Smith, 'South Africa's "Secrecy Bill" Attracts International Condemnation', 2012, www.theguardian.com/world/2012/jun/13/south-africa-secrecy-bill-un-condemnation.

[38] Paul Mashatile, 'Statement by the Minister Paul Mashatile on the Occasion to Announce Artists to Represent South Africa at the 55th International Art Exhibition – La Biennale di Venezia', 2013, Department of Arts and Culture www.dac.gov.za/media_releases/2013/18-03-2013.html.

and international relations. In *Imaginary Fact,* artists used the archive to engage political representation, especially around the subject of violence.[39]

Three key narratives about violence emerged from the exhibition: the unresolved violence of apartheid-era crimes, the structural violence of pervasive practices of discrimination, and the physical violence which people continue to be subjected. Examining these narratives draws attention to the political motivations of the artists to remember, to record, and to restore in order to not repeat the past, as well as the political implications which arise out of these approaches to archival knowledge.[40] This is important in order to understand *why* the artists are using archives.

The emphasis on representation and violence add new analytical dimensions to the existing conceptual framework of *Imaginary Fact* – outlined in the catalogue.[41] The curator uses five themes to construct this framework; these themes are administering the archive, performing the archive, spatialisation of the archive, post-independence media formations, and archival absences and surrogate collections of the African state. Largely based around the types of archives from which the artists draw stimuli and the methods they use, this framework predominantly focuses on *what* the artists are doing (exploring how the past affects the present through archives) and *how* they approach archives (using different media and artistic practices to preserve, perform, address, reproduce, and interrogate archival processes).

Three artworks stand out for the ways in which they emphasised that remembering violence, recording violence, and restoring violence engage issues around political representation in South Africa. These artworks were David Koloane's *The Journey,* Sue Williamson's *For Thirty Years Next to His Heart,* and Zanele Muholi's *Faces and Phases.* These artworks warn against the repetition of discrimination, document the structures of discrimination, and expose continuing practices of discrimination in the 'new' South Africa.

Each of these three artists is a highly influential figure within South African art. Koloane and Williamson were both deeply involved in resistance to apartheid, both have founded key arts organisations, and both are crucial contributors to contemporary arts discourse in their roles as practicing artists, curators, writers, and educators. In the 1970s, Koloane co-founded an art gallery in Johannesburg called The Gallery (the first gallery to provide a space for black artists) and in the early 1990s, he co-founded The Bag Factory – an

[39] This chapter contains ideas explored earlier in Eliza Garnsey, 'On Representation(s): Art, Violence and the Political Imaginary of South Africa', *Critical Review of International Social and Political Philosophy,* vol. 22, no. 5 (2019): reprinted by permission of Taylor & Francis.

[40] Bleiker and Hutchinson argue that representation 'tells us more about the values of those representing than the objects or events they portray'; Roland Bleiker and Emma Hutchison, 'Fear No More: Emotions and World Politics', *Review of International Studies,* vol. 34 (2008): 130.

[41] See Maart, *Imaginary Fact,* 11.

independent studio and gallery space in Johannesburg.[42] In 1997, Williamson founded *Art Throb* – South Africa's principal contemporary arts publication – and in 1999, she founded the arts organisation Public Eye; she has also written several important books on South African art and is heavily involved in scholarly debates.[43] Muholi's reputation has steadily increased over recent years, as her visual activism challenges ongoing practices of oppression within South Africa, regularly making news headlines. In 2002, Muholi co-founded the Forum for the Empowerment of Women (a non-profit organisation which defends the rights of black lesbians) and in 2009, she founded *Inkanyiso* – a non-profit visual arts and media advocacy platform which includes a website where she documents hate crimes against South Africa's lesbian, gay, bisexual, transgender, and inter-sex (LGBTI) community.[44] In the same year as exhibiting in the Biennale, Muholi won the international Freedom of Expression Award – awarded by Index on Censorship to 'individuals or groups who have had a significant impact fighting censorship anywhere in the world'.[45] All three artists regularly exhibit internationally, all are represented by major commercial galleries in South Africa, all have artworks in the permanent collections of major arts institutions around the globe, and between them they have won every major art award in South Africa.[46]

It is not the first time these specific artworks by Koloane, Williamson, and Muholi have been shown overseas. *The Journey* was first shown in 1999 in *Liberated Voices: Contemporary Art from South Africa,* an exhibition at the Museum for African Art in New York City. As a series of five, *For Thirty Years Next to His Heart* regularly shows outside of South Africa, having been exhibited in 1992 in the Sydney Biennale and the Havana Biennale, as well as in major exhibitions across Europe, and in 2011 in the exhibition *Impressions from South Africa: 1965 to Now* at the Museum of Modern Art in New York City. Prior to the Biennale, *Faces and Phases* was shown in several large-scale exhibitions, including in 2011 at Art Basel in Switzerland and in 2012 at Documenta in Kassel, Germany. Since the Biennale, the series has been exhibited in Canada in 2014, in 2015 at Muholi's solo exhibition entitled *Isibonelo/Evidence* at the Brooklyn Museum of Art in New York, and in 2017 at the Stedelijk Museum Amsterdam. The international exposure of these artworks reinforces their role in creating an external image of South Africa.

42 See Linda Chernis, 'David Koloane Biography', *David Krut*, http://davidkrutprojects.com/34459/david-koloane-biography.

43 See 'Art Throb', http://artthrob.co.za/about; Sue Williamson, *Resistance Art in South Africa* (Cape Town: Double Storey, 1989); Sue Williamson, *South African Art Now* (New York: Harper Collins, 2009).

44 See 'Forum for the Empowerment of Women', www.few.org.za; 'Inkanyiso', https://inkanyiso.org/about.

45 'Freedom of Expression Awards', https://awards.indexoncensorship.org/#about.

46 Koloane and Williamson are represented by the Goodman Gallery, and Muholi is represented by Stevenson Gallery. Also see profiles on Williamson and Koloane in Perryer, *10 years 100 artists.*

The established reputation of these artists and the exhibition history of their artworks is important in the context of *Imaginary Fact* where both the artists and their work are representing South Africa at the Biennale. Each of these artists wields influence beyond the art world; they are recognised activists with socially and politically motivated artistic practices. Koloane, Williamson and Muholi are heavyweight ambassadors, accustomed to competing in the international ring – both Koloane and Williamson also exhibited in South Africa's reentry into the Biennale in 1993. Each of their artworks in *Imaginary Fact* are also inherently critical of the South African government; governments both past and present. The artists' activism and critical approaches complicate the diplomacy of *Imaginary Fact* (discussed in Chapter 10).

Remembering Violence

David Koloane's *The Journey* 1998 (Fig. 9.1; see also Fig. 2.4) is a series of 19 oil pastel works on paper which reconstructs the sequence of events that lead to Steve Biko's death: from his arrest, interrogation, detention, and autopsy. Biko was leader of the Black Consciousness Movement and an anti-apartheid activist, whose murder in 1977 at the hands of members of the Security Branch became a discursive event in the fight against apartheid and remains a discursive event in the nation's transition – one that often arose in interviews and conversations with South African decision makers and artists.

The Journey engages multiple layers of representation. Firstly, by imagining the events of Biko's death Koloane is making a claim to represent a pivotal figure and moment in South Africa's struggle for humanity. Koloane created *The Journey* in response to observing the perpetrators of Biko's death seeking amnesty at the TRC. Having worked with Biko at Black Community Programmes – an organisation running development projects – in the 1970s, the process of making the artwork was a way for Koloane to remember Biko's murder and reflect on the subsequent process of amnesty: 'It left a deep impression in my mind, in my life in a way, to see how dangerous the apartheid government was, that people could just disappear and be killed like that.'[47] *The Journey* is deeply personal and at the same time highly political. The artwork depicts the intimate scenes of Biko's torturous journey; restoring 'the simplicity of the horror of torture and murder to a collective consciousness'.[48] It is a product of Koloane's emotional response to Biko's death:

> I recalled all those horrors of that period that I read about; what they did to him and how his body was driven for so many thousands of miles naked in the back of a police van. It was one of the most brutal things I've ever experienced

[47] Statement made in an interview with the author, attributed here with the consent of David Koloane, Artist.

[48] Maart, *Imaginary Fact*, 18.

Figure 9.1 David Koloane, *The Journey* (1998), acrylic and oil pastel on paper, each 29 x 42 cm (details). Images courtesy of the artist and Goodman Gallery

> emotionally. So that was why I started doing those series because I was trying to recall what had happened during that period.[49]

By drawing on his personal response to the murder in order to imagine the event, the artist memorialises Biko, representing his prominent legacy in the anti-apartheid struggles and continued legacy in the post-apartheid transition.

Secondly, the artwork bears witness to the contested truths which emerged during the perpetrators' testimonies at the TRC, questioning what it means to enact truth and reconciliation. In 1999 – the year after Koloane created *The Journey* and in the same year the artwork was first exhibited abroad – the five surviving policemen (Harold Snyman, Daniel Petrus Siebert, Jacobus Johannes Oosthuysen Beneke, Rubin Marx, and Gideon Johannes Nieuwoudt) responsible for Biko's death were denied amnesty on the grounds that they failed to disclose the full truth and that their version of how Biko died was 'so improbable and contradictory that it had to be rejected as false'.[50]

[49] Statement made in an interview with the author, attributed here with the consent of David Koloane, Artist.

[50] Truth and Reconciliation Commission, 'Amnesty Decision on Death of Steve Biko', 1999, www.justice.gov.za/trc/media/pr/1999/p990216a.htm. Also see this review of the exhibition in which *The Journey* was first exhibited; Holland Cotter, 'South Africans, Isolated No More', 1999, www.nytimes.com/1999/09/24/arts/art-review-south-africans-isolated-no-more.html?pagewanted=all.

Despite admitting to taking part in Biko's murder and being denied amnesty for it, the five men were never prosecuted. In 2003, the South African Justice Ministry announced it had insufficient evidence to prosecute for murder and that it would be unable to lay any other charges because the timeframe for prosecution had expired.[51] While the amnesty hearings afforded an important opportunity for public confession, the TRC has been criticised for not asking more detailed questions during these hearings which would facilitate criminal prosecution if amnesty was denied. The result of the TRC and the inability of the Justice Ministry to prosecute mean that Biko's killers have in effect received de facto amnesty.[52]

The lack of resolution around Biko's death remains an open wound in post-apartheid South Africa, particularly for Biko's family who challenged the constitutionality of the amnesty process at its initial stages.[53] Given Koloane created *The Journey* one year before Biko's killers were denied amnesty and six years before the Justice Ministry's decision not to prosecute, the commemoration of Biko's murder in the artwork takes on heightened political significance; it becomes an unintended symbol of the limitations of South Africa's transition, representing the unresolved issues which Biko's case has come to exemplify. *The Journey* complicates the progressive narrative of the TRC by drawing attention to its limitations, reflecting the ongoing claims for truth and justice which exist in South Africa.

Thirdly, the artwork is received by viewers as a warning against the repetition of such crimes: 'It's a constant reminder to say look this is where we were and we can't go back there.'[54] This claim aligns with Koloane's intention: 'to remind people that even if we have a black government it doesn't mean things are going to be rosy. This [Biko's death] could still happen with a black government.'[55] By remembering the events surrounding Biko's death, the artwork contemplates how those events came to be, but also how these circumstances are potentially not unique to apartheid.

It is not necessary to be familiar with Biko's story in order to access the politics of, and racial conflict within, *The Journey*. In the context of the South Africa Pavilion, *The Journey* is circumscribed by the nation's political tensions and oppressive past. The sequential images portray the torture of a black body at the hands of white bodies. The repeated figure of Biko is Christ-like, each

[51] Ford Associated Press, 'No Trial of Police in Biko Case', 2003, http://articles.latimes.com/2003/oct/08/world/fg-safrica8.

[52] Rosemary Nagy, 'Violence, Amnesty and Transitional Law: "Private" Acts and "Public" Truth in South Africa', *African Journal of Legal Studies*, vol. 1, no. 1 (2004): 25.

[53] See Nkosinathi Biko, 'Amnesty and Denial', in *Looking Back Reaching Forward: Reflections on the Truth and Reconciliation Commission of South Africa*, ed. Charles Villa-Vicencio and Wilhelm Verwoerd (Cape Town: University of Cape Town Press, 2000). Also see Mihai, *Negative Emotions and Transitional Justice*, 113.

[54] Exhibition management 7.

[55] Statement made in an interview with the author, attributed here with the consent of David Koloane, Artist.

frame becoming a station of the cross, progressing through the final days of life. This sense of martyrdom was increased by the artwork being hung in a low-lit area of the Pavilion. The imagery in *The Journey* is abstracted by the densely coloured layers of oil pastel. This style increases the tension; the artwork becomes more disturbing the more it is looked at: 'There is a quality in those works, an impressionistic quality that, for me, keeps it trembling and living now.'[56] The blurred lines between abstraction and realism in *The Journey* avoid sensationalising torture and death. The symbolism and style of the artwork, coupled with its deliberate installation, implicates Biko in a redemptive narrative. His sacrifice comes to symbolize South Africa's sins. Koloane represents the ongoing struggles of a nation and the people within its borders.

Several other artworks in *Imaginary Fact* also represent memories of violence. For instance, Nelisiwe Xaba's *The Venus in Venice* remembers the life of Sara Baartman, a South African woman who was exhibited in European circuses under the pseudonym 'Hottentot Venus' in the nineteenth century.[57] Xaba's performance imagines Baartman visiting Venice in the present day, exploring questions around the politics, practices, and violence of display, resonating with depictions of contemporary human rights struggles.

Recording Violence

Sue Williamson's *For Thirty Years Next to His Heart* (Fig. 9.2; see also Fig. 2.4) portrays evidence of the apartheid Pass Laws. The artwork depicts forty-nine colour laser prints of Ncithakalo John Ngesi's *dompas* (passbook) – a document required under the apartheid government to be carried by every black South African over the age of sixteen at all times.[58] The artist met Ngesi at an Advice Office (legal resources centre) where she went in search of a dompas to copy.[59] Dompas contained personal information – photographs, fingerprints, and addresses – employment history, employer's signatures and reports, travel and residential permissions, and other identification information. A person's rights to live and work in, and visit, certain areas – as well as their family's rights – were jeopardised if an employer did not endorse their dompas, regardless of the reason. Failure to produce a dompas on demand resulted in arrest – on average 600,000 people were arrested each year in the late 1960s for violating the Pass Laws[60]; around 18 million arrests for these violations occurred between when the *Pass Law Act* was introduced in 1952 and when

56 Curatorial team member 4.

57 Maart, *Imaginary Fact*, 16.

58 See Keith Breckenridge, 'Verwoerd's Bureau of Proof: Total Information in the Making of Apartheid', *History Workshop Journal*, vol. 59, no. 1 (2005).

59 Artist statement in Maart, *Imaginary Fact*, 163.

60 W T S Gould, 'Regional Labour Migration Systems in East Africa', in *The Cambridge Survey of World Migration*, ed. Robin Cohen (Cambridge: Cambridge University Press, 1995).

Figure 9.2 Sue Williamson, *For thirty Years Next to His Heart* (1990), mixed media, 196 × 262 cm. Photograph: Andrew Meintjes; Image courtesy of the artist and Goodman Gallery; Collection: MoMA, New York.

it was repealed in 1986.[61] As a document of oppression and control, the dompas was a hated symbol of apartheid.

Unlike *The Journey*, which reclaims space through the imaginative remembering of pivotal events, *For Thirty Years Next to His Heart* draws attention to the restriction of space through the recording of a document designed to deny people the right to move. The artwork becomes evidence of several claims about representation. This is not to say it only serves a mimetic function; rather, it captures the invasion of private life by public authorities. In doing so, the artwork subverts the apartheid claims on private life by making these claims public; enabling claims about the representation of structural violence to be made and received.

Firstly, *For Thirty Years Next to His Heart* represents a highly personal item carried by Ngesi in the inner pocket of his jacket for over three decades, recording aspects of his life; his movement, his employment, his earnings, his encounters with other people. As the title suggests, the dompas was held close to his heart. Yet it is not an object of love as the word 'heart' might imply, but an object forced upon Ngesi's body by the apartheid government; tellingly, Ngesi gave his dompas to Williamson, he did not want it back.[62] The dompas

[61] Michael Savage, 'The Imposition of Pass Laws on the African Population in South Africa 1916–1984', *African Affairs*, vol. 85, no. 339 (1986).

[62] Artist statement in Maart, *Imaginary Fact*, 163.

was highly personal, but at the same time it was also highly de-personalised, being an instrument of discrimination against the majority of the population, perpetrated by the state; controlling existence through the dompas was an act of state-sanctioned mass oppression. Ngesi's existence becomes an official record. The inhumanity of the apartheid system is exposed by its invasion into, and regulation of, Ngesi's personal life.

The tension between private and public, personal and political, is evident not only in the subject matter of *For Thirty Years Next to His Heart* but also in the way the artist depicts the dompas. Glimpses of Ngesi's jacket and hands connect the dompas to a person; the traces of human hands remind viewers that this document belongs to someone, it is about someone's life. By contrast, the highly gridded, ordered display of the artwork is symbolic of the bureaucratic control epitomised by the dompas. Each frame is made from material relating to the page pictured in the print. For instance, bank notes cover the frame of the taxes section and tin is used to make the frame of the employment section, referring to Ngesi's work in a mine. Using a colour photocopier to create the prints also reinforces the sense of officialdom in the artwork: 'It seemed to me appropriate in any case to use a photocopier to record it [the dompas] because photocopiers are so used to copy people's documents.'[63]

Secondly, *For Thirty Years Next to His Heart* is simultaneously evidence of Ngesi's life and evidence of apartheid's mechanisms of control; an indictment of the system and a warning against it. Williamson draws on this evidence to expose the gross injustices which the Pass Laws proliferated: the artwork testifies to this effect. The artist documented a dompas so people who never had to carry one did not 'forget about quite how horrific they were'.[64] Williamson is making dual representative claims about the people subjected to the dompas system and those who were not, preserving the dompas in order to prevent its return – a goal undermined by aspects of current identity card systems in South Africa which echo passbooks.

The artwork records the dompas system and it also becomes evidence of participation and complicity in that system. Names of companies and signatures of people are found on every page: 'One is implicated in the whole system of passbooks whether you want to be or not, because it's your signature, you as an employer have this power over the people that you wish to employ . . . you are validating their existence in this city for another month every time you sign.'[65] The artwork draws attention to the involvement of people beyond official levels, where so many ordinary people were complicit in proliferating an unjust system. It is not only evidence of Ngesi's life being circumscribed by

[63] Statement made in an interview with the author, attributed here with the consent of Sue Williamson, Artist.

[64] Statement made in an interview with the author, attributed here with the consent of Sue Williamson, Artist.

[65] Statement made in an interview with the author, attributed here with the consent of Sue Williamson, Artist.

state control, but it is also evidence of people observing and participating in that state control. The artwork implicates certain groups in the maintenance of apartheid, while revealing the structural violence of that system against other groups, divided along racial lines.

Thirdly, *For Thirty Years Next to His Heart* is a familiar visual vocabulary for viewers unfamiliar with the dompas. The dompas looks like a passport, which similarly allows and restricts freedom but on an international scale – an increasingly critical issue in current debates about statehood and migration. The artwork resonates with the restrictions states place on people's movements:

> The passport scans are something that I always wanted to do because I have what is rated the second worst passport in the world. It's not an apartheid passport but really it is. It is a document created by a government not of my choosing and it's a government of a colonising power. Probably the South African Pavilion, other than the Arab Pavilions, was the only Pavilion I could relate to as an Arab.[66]

This familiar imagery also makes the artwork tangible, or more graspable; an idea that arose when I witnessed a viewer from Australia almost in tears in front of *For Thirty Years Next to His Heart.* The viewer said they were teary because they had been previously unaware of the severity of the injustices under apartheid; a reality which their eyes were opened to by the images of the dompas.

There is also an inherent paradox of freedom in *For Thirty Years Next to His Heart*; it captures a false 'freedom' imposed by a repressive regime: 'It's a symbol of restriction and a symbol of freedom because if you had this passport you could go everywhere.'[67] The original un-freedom of the dompas is freely transported as an archive. The artwork is well travelled, being regularly exhibited outside of South Africa; one of the editions is also part of the permanent collection of the Museum of Modern Art in New York City. Its transformation into an artwork turns a hated symbol of apartheid into a public denunciation of that regime.

The recording of violence is found in several other artworks in *Imaginary Fact* but in more abstract ways. For instance, Sam Nhlengethwa's *Glimpses of the Fifties and Sixties* 2002–2003 uses photographs from *Drum* magazine – an important activist platform in South Africa during apartheid – and his family albums to recreate images of daily life in South Africa. Nhlengethwa's collages produce a kind of historical evidence which highlights the effects of apartheid on people's lives during those years. Joanne Bloch's *Hoard* combines reproductions of objects from three archives – the University of Cape Town's archive, the Mapungubwe Collection, and her personal collection – to produce

[66] Biennale staff member 3 from Iraq.
[67] Biennale staff member 4.

Figure 9.3 Zanele Muholi, *Faces and Phases* (2006–2013), series of 200 photographic prints, unframed black-and-white digital photographic prints, each 30.5 x 44cm.
Installation view of *Imaginary Fact*, 2013 Venice Art Biennale, photography by Giovanna Zen, courtesy of the National Arts Festival

a new historical record which questions how artefacts attain value and are used as evidence of the past. Penny Siopis's film *Obscure White Messenger* brings together a psychiatrist's interview with Demitrios Tsafendas (the man responsible for the death of Hendrik Frensch Verwoerd – the architect of apartheid) with found film footage of white South African families on holiday. By doing so the film reveals the complicity of ordinary people in the apartheid system.

Restoring Violence

Zanele Muholi's series of portraits of LGBTI people in South Africa, entitled *Faces and Phases* (Fig. 9.3), restores black queer visibility. The black-and-white photographs portray a marginalised segment of South African society; marginalised in terms of being erased from historical canons, and subjected to severe discrimination resulting from ingrained social attitudes towards heteronormativity and apartheid's major legacy of intolerance towards difference. Through the photographic series Muholi is restoring visual representation; creating 'images of people like me for reference point for posterity', restoring a legacy of queer identity in the 'new' South Africa.[68]

[68] Statement made in an interview with the author, attributed here with the consent of Zanele Muholi, Artist.

Ten gaps in the grid of 200 photographs signify the missing portraits of people who have been the victims of hate crimes. Homophobic violence is an ongoing problem in South Africa. In particular, the nation is experiencing a 'backlash of crimes targeted specifically at lesbian women, who are perceived as representing a direct and specific threat to the status quo'.[69] Violence often takes the form of corrective rape – where men rape women in order to 'cure' their lesbianism.[70] These crimes are not only underreported due to the stigma associated with them, but they are also under-recorded by the police and seldom prosecuted as hate crimes on the basis of sexual orientation; a situation that contributes to the silence around such prejudice-related violence.[71] The simultaneous presence and absence of the portraits draws attention to this violence.

Muholi defines herself as a visual activist rather than a visual artist.[72] Her artistic practice arises from activism, but it is also a lived imperative. She documents ongoing cases of rape, assault, and murder: 'I [go] from one place to the next place documenting, listening to people, their needs. If there is a case that needs to be referred to an organisation, I refer that case.'[73] By refusing to call herself an artist, Muholi is making a claim about the form of representation she is practising. Her visual activism is explicitly political representation, yet it is also artistic representation, as it is created and mediated through her photographic works which are exhibited in major art exhibitions.

While *Faces and Phases* restores black queer visibility, it is simultaneously an indictment of current discrimination in South Africa: a call to action. Muholi is advocating for equal rights and treatment, drawing attention to the violence and discrimination faced by the LGBTI community: 'The whole point is to educate the next person who is not a member of the LGBTI community.'[74] There is a deliberate element of didacticism in Muholi's work. However, for audiences unfamiliar with these issues, it is difficult to grasp them from the photographs alone, without accompanying text or information which explains who is being represented and why; in the context of the Biennale viewers 'needed to be guided into that process'.[75] *Faces and Phases* de-essentializes the gender of the people represented in and by the

[69] Andrew Martin et al., *Hate Crimes: The Rise of 'Corrective' Rape in South Africa* (London: Action Aid, 2009), 5.

[70] Statement by Jody Kollapen, Chair of the South African Human Rights Commission, in ibid., 3.

[71] See Lea Mwambene and Maudri Wheal, 'Realisation or Oversight of a Constitutional Mandate? Corrective Rape of Black African Lesbians in South Africa', *African Human Rights Law Journal*, vol. 15, no. 1 (2015).

[72] Williamson, *South African Art Now*, 130.

[73] Statement made in an interview with the author, attributed here with the consent of Zanele Muholi, Artist.

[74] Statement made in an interview with the author, attributed here with the consent of Zanele Muholi, Artist.

[75] Exhibition management 3.

photographs, yet it does so to such a degree that the claims being made about representation require further elaboration. The intention of the artist does not easily, or necessarily, align with the reception of the audience.

There is a tension between celebration and bereavement in *Faces and Phases*. Five per cent of the people represented in the artwork – whose portraits are absent – are the victims of fatal violence, while the remaining 95 per cent embody an enduring community. The missing photographs mourn absent people, while the existing photographs celebrate the people present. The direct gaze of each person looking out from each photograph creates a personal connection with viewers: 'Muholi's work really puts you in the moment of these women staring at you, being almost canonised in a way that makes you consider where they come from, who they are, and what they were subject to after all these years of democracy.'[76] This gaze also counter-exerts power; the photographs are of people, not of art objects to be looked at.[77] The series is about more than looking. It is about questioning why these faces are all in the one space; who these people are and why they are on display; and where the missing faces have gone. As much as *Faces and Phases* is about restoring and celebrating representation, it is also about challenging why the absence of representation exists in the first place – both regarding individual representation of victims of hate crimes and the collective representation of the LGBTI community.

For the artist *Faces* expresses the people in the photographs and her face-to-face encounters with them.[78] While *Phases* signifies 'the transition from one stage of sexuality or gender expression and experience to another',[79] there is also a more disturbing association to the word 'phase' which is sometimes used pejoratively to refer to sexuality as something that can be overcome or corrected. In the context of South Africa, phase also evokes a political association with the nation's transition.

Including *Faces and Phases* in the South Africa Pavilion draws attention to the politics within South Africa which surrounds Muholi's visual activism. In 2009, the then Arts and Culture Minister Lulama Xingwana refused to open *Innovative Women* – an exhibition featuring Muholi's work – on the basis that it was 'immoral' because it depicted images of lesbians, and in doing so the exhibition was against 'nation-building'; the minister has been widely quoted as saying, 'Our mandate is to promote social cohesion and nation building. I left the exhibition because it expressed the very opposite of this.'[80] This event sparked controversy in South Africa both within and outside of art circles,

[76] Curatorial team member 4.

[77] Idea raised in Maart, *Imaginary Fact*, 23.

[78] Zanele Muholi, *Faces and Phases* (Munich: Prestel Verlag, 2010), 6.

[79] Ibid.

[80] Brenna M. Munro, *South Africa and the Dream of Love to Come: Queer Sexuality and the Struggle for Freedom* (Minneapolis: University of Minnesota Press, 2012), 219.

becoming a discursive event noted by many interviewees when speaking about Muholi's work.

The minister's statement presupposes a vision of the nation circumscribed by heteronormativity.[81] This gendered form of political identity in the 'new' South Africa betrays its rainbow nationalism which appears to be slowly disintegrating as Mandela's legacy fades with time, but it also echoes apartheid-era strategies of silencing alterity. For the minister, social cohesion appears to be less about representing all of South Africa's citizens, and in the process of doing so addressing the struggles of marginalised communities, and more about constructing an image of the nation built on a narrow conception of citizenhood. The minister's actions are indicative of the discrimination experienced by the LGBTI community at some of the highest levels, emphasising the vast gap between the conceptual liberalness of South Africa's constitution and its political practice – amplified by the fact that the *Innovative Women* exhibition was located on Constitution Hill, the site of the Constitutional Court: 'On the face of it we have this very liberal constitution which forbids discrimination of any kind and in fact it's just not adhered to, even by the government itself'[82]; 'the gap between the diversity proposed in the Constitution or what's acceptable or allowable in the Constitution and reality on the ground is so radically enormous that it's good to have her [Muholi's] work at a big international [exhibition].'[83] The inclusion of Muholi's work in the 2013 South Africa Pavilion challenges the views of the former Arts and Culture minister. In opening *Imaginary Fact* the then Arts and Culture Minister Paul Mashatile described all the artists in the exhibition as 'immensely talented and, as a nation, we are proud of them and of the opportunity to showcase them to the world'.[84] The sentiment of this statement stands in opposition to the views expressed by the previous minister and it also stands in opposition to the longer-running history of discrimination against LGBTI people in South Africa. Despite Mashatile and Xingwana belonging to the same political party – the ANC – Mashatile's statement is a concerted effort to distinguish his leadership of arts and culture from his predecessor's.

While DAC ostensibly had little control over the inclusion of *Faces and Phases* in the South Africa Pavilion – the artist was selected and announced by the curatorial team at a late stage – it is significant that they did not intervene or distance themselves from the exhibition in light of the previous minister's actions in 2009. Arguably, the South African government was prevented from intervening because the curatorial team was selected by an independent jury in

[81] The link between nationalism and heteronormativity is established across many contexts; see, for example, Henriette Gunkel, *The Cultural Politics of Female Sexuality in South Africa* (New York: Routledge, 2010).

[82] Artist 24.

[83] Artist 15.

[84] Mashatile, 'Speech on Occasion of the Opening of South African Pavilion at the 55th Venice Biennale'.

order to keep decisions at relative arm's length from DAC, and nor could it politically afford another controversy over the Pavilion after the events of 2011. Rather the government embraced Muholi and her work as an example of South Africa's liberal development. The Commissioner (who is also the Consul-General of South Africa to Milan) indicated that the government wanted the inclusion of Muholi's work to signal that South Africa is accepting of homosexuality: 'To destroy the myth that Africa as a whole persecute people because of their sexual orientation. We are trying to bring it into the mainstream to say with us your sexual orientation doesn't necessarily matter to us.'[85] The inclusion of *Faces and Phases* in this international context is intended to demonstrate South Africa's willingness to acknowledge these struggles and by doing so to differentiate the state from other nations on the African continent who criminalise homosexuality. However, although homosexuality is not criminalised in South Africa, it is far from accepted. Muholi's artwork complicates the government's diplomatic narrative by exposing the ongoing struggle for representation in a society plagued by prejudice.

The inclusion of *Faces and Phases* in the South Africa pavilion stems from two competing attempts to restore representation: the government's claim to restore South Africa's representation in the international community, seeking to cultivate an image of the state's inclusivity and to distinguish it from other states; and the artist's and the curatorial team's claim to expose the continuing practices of discrimination in the 'new' South Africa and, in doing so, to restore representation of the black queer community. There is also a third dimension of restoring representation at stake. By exhibiting in *Imaginary Fact* Muholi is representing South Africa. This signals support for her artwork as one of the representatives of the state at the Biennale – which would not have been possible under the apartheid regime (or arguably under the former minister). The inclusion is actively redressing the imbalances of representation directly resulting from apartheid.

Beyond its specific relationship to South Africa, *Faces and Phases* opens up a wider discussion about LGBTI representation in other nations, particularly the member states of the Biennale: 'The reaction in front of Zanele Muholi's work is really different from all the rest. People don't think about the past, as in all the other works, because it's something they immediately recognized as current and contemporary, a universal theme that is a social issue also in Italy.'[86] Although *Faces and Phases* is focused on practices of discrimination in South Africa, it also responds to broader practices of discrimination which are not unique to South Africa: 'Internationally there's an upsurge of hate for homosexual people. I didn't see much around the rest of the Biennale about

[85] Statement made in an interview with the author, attributed here with the consent of Saul Kgomotso Molobi, *Imaginary Fact* Commissioner and Consul-General of South Africa to Milan.

[86] Biennale staff member 5.

these issues. I'm very glad that we [South Africa] touched on that incredibly important human issue.'[87] In the context of the Biennale, Muholi's visual activism provokes reflection on the practices of other nation-states. This fourth dimension of representation is especially significant given that *Faces and Phases* is widely exhibited internationally.

Other artworks in *Imaginary Fact* lacked the sense of life-and-death urgency which *Faces and Phases* emphasised; however, several artworks also sought to restore representation in various ways. For instance, Athi-Patra Ruga's performance piece entitled *The Future White Women of Azania* entailed the artist – dressed in balloons and accompanied by four performers veiled in gold robes – sailing down the Grand Canal; an unexpected intervention in the Venetian landscape. The Azanian People's Organisation (AZAPO) (an offshoot of the Black Consciousness Movement) campaigns for South Africa to be renamed Azania, to free the state from its colonial past.[88] For Ruga, Azania exists in 'the form of a utopian identity/nationality . . . made alive with an AZAPO liberation agenda'.[89] *The Future White Women of Azania* raises questions about race, nationality, and what it means to belong to, and represent, an Azanian nation; to restore a utopian identity by queering an 'ostensibly masculine history'.[90]

Violence reverberates throughout the artworks by Koloane, Williamson, and Muholi. By remembering, recording, and restoring violence, each artist questions what it means to represent a state that is in flux. They capture three ways in which the pervasive practices of discrimination live on in South Africa, leaving a sense that the process of political transition is not only unfinished but must be remembered, recorded, and restored so as not to be repeated.

87 Exhibition management 4.
88 Maart, *Imaginary Fact*, 16.
89 Artist statement in ibid., 149.
90 Brenton Maart, 'Venice Distilled', *Archive and Public Culture*, www.apc.uct.ac.za/news/venice-distilled.

10

The Cultural Diplomacy of *Imaginary Fact*

> In the long course of history, having people who understand your thought is much greater security than another submarine.[1]

> Our participation [in the Biennale] is a means of reasserting the importance of Art as a universal language through which we can reach the whole world.[2]

> Any cabinet minister is always looking for artwork that does have political substance. But this [Imaginary Fact] wasn't political substance in terms of propaganda, it was political substance that was meaningful and could advocate for discussion.[3]

> I didn't know the country [South Africa], but now I know they have art, I understand it.[4]

Being invited to stage a national pavilion by the Biennale is the art world's equivalent of being offered membership of the United Nations General Assembly. At least that is the perception and the reputation that the Biennale Foundation strives to foster: 'For you as a nation to exhibit at the Venice Biennale, it's a strong brand to put on the cultural portfolio of a country.'[5] The Biennale is exclusive: states bid to get a seat at the table; it is orchestrated around historical relationships and balances of powers; the Foundation President presides over a bureaucracy tightly controlled by relationships and codes of conduct; and the event wields influence – both symbolic and economic – over the art and diplomatic worlds. The Biennale is a hegemonic machine which links the 'local to the global within the field of symbolic struggles for legitimation'.[6] Artists are legitimated through state membership; states are

[1] As quoted in Geoffrey Cowan and Amelia Arsenault, 'Moving from Monologue to Dialogue to Collaboration: The Three Layers of Public Diplomacy', *The Annals of the American Academy of Political and Social Science*, vol. 616, no. 1 (2008): 19.

[2] Mai bint Mohammed Al Khalifa, Minister of Culture of the Kingdom of Bahrain, statement in Melissa Enders-Bhatia and Elie Flouty, *In a World of Your Own*, ed. La Biennale di Venezia (Kingdom of Bahrain Ministry of Culture, 2013), 2.

[3] Statement made in an interview with the author, attributed here with the consent of Saul Kgomotso Molobi, *Imaginary Fact* Commissioner and Consul-General of South Africa to Milan.

[4] Biennale staff member 6.

[5] Biennale staff member 3.

[6] Oliver Marchart, 'The Globalization of Art and the "Biennials of Resistance": A History of the Biennials from the Periphery', *World Art*, vol. 4, no. 2 (2014): 264.

legitimated through membership of the international community; and the international community is legitimated by member states.

At the 2013 Biennale, France and Germany staged an art coup – they swapped pavilions. It was the first time in the Biennale's history that two states took this course of action. It was a like-for-like temporary trade of two prominent purpose-built neo-classical pavilions. France exhibited *Ravel Ravel Unravel* by Albanian artist Anri Sala in the Germany Pavilion, while Germany exhibited in the France Pavilion the work of four artists from different nations who were all affirmed as being active in the German art scene – Ai Weiwei from China, Romuald Karmarkar from France, Santu Mofokeng from South Africa, and Dayanita Singh from India. Both pavilions downplayed nationalism by emphasising the non-German and non-French identity of artists they displayed – indicative of a contemporary trend at the Biennale where national pavilions exhibit the work of artists from other nations.[7] The swap was also ostensibly a gesture by the curators of the two pavilions to destabilise the idea of national representation at the Biennale. However, these two exhibitions also reinforced notions of national representation and identity by emphasising the home nations of artists on display – particularly by giving prominence to nations without official pavilions (for example, Albania and India) and to artists who have a tense relationship with their home nations for reasons of political dissonance (for example, Ai Weiwei).[8] Arguably, France and Germany's swap could only be performed by established nations at the Biennale – nations which are already secure enough in their own identities to exhibit those of other states. The pavilion trade was also an exchange orchestrated by the respective foreign ministries to mark the fiftieth anniversary of the Élysée Treaty on Franco–German friendship, which one art critique described as more than an 'organizational detail in the art world, the exchange is actually part of a global policy to strengthen friendly relations between France and Germany during these troubled economic times'.[9] By trading one set of neo-classical columns for another, France and Germany's symbolic act of friendship was applauded for challenging conceptions of nationhood which pervade the Biennale, while at the same time it was a politically savvy act of diplomacy.[10]

7 See Wei, 'From National Art to Critical Globalism,' 470.

8 Ai Weiwei is outspokenly critical of the Chinese government, and at the time of the 2011 Biennale he was imprisoned in China on charges of 'economic crimes'; see Shirong Chen, 'Chinese Artist Ai Weiwei Held for "Economic Crimes"', 2011, BBC, www.bbc.co.uk/news/world-asia-pacific-12994785. At the 2013 Biennale Weiwei held a collateral exhibition entitled *SACRED* in which he displayed recreations of his prison cell.

9 Céline Piettre, 'France and Germany Will Trade Pavilions at the 2013 Venice Biennale', 2012, http://blogs.artinfo.com/artintheair/2012/11/21/france-and-germany-will-trade-pavilions-at-the-2013-venice-biennale/. Also see Susanne Gaensheimer, 'Interview: There's No National Culture Anymore', 2013, www.goethe.de/en/kul/bku/20374620.html.

10 An example of this positive reception of the pavilions swap can be seen in the following review by Christopher Mooney, 'Anri Sala', 2013, http://artreview.com/features/feature_anri_sala/.

The French and German (pavilion) borders were temporarily redrawn, not to dramatically destabilise the geo-politics of the Biennale, but to draw attention to how the set-up of the Biennale is an important site of cultural diplomacy. This *site* and *sight* of cultural diplomacy is largely neglected by scholars of international relations, despite the emphasis by art theory scholars on the relationships between global politics and biennials.[11] The geo-political structure of the Biennale (discussed in Chapter 8) fosters relationships and forces comparisons between nations. The pavilions function as slices of territory, in which nations present an image of themselves and negotiate their place in the international community through art.[12] At the Biennale, art carries the 'burden of national representation, [among] the politics of national prestige'.[13]

Staging a Vision of the Nation

At the time of the 2013 Biennale, South Africa's *White Paper on Arts Culture and Heritage* was being revised. The *2013 White Paper* included a small but significant section on cultural diplomacy which embedded it within the framework of national security:

> Cultural diplomacy seeks to induce greater co-operation between two nations; aid in changing the policies or political environment of the target nation; prevent, manage and mitigate conflict with the target nation, develop a positive view of the country's people, culture and policies; increase tourism and investment opportunities. It also helps a country to better understand the foreign nation it is engaging with and consequently improves collaboration through mutual understanding and respect. Cultural diplomacy has the added advantage of reaching so called ordinary people outside of the traditional international relations circuit. It also has the potential to demonstrate national power, create an environment conducive to support, and assist in the collection and interpretation of information. This, in turn, aids in the interpretation of intelligence, enhances a nation's prestige and aids in garnering support for policies abroad. All of these factors affect a nation's security, thus, cultural diplomacy has an effect on, and a role to play, in regards to national security.[14]

[11] See Elena Filipovic, Marieke van Hal, and Solveig Øvstebø, eds., *The Biennial Reader* (Bergen: Hatje Cantz, 2010).

[12] Madra theorises that the Biennale is undergoing a transition from a nation-state/imperial mode to a transnational mode; see Madra, 'From Imperialism to Transnational Capitalism.' While this idea is seen reflected in some exhibitions – such as Germany showing artworks by non-German citizens – I contend that on the whole, the Biennale continues to uphold the nation-state model which it is architecturally and conceptually founded on. Efforts to transform this model are cursory and lacking the substantial impetus which such transformation requires. This is seen in the continued emphasis on nationality and national pavilions which occurs at the Biennale.

[13] Nicholas J Cull, 'Africa's Breakthrough: Art, Place Branding and Angola's Win at the Venice Biennale, 2013', *Place Branding and Public Diplomacy*, vol. 10, no. 1 (2014): 1.

[14] Department of Arts and Culture, 'Revised White Paper on Arts, Culture and Heritage', 2013, http://heritagesa.org/wp/2194-2/. DAC withdrew this October 2013 draft and resumed writing the white paper. See the information provided by DAC about the difficulties regarding the white

This interpretation of cultural diplomacy raises two concerns. First, by viewing cultural diplomacy as something that can be wielded for political purposes and to demonstrate national power, the government reduces cultural interlocutors (artists, performers, musicians, actors) to political agents. Under this interpretation, culture is something that can be instrumentalised by government to achieve specific goals, beyond the general goal of influencing 'hearts and minds'.[15] This view of cultural diplomacy conflates it with public diplomacy, which is responsible for garnering support for specific policies, such as going to war.[16] One of the distinguishing cornerstones of cultural diplomacy is that it is intended to be at arm's-length from the government; a stance that strengthens its legitimacy.[17] It also ignores one of the key benefits of cultural diplomacy where the dissent of cultural interlocutors may actually work in a nation's favour because it can attract support for people, rather than politics and policies, over a longer period of time.[18]

The second concern is the direct link to national security. While mutual understanding is the key goal of cultural diplomacy and may ultimately make nations less likely to enter into conflict with one another, the direct securitisation of culture has troubling implications for what culture gets shown abroad. Embedding culture in a national security framework where cultural diplomacy becomes part of a strategy to demonstrate national power implies that the government will censor culture:

> The role of arts in projecting a particular view of the country, will be limited to those that have a 'good story to tell'. International opportunities will be limited to those who do not critique the political status quo; those that do, may be deemed to be threats to national security.[19]

Subsuming cultural diplomacy explicitly under national security is problematic because it risks impinging on freedom of expression, facilitating hegemonic voices which support the government's national security goals to silence those of opposition. This would be a worrying precedent to set, especially in a new democracy such as South Africa. Given the government's budding antagonism towards artistic freedom – demonstrated by the case of *The Spear* and by the appointment of the former police commissioner to the position of arts minister discussed in Chapter 5 – it is unsurprising that similar

paper process in Department of Arts and Culture, 'Project Plan for Revised White Paper on ACH', 2015, https://artsculturesa.files.wordpress.com/2015/10/2015-october-11-internal-consultation-presentation-cultural-diplomacy.pdf.

15 Elsewhere I have discussed the concept of 'hearts and minds'; see this brief article Eliza Garnsey, 'The Battle for HeARTs and Minds: Art and the War on Terror', *The Diplomatic Courier*, February 2012.

16 See Jan Melissen, 'The New Public Diplomacy: Between Theory and Practice', in *The New Public Diplomacy*, ed. Jan Melissen (Hampshire: Springer, 2005).

17 Zaugg and Nishimura, 'Angola and Kenya Pavilions in the 2013 Venice Biennale,' 145.

18 Schneider, 'Cultural Diplomacy', 102.

19 Mike van Graan, 'Revised White Paper on Arts, Culture, Heritage: A Critique' (2013).

restrictions are appearing in the state's diplomatic outlook; a sentiment reflected by the Department of International Relations and Cooperation (DIRCO) which views cultural diplomacy as a direct 'externalisation of our domestic policy'.[20]

While participation in the Biennale forms part of DAC's strategic plan to 'highlight the importance of cultural diplomacy in our international relations and expand South Africa's network with the world',[21] the view of cultural diplomacy articulated in the *2013 White Paper* complicates South Africa's participation.[22] In the 2013 Biennale, South Africa reinvented its image both in its own eyes and, more importantly, in the eyes of the international community.

The South Africa Pavilion at the 2013 Biennale was an important instance of cultural diplomacy. *Imaginary Fact* played a paradoxical role in the process of nation building because it presented a dual image of South Africa re-asserting itself in the international community while simultaneously exploring its own identity:

> I don't think our nation-building is complete in this country [South Africa], we're far from defining what the nation is, or being able to claim that we are a nation. We're groupings of communities making a nation ... The Biennale does open up that conversation for us. I think it advances cultural diplomacy, it allows people to begin to engage with who we are. The key thing for me of exhibiting at the Biennale should be for the world to take notice that we have artists that can play on the global stage, and they can play on the global stage because of their art.[23]

As a zone of cultural diplomacy, the Biennale enables South Africa to test and form its new identity. Exhibiting in this zone opens up the conversation on what it means for South Africa to represent itself as a nation. It also confers prestige on South Africa – meeting the objectives of cultural diplomacy as stated in the *2013 White Paper* – where artists can compete on the global stage. The South African state is validated by competing on equal terms with other nations. Artistic representation is important if South Africa is to compete on

[20] Marius Fransman, 'Keynote Address by Deputy Minister Marius Fransman on the Topic of "Cultural Diplomacy and Sports as Tools for Nation Building and Development" on the Occasion of DIRCO's Annual Conference', 2010, www.dirco.gov.za/docs/speeches/2010/frans1119.html.

[21] Department of Arts and Culture, 'Strategic Plan 2011–2016', 11.

[22] Notably, the three revisions of the White Paper issued post-2015 omit any mention of national security. See Department of Arts and Culture, 'Revised White Paper on Arts, Culture and Heritage: Second Draft', 2016, www.dac.gov.za/content/second-draft-revised-white-paper-arts-culture-and-heritage-1; Department of Arts and Culture, 'Revised White Paper on Arts, Culture and Heritage: Third Draft', 2017, www.dac.gov.za/content/third-draft-revised-white-paper-arts-culture-and-heritage; Department of Arts and Culture, 'Revision of the Department of Arts and Culture 1996 White Paper: Fourth Draft', 2017, www.dac.gov.za/content/revised-white-paper-arts-culture-and-heritage-fourth-draft-0.

[23] Exhibition management 3.

the global stage, and at the same time, artistic representation enables South Africa to compete in this capacity, performing a particular image of the state.

For South Africa, participation in the Biennale is a question of access: '[The Biennale] makes South Africa part of this great community, it gets South Africa closer to us'[24]; 'I probably won't be able to visit South Africa so this would be the closest thing I would ever get to South Africa and meeting or seeing South African production or culture.'[25] Being able to access the Biennale means being able to access the international community – the member states and their representatives, as well as visitors to the exhibition – a community from which South Africa was previously isolated. In 2013, nearly half a million people visited the Biennale, including three Heads Of State, forty-seven government ministers, and forty-eight ambassadors and vice ambassadors.[26] In turn, it also meant that this community was able to access South Africa, albeit a selected image of South Africa:

> As a group exhibition that happens overseas, it carries the nation and it says who we are. It can tell the true story about who South Africa is to somebody who doesn't have a clue, who just knew that there were injustices.[27]
>
> *Imaginary Fact* provides people with some glimpse of what our country is, where we are at, where our democracy is at and just how far we've come. Elements of that exhibition do speak to nationhood in a very, very, strong way. But I'm not talking of nationhood in this patriotic sense . . . it echoes some of the pain and some of the triumph of a nation through the artworks.[28]

Imaginary Fact was perceived as opening up South Africa for people less familiar with its history and politics. This element of didacticism was reinforced by the exhibition being included in the Biennale's Education Department tour of 'images as sources of cultural identity'.[29] *Imaginary Fact* was included in the tour to give visitors insight into how South African identity had been shaped by its history:

> There's not a deep knowledge about Apartheid and to discover about dompas, police repression, the Truth and Reconciliation Commission . . . is something really interesting for the main part of the people. Pretty often people created historical connection with the Second World War (between the Truth and Reconciliation Commission and the Nuremberg Trials for example).[30]
>
> Many of my students didn't know about South African politics and they know now because of the artwork and they got interested more and more to read about it.[31]

[24] Visitor 24 from Switzerland.
[25] Biennale staff member 3.
[26] La Biennale, 'Final Day Press Release'.
[27] Artist 28.
[28] Exhibition management 3.
[29] Biennale staff member 5.
[30] Biennale staff member 5.
[31] Biennale staff member 3.

The level of didacticism of the exhibition serves as an advantage for South Africa because this communication reinserted its absent past back into the Biennale.

Statements made by visitors indicate that the exhibition was informative about South Africa:

> I didn't know the country, but now I know they have art I understand.[32]
>
> This was very close to news, it was very direct, the political context was very direct.[33]
>
> It makes you think a lot about apartheid ... you think about justice in a way.[34]
>
> Everything tells you about the pain in this country; every artist tries to communicate the suffering in their way.[35]
>
> It's easy to understand and not so conceptual – that's the strength of the exhibition.[36]
>
> As a newcomer to South Africa, I learned from it.[37]
>
> We love the fact that you make people aware of the real problems in Africa.[38]
>
> Thank you so much for an amazing representation of South African artists – incredibly powerful, diverse, deep, visually coherent and striking, and also giving a real insight in your history, mentality, art. From Russia.[39]

In being informative, the exhibition was perceived as instructive in thinking about crosscutting themes which affect all of humanity:

> Art usually helps to have a big view about the political situation, the social situation ... the visual in this case is the best way to show how a country can live.[40]
>
> We have many problems with justice in Europe, South Africa too ... there is not for me a big difference between countries, this is a human problem.[41]
>
> The exhibition itself, the fact it was shown here [at the Biennale] was probably not possible during apartheid era ... it's an advantage.[42]
>
> That was South Africa, that's a particular story, that's a particular history and it tells me something more about my own history in Europe.[43]
>
> Incredible, never want to leave; so inspired and conscious to the state of the world, not self-indulgent. From USA.[44]

32 Biennale staff member 4.
33 Visitor 13 from France.
34 Visitor 0 from Australia.
35 Biennale staff member 3.
36 Visitor 22 from the Netherlands.
37 Comment written in visitors' books, June–November 2013.
38 Comment written in visitors' books, June–November 2013.
39 Comment written in visitors' books, June–November 2013.
40 Visitor 28 from Italy.
41 Visitor 13 from France.
42 Visitor 31 from China.
43 Artist 3.
44 Comment written in visitors' books, June–November 2013.

These two key didactic elements of *Imaginary Fact* – being informative about South Africa while simultaneously connecting with wider human problems about justice and not repeating history – situates the exhibition in an idea of nation-building that is predicated on access, both visitors' access to information and South Africa's access to the Biennale.

Some comments made by visitors also expressed a level of anger at South Africa's examination of the past: '[V]ery disappointing and backward looking. SA is also white, Asian, Malaysian faces. Embrace the present, do not wallow in the past'; 'Is SA over it yet? Will SA get over it? Is it over yet in SA? Get over it SA! Please!'[45] By inspiring these comments, the exhibition touches upon the tensions within South Africa concerning whether apartheid is something which can just be 'gotten over' or moved beyond:

> The Apartheid project in this country remains a dirty little secret from the past and whenever it comes back in any shape or form, generally, people don't have the power to articulate it or write about it, and then they complain why are we talking about Apartheid again? We've been talking about the Holocaust for decades. We've been talking about world wars for decades. We're talking about atrocities committed and the effects on subsequent societies for a long time. We had the Truth and Reconciliation Commission and then we packed it away neatly.[46]

The TRC is often criticised for the way in which it drew a line under the past, although this criticism is not unique to the TRC but indicative of the limitations of time-limited transitional justice processes.[47] *Imaginary Fact* draws attention to the ongoing debate in South Africa about looking back or moving forward. However, the exhibition reimagines this dichotomy so that it is not one *or* the other, but rather one *and* the other showing how the past intervenes in the present: it is necessary to look back in order to look forward.

In the same way that individual artworks within *Imaginary Fact* engaged issues of representation around remembering, recording, restoring violence, the exhibition as a whole offered a fourth narrative, that of rethinking representation. By bringing together an array of artworks, new and old, the exhibition became an archive in and of itself. An archive which revealed 'a country with a very split identity . . . on the edge of two worlds'[48]:

> It's kind of like two countries; people constantly talk about two countries. You're getting the kind of artwork that's technically superb, that's extremely well put-together, that's aesthetically very superior, but shows a certain naivety around its placement in South Africa. Then you get the kind of work that's taking on the complexities of South African society: issues of poverty or unemployment, or

[45] Comments written in visitors' books, June–November 2013.
[46] Exhibition management 4.
[47] See, for example, van Der Merwe and Chapman, *Truth and Reconciliation in South Africa.*
[48] Visitor 19 from Belgium.

> issues of violence, the continued economic asymmetry, issues of land, restitution and all that.[49]
>
> What comes to us about South Africa from *Imaginary* Fact is still a picture of an avant-garde, developed nation, but actually what it looks like to me is that they're still in a stalemate.[50]

The exhibition presented an image of the nation at a junction: a vision of South Africa rethinking itself, facing ongoing complexities in need of attention, while trying to move past those same complexities in order to participate on the global stage.

This rethinking complicates the cultural diplomacy of the South Africa Pavilion. As discussed in Chapter 7, South Africa's participation in the Biennale confers a sense of prestige on the state, a sense that it can compete in this context, and do so without help from other states. The government re-establishes its status within the international community by presenting an image of South Africa as an archetype of political transition; having gone through intense conflict, it has successfully emerged out the other side to become a member state of the Biennale. At the same time the content of *Imaginary Fact* exposes the nation's ongoing internal struggles. The artworks portray how the past continues to impact on the present and how the ramifications of apartheid and violent conflict live on, creating an image of a nation circumscribed by disparity and uncertainty. The official image of South Africa as a global competitor – a transitioned nation – sits in tension with the artists' image of South Africa as an unsettled nation – a transitioning nation circumscribed by ongoing challenges to human rights.

At first look the tension created by these two opposing images of South Africa undermines its soft power stemming from the state's 'successful democratic transition, progressive constitution grounded in the steadfast protection of human rights, and preference for negotiated settlements to conflict rather than military resolutions'.[51] However, on closer inspection, exposing some of the nation's ongoing struggles may prove to work in South Africa's favour:

> It's very interesting and brave for a country [South Africa] to admit it made a mistake, regardless of what the country is doing now. I'm sure things haven't changed dramatically for the best, but to admit in an international art exhibition, saying okay, this is the history of the country and it's an ugly history, and we're going to promote it and we're going to show it and we're not ashamed of it. I think that's very brave. I come from a culture that is hush hush about the history. Don't talk about the ugliness just show the beauty.[52]

49 Curatorial team member 4.
50 Biennale staff member 5.
51 Mills Soko and Neil Balchin, 'South Africa's Quest for Leadership in Africa: Achievements, Constraints and Dilemmas', in *Global and Regional Leadership of BRICS Countries*, ed. Stephen Kingah and Cintia Quiliconi (Cham: Springer, 2015).
52 Biennale staff member 3 from Iraq.

By drawing attention to its internal struggles, South Africa is admitting that its transition is unfinished. This is a level of political honesty created by the artists and curatorial team but endorsed by the state; an endorsement which demonstrates the state's assent to support certain art to be shown at the Biennale, in order to achieve a particular image of itself. After all, not all states have been known to endorse their own national pavilions.[53]

However, the cultural diplomacy of South Africa at the Biennale sits uncomfortably with one aspect of the state's foreign policy agenda, which has followed three central objectives since 1994: 'national interests and values, the African Renaissance and the creation of a better world for all'.[54] The tenet of an African Renaissance – the pan-Africanist viewpoint which has figured so prominently in South African foreign policy discourse – is challenged by South Africa's participation in the Biennale.

The geo-political set-up of the Biennale emphasises the separateness of national pavilions and in so doing instils a false sense of rigidity around states' borders, making it next to impossible to foster any sort of pan-identity in this context, unless exhibiting under the auspices of a regional pavilion such as the Latin America Pavilion. In 2013, only six nations from the African continent had national pavilions at the Biennale – Angola (which was awarded the Golden Lion for best pavilion), Egypt, Ivory Coast, Kenya, South Africa, and Zimbabwe.[55] Of these, Egypt and South Africa were the only states to have national pavilions inside the main Biennale venues, the Giardini and Arsenale, respectively; locations which confer degrees of status in the event. Adding to this, South Africa's commitment to the Biennale (signalled by its long-term lease on a pavilion space) shifts its emphasis outside of Africa, away from, for example, the Johannesburg Biennale (which is now defunct), towards this hegemonic and Eurocentric art space. This shift is also evident in the *2013 White Paper* where the cultural diplomacy institutions of several key, mainly European, Biennale member states – including the British Council, the French Cultural Institutes, and Germany's Goethe Institute – are offered as examples for South Africa to follow; and in the two-year collaboration between South Africa and France which resulted in 250 artistic projects and exchanges.[56] This is in marked contrast to the previous *1996 White Paper* which firmly declared that looking to European nations was no longer a priority.[57] While South

53 For example, the Kenyan government disavowed the Kenyan Pavilion scheduled for the 2015 Biennale; see Zaugg and Nishimura, 'Angola and Kenya Pavilions in the 2013 Venice Biennale,' 147.

54 Department of International Relations and Cooperation, 'Annual Report' (2013–2014).

55 Elsewhere described as 'a record six' in Zaugg and Nishimura, 'Angola and Kenya Pavilions in the 2013 Venice Biennale,' 135.

56 These examples are offered, respectively, in Department of Arts and Culture, 'Revised White Paper on Arts, Culture and Heritage'; Department of Arts and Culture, 'Annual Report 2013–2014', 15.

57 Department of Arts Culture Science and Technology, 'White Paper on Arts, Culture and Heritage'.

Africa may be validated as an individual state by participating in the Biennale, the ways in which this event enforces state borders and rigid nationalism arguably undermines the state's foreign policy agenda towards its own region.

The emphasis by the organisers of the South Africa Pavilion on participating in the Biennale on 'the same terms', 'not as a token country from Africa', without 'outside' help, reinforces a sense of separation between South Africa and other nations in Africa – a position also reflected by the Commissioner's comments about South Africa being more accepting of homosexuality than the rest of Africa (discussed in Chapter 9).[58] As one artist said, 'I look at other countries on the continent, they haven't moved forward but in our little space, in our short period I think we've done pretty well.'[59] The implication is that South Africa is further ahead than other African states which are unable to participate in the Biennale, or uninterested in doing so, either for political or economic reasons. By emphasising its ability to compete in this arena, South Africa is presenting its 'superiority' and distinguishing itself from the rest of Africa. This perspective is reinforced by the 'big-brother' image that the state adopts in representing the region in both multilateral forums and exhibitions of African art.[60] Although South Africa fosters policies of pan-Africanism within the continent, it uses the platform of the Biennale to carve out a distinct national status which separates it from the rest of the continent: this is diplomacy premised on assumptions about modernity and development.[61] This status is reinforced by the organisational structures and the 'global competition hysteria'[62] of the Biennale, where national specificity is instrumental. 'The international art system is a good terrain on which to envisage and to install new projects of political sovereignty'.[63]

Imaginary Fact was not a straightforward promotion of 'South Africa in a positive light'[64] as one former South African ambassador claimed. Rather, it inhabits a more contested and complicated narrative – which may explain why the Biennale received little mention in DAC's Annual Review for 2013 and why DAC is reluctant to discuss the Biennale.[65] By rethinking representation,

58 Exhibition management 3.

59 Artist 28.

60 Soko and Balchin, 'South Africa's Quest for Leadership in Africa', 231; Raphael Chikukwa, 'Curating Contemporary African Art: Questions of Mega-Exhibitions and Western Influences', *African Identities*, vol. 9, no. 2 (2011): 227.

61 Von Eschen makes a similar point about the cultural diplomacy of the United States against that of Russia in Penny Von Eschen, *Satchmo Blows Up the World: Jazz Ambassadors Play the Cold War* (Cambridge, MA: Harvard University Press, 2009), 25.

62 Pascal Gielen, 'The Biennale: A Post-institution for Immaterial Labour', *Open: The Art Biennial as a Global Phenomenon*, vol. 8, no. 16 (2009): 17.

63 Groys, 'From Medium to Message,' 65. By contrast the 2013 Kenya Pavilion adopted a comparative approach between Africa and China, see Zaugg and Nishimura, 'Angola and Kenya Pavilions in the 2013 Venice Biennale,' 141.

64 Sheila Camerer, 'SA Art at Venice Biennale Makes Me Proud', 2013, www.thoughtleader.co.za/sheilacamerer/2013/08/12/sa-art-at-venice-biennale-makes-me-proud/.

65 Department of Arts and Culture, 'Annual Report 2013–2014', 35.

Imaginary Fact is a unique instance of cultural diplomacy: one which bore witness to the internal struggles of coming to terms with the past, of redressing wrongs, and reconciling cases of suffering which are ongoing within South Africa, while simultaneously projecting a collective narrative of a state that has undergone a difficult transition and come out the other side to take its place and membership in the international community. This split identity is indicative of South Africa's glocal transitional justice narrative, discussed in Chapter 2. That is, one that is simultaneously local – being focused inwards on national reconciliation – and global – being directed outwards for diplomatic purposes. In its wake, *Imaginary Fact* left a dual image of a state grappling with the past and at the same time trying to re-establish itself on the global stage, in the diplomatic zone of the Biennale.

11

Conclusion

> Justice is still transitional . . . it's being made all the time and that is in some way the kind of extraordinariness of South Africa.[1]

> South African art will be successful if it is able to show us a new South African society.[2]

At the beginning of this book I posed three broad questions to help shape the enquiry. First, how can the meeting point between visual art and transitional justice be best understood? Second, why should the relationship between visual art and transitional justice be considered? Third, what is the nature and extent of the role played by visual art within state-sponsored institutions emerging out of South Africa's transition? While discussions in each chapter have already presented conclusions to these overlapping questions, it is worth briefly clarifying my response.

Most importantly, the sentiment, agency, encounters, and spaces created by visual art open up new political possibilities which empower and support transitional justice. Art positions seeing, speaking, listening, and creating as important actions in transitional justice. Art enables individual and collective identities to be imagined, tried out, challenged, and created. Art is a radical form of political participation in times of transition.

In the case of South Africa, the relationship between transitional justice and visual art plays out at both national and international levels. The Constitutional Court is focused on justice, and *founded on* art. When establishing the most significant institution to emerge out of South Africa's transition, judges were not on the side line as mere future inhabitants of the courtrooms; rather, they were on the front line pushing and prioritising art to be at the heart of this justice institution. The close relationship between visual art and the Court establishes an important precedent. Art is fundamental to the appearance, understanding, and provision of justice in South Africa and of South African justice at the highest judicial level.

[1] Artist 3. Also expressed by Artist 18.

[2] Statement made in an interview with the author, attributed here with the consent of Saul Kgomotso Molobi, *Imaginary Fact* Commissioner and Consul-General of South Africa to Milan.

Firstly, the art collection reflects South Africa's transition: it gives the Court a direction. Chapter 3 introduced the symbolic and physical significance of the Court; representing South Africa's transition at the same time as it transforms the site of justice. By contextualising the development of the Court, the art collection emerges as an important precedent in South Africa's post-apartheid justice system. Secondly, the art collection shapes how justice is understood: it delineates the Court. Chapter 4 unpacked the symbolic intentions and material interventions represented by, and captured in, the art collection at the Court. These pairings draw attention to the dominant themes in the spatial politics of the Court which are directly connected to the constitutional project and how justice is understood in post-apartheid South Africa. Thirdly, the art collection shapes the appearance of justice: it gives the Court a character. Chapter 5 explored three narratives about recognition in the art collection: the recognition of personality, community, and temporality. By emphasising particular individuals, groups, and junctures, these narratives play an important role in creating the larger transitional justice narrative of the Court. Finally, the art collection is a unique instance of visual jurisprudence: it indirectly influences justice. Chapter 6 examined two claims about the artworks regarding normative instruction and affective understanding which are embedded in the judicial consciousness and the wider rhetoric of the Court. The art collection inhabits a unique position in which the assumptions of justice (and Justices) and what it means to uphold the Constitution can be probed, creating a visual jurisprudence of the Court which reflects both the values which underpin it as well as ways of practicing justice in post-apartheid South Africa; values and practices which are circumscribed by a global human rights discourse.

The Biennale is focused on art, and is *the founder of* a new form of transitional justice. South Africa's participation in this key space of cultural diplomacy re-establishes the state's membership of the international community. Art is critical to how South Africa engages in international relations by asserting its successful transition while acknowledging that justice is ongoing.

Firstly, the history of the ban on South Africa from the Biennale resonates in the return of the nation to the exposition. Chapter 7 introduced how South Africa's participation in 2013 was as much about re-injecting the state's identity back into the Biennale – back onto the artistic global stage – as it was about exploring the archival movement in South African contemporary art. Secondly, the geo-political set-up of the Biennale – where the visual contrasts and spatial relationships between states are emphasised – implicates the South Africa Pavilion in a zone of cultural diplomacy. Chapter 8 examined how, in this context, South Africa is presenting an image of itself for the consumption of the international community. Thirdly, the form of *Imaginary Fact* is both a product and proliferation of South Africa's transition. Chapter 9 explored how the ramifications of apartheid and the processes of transition impact on the way in which artworks within the exhibition engage issues of representation around remembering, recording, and restoring violence. Finally, as a whole, the exhibition engages a dual image of South Africa as a nation-state struggling to reconcile the deep rifts of exclusion and discrimination which continue to plague it, while also having come through a difficult transition to compete at the Biennale – a glocal image which is examined in Chapter 10. The Biennale frames the state's ongoing transition, at the same time that the state's participation in the Biennale becomes an important part of that transition.

The South African case study reveals that the meeting point and relationship between transitional justice and visual art creates new critical spaces of political recognition and representation. Art is embedded in creative state-building, both internally and externally. The state uses visual art from the inside out to reconceptualise the South African justice system, and from the outside in to re-engage the international community with the South African state.

Potential Criticisms

Before outlining the key implications and contributions of the book, I want to address two potential criticisms. First, some scholars might claim that what I have discussed does not count as transitional justice. This criticism arises from two interconnected schools of thought: those who believe transitional justice only pertains to specific quasi-legal mechanisms utilised in the aftermath of conflict, and those who argue that other types of justice might better address the kinds of socio-political relationships discussed in the book.

From the outset I – like many transitional justice scholars – adopted the normative position that an holistic perspective of transitional justice should include legal, social, and cultural measures, precisely because of the wide-ranging practical and ideological challenges that societies face in the aftermath of conflict. I proceeded to argue that transitional justice is circumscribed by feelings of justice, and as a consequence, art plays an important role in animating and activating the narratives of individuals so that they take on collective importance. Both these positions reject a narrow conception of transitional justice, as referring only to a quasi-legal tool kit; a position predominantly associated with early developments in the field being focused on the rule of law.[3]

At the beginning of this book I also outlined how transitional justice is specifically associated with periods of political change following mass conflict. Other types of justice, such as restorative, transformative, retributive, criminal, and social, are not embedded with the same salient association. While all these types of justice can potentially occur in transitional contexts – for instance, the South African TRC is based upon a restorative approach to justice – they also

[3] For an overview of debates about what is included in the field of transitional justice, see Christine Bell, 'Transitional Justice, Interdisciplinarity and the State of the "Field" or "Non-field"', *International Journal of Transitional Justice*, vol. 3, no. 1 (2009); Rama Mani, 'Dilemmas of Expanding Transitional Justice, or Forging the Nexus between Transitional Justice and Development', ibid. 2, no. 3 (2008); Rosemary Nagy, 'Transitional Justice as Global Project: Critical Reflections', *Third World Quarterly*, vol. 29, no. 2 (2008).

occur in non-transitional settings. Art is often associated with restorative justice, such as in therapeutic or peacebuilding practices, and in the context of South Africa it can be associated with aspects of transformative justice (for instance, the transformation of the justice system by the Court).[4] However, given the visual art in this book arises directly out of, and in response to, South Africa's transitional context, and given the range of socio-political implications discussed which span different approaches to justice, the concept of transitional justice is deliberately adopted to capture the spectrum of possibilities created in relation to this ongoing period of change.

The second anticipated criticism relates to whether art really matters in post-conflict settings in the face of urgent human need, such as food, security, housing, health care, and income, since it cannot materially solve these issues. Like other transitional justice scholars, I would not argue for the ante-position of arts initiatives, but this book strongly defends their concomitant effect: 'I agree with such prudential concerns, but I would argue that they only justify the postponing, but not the irrelevance.'[5] This postponement is reflected in how visual art has emerged in relation to transitional justice in South Africa; formative from the beginning then increasingly prominent as time has passed. Art may not be able physically to protect people, but this does not mean that it is not, or should not be, an important element in initiatives to address human rights concerns. Indeed, art often draws attention to these issues in unexpected yet significant ways. Furthermore, artistic expression is an important index within societies moving away from authoritarian rule, especially since it is often the first of many endeavours to be silenced under such rule.[6]

Key Implications and Contributions

This book has shown that an in-depth study of post-apartheid visual art can offer important insight into the relationship between transitional justice and art. There are a number of key implications and contributions which can be drawn from the research. First, the findings should persuade a broad range of academics and practitioners that there are aesthetic and creative ways to pursue transitional justice. The theoretical framework developed in Chapter 2 accounts for the role of visual art in pursuing transitional justice. It is supported by extensive empirical research which not only expands the horizons of

[4] See for example Cohen, Varea, and Walker, *Acting Together*; Rosemarie Buikema, 'Restorative Justice and the Arts', in *Eighty Eight Mieke Bal PhD's 1983–2011*, ed. Murat Aydemir (Amsterdam: ASCA, 2011). For an overview of transitional justice versus transformative justice especially in the context of South Africa, see Matthew Evans, 'Structural Violence, Socioeconomic Rights, and Transformative Justice', *Journal of Human Rights*, vol. 15, no. 1 (2016).

[5] Mihai, 'Democratic "Sacred Spaces"', 178.

[6] For example, see the threats to artistic freedom documented by 'The Index on Censorship', www.indexoncensorship.org.

the framework but mitigates against any potential dismissal of the research by social scientists and policy-makers on the basis of it not being grounded in 'real world' applications and experiences.

Second, the book begins to develop a unique theory of art as visual jurisprudence, as well as novel conceptions of visual jurisprudence and cultural diplomacy as forms of transitional justice. These offer two new and distinct research agendas for transitional justice scholarship in addition to art; facilitating the search for holistic, alternative, and innovative ways to pursue justice in the aftermath of mass conflict. These also present new research possibilities for other fields, such as jurisprudential and diplomatic studies. The book also demonstrates that transdisciplinary research across IR and art theory generates productive and insightful contributions for transitional justice and social science more broadly.

Third, the book reveals the importance of the *movement between* generality and particularity for transitional justice. Both are necessary in order to legitimate practices at a local level and observe norms at a global level. The book highlights the continuous movement between the individual and the collective, the internal and the external, the local and the global, the universal and the singular, the national and the international, in post-apartheid visual art. Art accommodates the tension between shared visions of humanity which organise justice and visions of difference which mobilise struggles against injustice. This accommodation is significant in light of how transitional justice measures face difficulty negotiating the balance between endogenous and universal models of how to perform justice.

To be clear, this book is *not* claiming that art should or could drive transitional justice, nor is it claiming that art should or could replace legal mechanisms; nor is it advocating for art to be instrumentalised in the pursuit of justice. The book *is* claiming that:

- art enables and supports transitional justice;
- art communicates justice in powerful and meaningful ways;
- art embeds justice on different political levels – both local and global;
- art becomes a radical form of political participation in times of transition;
- art is critical to the *perception* and *provision* of justice in South Africa; and
- art needs to be more widely considered by political institutions.

Without the proper recognition of the relationship between visual art and transitional justice, and without a deeper understanding of how and where this relationship occurs, the ability to comprehend the complex ways in which the past haunts the present is impeded. The danger is that without art, transitional justice will fail to fully comprehend and respond to the injustices which are the long-term causes of conflict: 'Human understanding and the need for human understanding is actually the true link between art and justice.'[7]

[7] Judge 4.

References

Adam, Georgina. 'Trading Places'. *Financial Times*, 6 June 2009.

Allo, Awol. 'The Courtroom as a Space of Resistance Reflections on the Legacy of the Rivonia Trial'. In *The Courtroom as a Space of Resistance: Reflections on the Legacy of the Rivonia Trial*, edited by Awol Allo, 1–20. Surrey: Ashgate, 2015.

Alloway, Lawrence. *The Venice Biennale, 1895–1968: From Salon to Goldfish Bowl.* Greenwich: New York Graphic Society, 1968.

Anderson, Benedict. *Imagined Communities: Reflections on the Origin and Spread of Nationalism*. London: Verso, 2006.

Appadurai, Arjun. *Modernity at Large: Cultural Dimensions of Globalization*. Minneapolis: University of Minnesota Press, 1996.

'Art Throb'. http://artthrob.co.za/about/. 1 June 2016.

ARTAFRICA. 'DAC Provides Documentation on South African Pavilion at 2011 Venice Biennale', 2012, https://artafricamagazine.org/dac-provides-documentation-on-south-africa-pavilion-at-2011-venice-biennale/. 3 November 2015.

ARTREVIEW. 'Gulf Labor Occupies Israeli Pavilion and Calls for Cultural Boycott'. 2015, http://artreview.com/news/news_4_aug_2015_gulf_labor_occupies_israel_pavilion/. 30 October 2015.

ARTSMART. 'NAF Curators of SA Pavilion'. 2013, http://news.artsmart.co.za/2013/02/naf-curators-of-sa-pavillion.html. 3 November 2015.

Ashcroft, Bill. 'Constitution Hill: Memory, Ideology and Utopia'. *Tydskrif vir letterkunde*, vol. 51, no. 2 (2014): 94–114.

Awad, Ammar. 'Italian Lawmakers Urge Recognition of Palestinian State'. 2015, Reuters, www.reuters.com/article/us-italy-palestinians-vote-idUSKBN0LV1FY20150227. 1 May 2016.

Bahun, Sanja. 'Transitional Justice and the Arts: Reflections on the Field'. In *Theorizing Transitional Justice*, edited by Claudio Corradetti, Nir Eisikovits, and Jack Volpe Rotondi, 153–166, Oxford: Routledge, 2015.

Bambanani Women's Group. 'Background History of the Bambanani Women's Group'. www.memorybox.co.za/index.php?option=com_content&task=view&id=12&Itemid=53. 17 April 2016.

Basilico, Gabriele, ed. *Common Pavilions: The National Pavilions in the Giardini of the Venice Biennale in Essays and Photographs*. Zurich: Scheidegger and Spiess, 2013.

Beaubien, Michael C. 'The Cultural Boycott of South Africa'. *Africa Today*, vol. 29, no. 4 (1982): 5–16.

Becker, Carol. 'The Art of Law'. *In These Times*, 15 March 2003.

Bell, Christine. 'Transitional Justice, Interdisciplinarity and the State of the "Field" or "Non-field"'. *International Journal of Transitional Justice*, vol. 3, no. 1 (2009): 5–27.

Bell, Duncan. 'Agonistic Democracy and the Politics of Memory'. *Constellations*, vol. 15, no. 1 (2008): 148–166.

Bell, Vikki. *The Art of Post-Dictatorship: Ethics and Aesthetics in Transitional Argentina*. Abingdon: Routledge, 2014.

'Contemporary Art and Transitional Justice in Northern Ireland: The Consolation of Form'. *Journal of Visual Culture*, vol. 10, no. 3 (2011): 324–353.

Bell, Vikki, and Mario Di Paolantonio. 'The Haunted Nomos: Activist-Artists and the (Im)possible Politics of Memory in Transitional Argentina'. *Cultural Politics*, vol. 5, no. 2 (2009): 149–178.

Bennett, Jill. *Empathic Vision: Affect, Trauma, and Contemporary Art*. Stanford: Stanford University Press, 2005.

Practical Aesthetics. New York: IB Tauris, 2012.

Berns, Marla C. 'Africa at the Venice Biennale'. *African Arts*, vol. 36, no. 3 (2003): 1–8.

Biber, Katherine. *Captive Images: Race, Crime, Photography*. Cavendish: Routledge, 2007.

Biko, Nkosinathi. 'Amnesty and Denial'. In *Looking Back Reaching Forward: Reflections on the Truth and Reconciliation Commission of South Africa*, edited by Charles Villa-Vicencio and Wilhelm Verwoerd, 193–198. Cape Town: University of Cape Town Press, 2000.

Bilbija, Ksenija, Jo Ellen Fair, Cynthia E Milton, and Leigh A Payne. *The Art of Truth-Telling about Authoritarian Rule*. Wisconsin: University of Wisconsin Press, 2005.

Blackman, Matthew. 'Department Mum on Venice Biennale Exhibition'. 2012, www.misa.org/media-and-children/item/328-department-mum-on-venice-biennale-exhibition. 3 November 2015.

'Department States It Has No Reason to Doubt Faked Invoices'. 2013, http://artthrob.co.za/News/Department_states_it_has_no_reason_to_doubt_faked_invoices_by_M_Blackman_on_30_July.aspx. 11 May 2016.

'Open Letter to the Minister of Arts and Culture Regarding the Venice Biennale 2011'. *South African Art Times*, 2012, 7.

'Silence from South African Art World Following Venice Biennale Controversy' 2011, www.theartnewspaper.com/articles/Silence+from+South+African+art+world+following+Venice+Biennale+controversy/24634. 23 March 2013.

'Taxpayers Dish Out R10m for "Private" Exhibition'. 2012, http://mg.co.za/article/2012-04-02-taxpayers-dish-up-for-private-initiative-exhibition. 11 May 2016.

Bleiker, Roland. *Aesthetics and World Politics*. Hampshire: Palgrave MacMillan, 2009.

Bleiker, Roland, and Emma Hutchison. 'Fear No More: Emotions and World Politics'. *Review of International Studies*, vol. 34 (2008): 115–135.

Bokhorst, Mattys. *South Africa: Venice Biennale 1968*. Exhibition catalogue. Cape Town: Disa Printers, 1968.

Brand, Stewart. *How Buildings Learn: What Happens after They're Built*. London: Pheonix Illustrated, 1994.

Breckenridge, Keith. 'Verwoerd's Bureau of Proof: Total Information in the Making of Apartheid'. *History Workshop Journal*, vol. 59, no. 1 (2005): 83–108.

Brenner, Neil. 'Global Cities, Glocal States: Global City Formation and State Territorial Restructuring in Contemporary Europe'. *Review of International Political Economy*, vol. 5, no. 1 (1998): 1–37.

British Council. 'From the Outside In'. 2013, http://venicebiennale.britishcouncil.org/media/album/item/from-the-outside-in. 1 July 2016.

Brunschwig, Colette R. 'On Visual Law: Visual Legal Communication Practices and their Scholarly Exploration'. In *Zeichen und Zauber des Rechts: Festschrift für Friedrich Lachmayer*, edited by Erich Schweihofer, Meinrad Hanstanger, Hofmann Harald, Franz Kummer, Edmund G Pimosch, Günther Schefbeck, and Gloria Withalm, 899–933. Bern: Editions Weblaw, 2014.

Buikema, Rosemarie. 'Monumental Dresses. Coming to Terms with Racial Repression'. In *Teaching Race with a Gendered Edge*, edited by Brigitte Hipfl and Kristín Loftsdóttir, 43–61. Budapest: Central European University Press, 2012.

'Performing Dialogical Truth and Restorative Justice: The Role of Art in the Becoming Post-apartheid of South Africa'. *Journal of Memory Studies* vol. 5, no. 3 (2012): 282–293.

'Restorative Justice and the Arts'. In *Eighty Eight Mieke Bal PhD's 1983–2011*, edited by Murat Aydemir, 51–59. Amsterdam: ASCA, 2011.

Bydler, Charlotte. 'The Global Art World, Inc.: On the Globalization of Contemporary Art'. In *The Biennial Reader*, edited by Elena Filipovic, Marieke van Hal, and Solveig Øvstebø, 378–405. Bergen: Hatje Cantz, 2010.

Camerer, Sheila. 'SA Art at Venice Biennale Makes Me Proud'. 2013, www.thoughtleader.co.za/sheilacamerer/2013/08/12/sa-art-at-venice-biennale-makes-me-proud/. 3 November 2015.

Cameron, Edwin. 'Report: Pollsmoor Correctional Centre – Remand Centre and Women's Centre'. Constitutional Court of South Africa, 2015.

Cameron, Edwin, and Albie Sachs. 'Celebrating Transition: Apartheid to Democracy'. In World Policy Blog: World Policy Institute, 2014.

Caney, Simon. 'Cosmopolitanism'. In *Ethics and World Politics*, edited by Duncan Bell, 146–163. Oxford: Oxford University Press, 2010.

Cascone, Sarah. 'Ukrainian Guerrilla Art Group Protests Occupation with a Vacation'. 2015, https://news.artnet.com/art-world/on-vacation-ukraine-protest-contest-306633. 30 October 2015.

Castillejo-Cuéllar, Alejandro. 'Knowledge, Experience, and South Africa's Scenarios of Forgiveness'. *Radical History Review*, vol. 97 (2007): 11.

Chen, Shirong. 'Chinese Artist Ai Weiwei Held for "Economic Crimes"'. 2011, BBC, www.bbc.co.uk/news/world-asia-pacific-12994785. 1 June 2016.

Chernis, Linda. 'David Koloane Biography'. David Krut Projects, http://davidkrutprojects.com/34459/david-koloane-biography. 1 June 2016.

Chikukwa, Raphael. 'Curating Contemporary African Art: Questions of Mega-Exhibitions and Western Influences'. *African Identities*, vol. 9, no. 2 (2011): 225–229.

Clark, Toby. *Art and Propaganda in The Twentieth Century: The Political Image in the Age of Mass Culture*. New York: Harry N. Abrams, 1997.

Clark-Brown, Gabriel. 'Cause for Alarm: The DAC Shady Dealings: Venice Biennale Debacle 2011'. *South African Art Times*, 2011, 8–11.

Clarkson, Carrol. 'Drawing the Line: Justice and the Art of Reconciliation'. In *Justice and Reconciliation in Post-Apartheid South Africa*, edited by Antje du Bois-Pedain and François du Bois, 267–288. Cambridge: Cambridge University Press, 2008.

Drawing the Line: Toward an Aesthetics of Transitional Justice. New York: Fordham University Press, 2014.

'Photo Essay: Welcome to Our Hillbrow'. *Safundi: The Journal of South African and American Studies*, vol. 10, no. 2 (2009): 215–222.

Cohen, Cynthia E, Roberti Gutiérrez Varea, and Polly O Walker, eds. *Acting Together: Performance and the Creative Transformation of Conflict*. Oakland: New Village Press 2011.

Cole, Catherine M. *Performing South Africa's Truth Commission: Stages of Transition*. Bloomington: Indiana University Press, 2010.

'Reverberations of Testimony: South Africa's Truth and Reconciliation Commission in Art and Media'. In *Transitional Justice, Culture, and Society: Beyond Outreach*, edited by Clara Ramírez-Barat, 397–432. New York: Social Science Research Council, 2014.

Combrinck, Lisa. 'Press Release: Participation of South Africa at the 55th la Biennale di Venezia'. Department of Arts and Culture, 2013.

'Come Back Africa'. https://comebackafrica.com/about/. 11 May 2016.

Constitutional Assembly. 'The Constitution'. 1996.

Constitutional Assembly. 'Interim Constitution'. 1994.

'Constitutional Court Art Collection: Foundation'. 2014, https://ccac.org.za/foundation/. 11 April 2016.

Constitutional Court of South Africa. 'August and Another v Electoral Commission and Others'. In *Case No. CCT 8/99*, 1999.

Constitutional Court of South Africa. *The Constitutional Court of South Africa: The First Ten Years*. Pretoria: Constitutional Court of South Africa, 2004.

Constitutional Court of South Africa. 'Economic Freedom Fighters v Speaker of the National Assembly and Others and Democratic Alliance v Speaker of the National Assembly and Others'. In *Case CCT 143/15 and CCT171–15*, 2016.

Constitutional Court of South Africa. 'Government of the Republic of South Africa and Others v Irene Grootboom and Others'. In *Case No. CCT 11/00*, 2000.

Constitutional Court of South Africa. 'Minister of Health and Others v Treatment Action Campaign and Other'. In *Case No. CCT 8/02*, 2002.

Constitutional Court of South Africa. 'Pheko and Others v Ekurhuleni Metropolitan Municipality (No 2) Media Summary'. In *Case No. CCT 19/11*, 2015.

Constitutional Court of South Africa. 'The State v T Makwanyane and M Mchunu'. In *Case no. CCT3/94*, 1995.

Cooke, Rachel. 'The Daring Art of Marlene Dumas: Duct-Tape, Pot Bellies and Bin Laden'. *The Guardian*, 11 January 2015.

Coombes, Annie E. *History after Apartheid: Visual Culture and Public Memory in a Democratic South Africa*. Durham: Duke University Press, 2003.

Corradetti, Claudio. 'Transitional Times, Reflective Judgement and the "Hōs mē" Condition'. In *Theorizing Transitional Justice*, edited by Claudio Corradetti, Nir Eisikovits, and Jack Volpe Rotondi, 185–198. Oxford: Routledge, 2015.

Cotter, Holland. 'South Africans, Isolated No More'. 1999, www.nytimes.com/1999/09/24/arts/art-review-south-africans-isolated-no-more.html?pagewanted=all. 1 June 2016.

Cowan, Geoffrey, and Amelia Arsenault. 'Moving from Monologue to Dialogue to Collaboration: The Three Layers of Public Diplomacy'. *The Annals of the American Academy of Political and Social Science*, vol. 616, no. 1 (2008): 10–30.

Cowell, Alan. 'South African Artists on Show at the Biennale'. 1993, *The New York Times*, www.nytimes.com/1993/06/26/arts/south-african-artists-on-show-at-the-biennale.html. 25 September 2015.

Cull, Nicholas J. 'Africa's Breakthrough: Art, Place Branding and Angola's Win at the Venice Biennale, 2013'. *Place Branding and Public Diplomacy*, vol. 10, no. 1 (2014): 1–5.

D'costa, Bina. 'Marginalized Identity: New Frontiers in Research for IR?' In *Feminist Methodologies for International Relations*, edited by A Brooks, Maria Stern, and Jacqui True, 129–152. New York: Cambridge University Press, 2006.

Dahlberg, Leif, ed. *Visualizing Law and Authority: Essays on Legal Aesthetics Law and Literature*. Berlin: De Gruyter, 2012.

Daniel, John, and Peter Vale. 'South Africa: Where Were We Looking in 1968'. In *1968: Memories and Legacies of a Global Revolt*, edited by Philipp Gassert and Martin Klimke, 137–146. Washington, DC: German Historical Institute, 2009.

David Krut Projects. 'Zwelethu Mthethwa Pulls Out of South Africa's Venice Biennale Pavilion'. 2011, http://davidkrut.bookslive.co.za/blog/2011/06/01/zwelethu-mthethwa-pulls-out-of-south-africas-venice-biennale-pavilion/. 3 November 2015.

Department of Arts and Culture. 'Annual Report 2013–2014'. South African Government, 2013–2014.

'Participation of South Africa at the 55th la Biennale di Venezia', news release, 27 February 2013, www.dac.gov.za/media_releases/2013/27-02-2013.html.

'Project Plan for Revised White Paper on ACH'. 2015, https://artsculturesa.files.wordpress.com/2015/10/2015-october-11-internal-consultation-presentation-cultural-diplomacy.pdf. 11 July 2016.

'Revised White Paper on Arts, Culture and Heritage'. 2013, http://heritagesa.org/wp/2194-2/. 1 June 2016.

'Revised White Paper on Arts, Culture and Heritage: Second Draft'. 2016, www.dac.gov.za/content/second-draft-revised-white-paper-arts-culture-and-heritage-1. 1 December 2018.

'Revised White Paper on Arts, Culture and Heritage: Third Draft'. 2017, www.dac.gov.za/content/third-draft-revised-white-paper-arts-culture-and-heritage. 1 December 2018.

'Revision of the Department of Arts and Culture 1996 White Paper: Fourth Draft'. 2017, www.dac.gov.za/content/revised-white-paper-arts-culture-and-heritage-fourth-draft-0. 1 December 2018.

'Strategic Plan 2011–2016'. 2011.

Department of Arts Culture Science and Technology. 'White Paper on Arts, Culture and Heritage'. 1996, www.dac.gov.za/content/white-paper-arts-culture-and-heritage-0#CHAP6. 1 July 2016.

Department of International Relations and Cooperation, 'Annual Report', 2013–2014.

Dewey, John. *Art as Experience*. New York: Penguin, 2005.

Di Stefano, Chiara. 'The 1968 Biennale: Boycotting the Exhibition'. In *Starting from Venice*, edited by Clarissa Ricci, 130–133. Milan: EtAl, 2010.

Dlamini, Jacob. *Askari: A Story of Collaboration and Betrayal in the Anti-Apartheid Struggle*. Auckland Park: Jacana, 2014.

Dlamini, Victor. 'Press Release, Desire'. South African Pavilion, 2013.

Dobson, Andrew. *Listening for Democracy: Recognition, Representation, Reconciliation*. Oxford: Oxford University Press, 2014.

Donnelly, Jack. *Universal Human Rights in Theory and Practice*. Ithaca: Cornell University Press, 2013.

Douglas, Stacy. 'Between Constitutional Mo(nu)ments: Memorialising Past, Present and Future at the District Six Museum and Constitution Hill'. *Law and Critique*, vol. 22, no. 2 (2011): 171–187.

Douzinas, Costas, and Lynda Nead. *Law and the Image: The Authority of Art and the Aesthetics of Law*. Chicago: University of Chicago Press, 1999.

Du Plessis, Lourens. 'Affirmation and Celebration of the "Religious Other" in South Africa's Constitutional Jurisprudence on Religious and Related Rights: Memorial Constitutionalism in Action?' *African Human Rights Law Journal*, vol. 8, no. 2 (2008): 376–408.

Dumas, Marlene, and Emma Bedford. *Marlene Dumas: Intimate Relations*. Edited by Standard Bank Art Gallery. Johannesburg: Roma Publications, 2007.

Durbach, Andrea, and Lucy Geddes. '"To Shape Our Own Lives and Our Own World": Exploring Women's Hearings as Reparative Mechanisms for Victims of Sexual Violence Post-Conflict'. *The International Journal of Human Rights*, vol. 21, no. 9 (2017): 1261–1280.

Enders-Bhatia, Melissa, and Elie Flouty. *In a World of Your Own*. Edited by La Biennale di Venezia. Kingdom of Bahrain Ministry of Culture, 2013.

Enwezor, Okwui. 'Mega-exhibitions: The Antinomies of a Transnational Global Form'. In *Other Cities, Other Worlds: Urban Imaginaries in a Globalizing Age*, edited by Andreas Huyssen, 147–180. Durham: Duke University Press, 2008.

'A Space of Encounter: Interview with Victoria Lynn'. *Art and Australia*, vol. 46, no. 2 (2008): 216–218.

Evans, Martha. 'Mandela and the Televised Birth of the Rainbow Nation'. *National Identities*, vol. 12, no. 3 (2010): 309–326.

Evans, Matthew. 'Structural Violence, Socioeconomic Rights, and Transformative Justice'. *Journal of Human Rights*, vol. 15, no. 1 (2016): 1–20.

Fadda, Reem, ed. *Mohammed Kazem*. Bologna: Damiani, 2013.

Feigenson, Neal. 'The Visual in Law: Some Problems for Legal Theory'. *Law, Culture and the Humanities*, vol. 10, no. 1 (2014): 13–23.

Ferguson, Bruce, and Rawan Sharaf. 'Otherwise Occupied'. 2013, www.palestineatvenice.com/curatorialstatement.html.

'Otherwise Occupied (exhibition handout)'. Edited by La Biennale di Venezia, 2013.

Filipovic, Elena, Marieke Van Hal, and Solveig Øvstebø, eds. *The Biennial Reader*. Bergen: Hatje Cantz, 2010.

Ford Associated Press. 'No Trial of Police in Biko Case'. 2003, http://articles.latimes.com/2003/oct/08/world/fg-safrica8. 1 June 2016.

'Forum for the Empowerment of Women'. www.few.org.za. 1 June 2016.

Fransman, Marius. 'Keynote Address by Deputy Minister Marius Fransman on the Topic of "Cultural Diplomacy and Sports as Tools for Nation Building and Development" on the Occasion of DIRCO's Annual Conference'. 2010, www.dirco.gov.za/docs/speeches/2010/frans1119.html. 1 July 2016.

Freedberg, David. 'The Case of the Spear'. *Art South Africa*, vol. 11, no. 1 (2012): 36–41.

'Freedom of Expression Awards'. https://awards.indexoncensorship.org/#about. 1 June 2016.

Freschi, Federico. 'Postapartheid Publics and the Politics of Ornament: Nationalism, Identity, and the Rhetoric of Community in the Decorative Program of the New Constitutional Court, Johannesburg'. *Africa Today*, vol. 54, no. 2 (2007): 27–49.

'From the '70s to the reforms of 1998'. www.labiennale.org/en/biennale/history/vb3.html?back=true. 1 May 2016.

Gaensheimer, Susanne. 'Interview: There's No National Culture Anymore'. 2013, www.goethe.de/en/kul/bku/20374620.html. 30 September 2015.

Garnsey, Eliza. 'The Battle for HeARTs and Minds: Art and the War on Terror'. *The Diplomatic Courier*, February 2012.

'Framing Human Dignity: Visual Jurisprudence at South Africa's Constitutional Court'. *Australian Journal of Human Rights*, vol. 22, no. 2 (2016): 81–102.

'On Representation(s): Art, Violence and the Political Imaginary of South Africa'. *Critical Review of International Social and Political Philosophy*, vol. 22, no. 5 (2019): 598–617.

'Rewinding and Unwinding: Art and Justice in Times of Political Transition'. *International Journal of Transitional Justice*, vol. 10 (2016): 471–491.

'The Site and Sights of Transitional Justice: Art at the Constitutional Court in Johannesburg'. In *New Critical Spaces in Transitional Justice: Gender, Art, and Memory*, edited by Arnaud Kurze and Christopher K. Lamont, 44–62. Bloomington: Indiana University Press, 2019.

'South Africa's Blue Dress: (Re)imagining Human Rights through Art'. *Angelaki*, vol. 24, no. 4 (2019): 38–51.

Gaut, Berys Nigel. *Art, Emotion and Ethics*. Oxford: Oxford University Press, 2007.

Gevisser, Mark, and Sarah Nuttall. 'From the Ruins: The Constitution Hill Project'. *Public Culture*, vol. 16, no. 3 (2004): 507–519.

Ghiu, Bogdan. 'The Myth of Place'. 2013, http://commonpavilions.com/pavilion-romania.html. 3 October 2015.

Gielen, Pascal. 'The Biennale: A Post-institution for Immaterial Labour'. *Open: The Art Biennial as a Global Phenomenon*, vol. 8, no. 16 (2009): 8–17.

Gienow-Hecht, Jessica C E. 'What Are We Searching For? Culture, Diplomacy, Agents, and the State'. In *Searching for a Cultural Diplomacy*, edited by Jessica C.E. Gienow-Hecht and Mark C. Donfried, 3–12. New York: Berghahn, 2010.

Gioni, Massimiliano. *Il Palazzo Enciclopedico*. Vol. I and II. Venice: Fondazione La Bienale di Venezia, 2013.

'Giving Voice to the Past, Hope to the Future'. *City Press*, 19 May 2008.

Global Project. 'Occupied Turkish Pavilion at the Venice Biennale (flyer)'. 2013.

Gobodo-Madikizela, Pumla, Jennifer Fish, and Tamara Shefer. 'Gendered Violence: Continuities and Transformation in the Aftermath of Conflict in Africa'. *Signs*, vol. 40, no. 1 (2014): 81–99.

Goniwe, Thembinkosi. *Desire: Ideal Narratives in Contemporary South African Art*. CulArt Productions, 2011.

'DESIRE: Ideal Narratives in Contemporary South African Art South Africa's Exhibition at the Venice Biennale, 4 June–27 November 2011'. *African Identities*, vol. 9, no. 2 (2011): 247–248.

Goodale, Mark. 'Locating Rights, Envisioning Law between the Global and the Local'. In *The Practice of Human Rights: Tracking Law between the Global and the Local*, edited by Mark Goodale and Sally Engle Merry, 1–38. Cambridge: Cambridge University Press, 2007.

Gould, W T S. 'Regional Labour Migration Systems in East Africa'. In *The Cambridge Survey of World Migration*, edited by Robin Cohen. Cambridge: Cambridge University Press, 1995.

Green, Charles Rick, and Anthony Gardner. *Biennials, Triennials, and Documenta: The Exhibitions That Created Contemporary Art*. Chichester: Wiley, 2016.

Green, Jeffrey Edward. *The Eyes of the People: Democracy in an Age of Spectatorship*. Oxford: Oxford University Press on Demand, 2010.

Greiff, Pablo De. 'On Making the Invisible Visible: The Role of Cultural Interventions in Transitional Justice Processes'. In *Transitional Justice, Culture, and Society: Beyond Outreach*, edited by Clara Ramirez-Barat, 11–24. New York: Social Science Research Council, 2014.

Groys, Boris. 'From Medium to Message: The Art Exhibition as Model of a New World Order'. *Open: The Art Biennial as a Global Phenomenon*, vol. 8, no. 16 (2009): 56–65.

Grynsztejn, Madeleine, and Adriana Valdes. 'Pavilion of Chile: Alfredo Jaar Venezia, Venezia'. edited by La Biennale di Venezia: National Council for Culture and the Arts, 2013.

Gulf Labor Artist Coalition. 'An Intervention at the Biennale: G.U.L.F and Gulf Labor at Venice'. 2015, http://gulflabor.org/2015/an-intervention-at-the-biennale-g-u-l-f-and-gulf-labor-at-venice/#more-2068. 30 October 2015.

Gunkel, Henriette. *The Cultural Politics of Female Sexuality in South Africa*. New York: Routledge, 2010.

Hamilton, Lawrence. *Are South Africans Free?* London: Bloomsbury, 2014.

Hardin, Debbie, and Migs Grove. 'Claiming Art Reclaiming Space: Post-Apartheid Art From South Africa'. Edited by National Museum of African Art, 1999.

Hayner, P B. *Unspeakable Truths: Transitional Justice and the Challenge of Truth Commissions*. London: Routledge, 2011.

Himonga, Chuma, Max Taylor, and Anne Pope. 'Reflections on Judicial Views of Ubuntu'. *PER: Potchefstroomse Elektroniese Regsblad*, vol. 16, no. 5 (2013): 1–61.

Hobbs, Philippa, and Elizabeth Rankin. *Rorke's Drift: Empowering Prints*. Cape Town: Juta, 2003.

Human Rights Watch. 'South Africa'. In World Report, 2014.

Hutchison, Emma. *Affective Communities in World Politics*. Cambridge: Cambridge University Press, 2016.

Ignatieff, Michael. *Human Rights as Politics, Human Rights as Idolatry*. The Tanner Lectures on Human Values. Princeton University, 2000.

'Imaginary Fact'. 2013, www.imaginaryfact.co.za. 20 November 2013.

Incroci del Sud: Affinities. Venice: Palazzo Giustinian Lolin, 1993.

'Inkanyiso'. https://inkanyiso.org/about/. 1 June 2016.

Jachec, Nancy. *Politics and Paintings at the Venice Biennale 1948–64: Italy and the 'Idea of Europe'*. Manchester: Manchester University Press, 2007.

Jason, Stefanie. 'Venice Biennale: SA Pavilion Finally Announces Artists'. 2015, http://mg.co.za/article/2015-04-16-venice-biennale-sa-pavilion-finally-announces-artists. 1 May 2015.

Jeffrey, Alex, and Michaelina Jakala. 'Using Courts to Build States: The Competing Spaces of Citizenship in Transitional Justice Programmes'. *Political Geography*, vol. 47 (2015): 43–52.

'Judicial Space and Architecture'. http://judicialimages.org/resources/publications-key-readings.html#resources_court_room_architecture. 1 July 2016.

Keegan, Tim. *Colonial South Africa: Origins Racial Order*. Charlottesville: University Press of Virginia, 1996.

Khoza, Amanda. 'I am going to throttle Ayanda Mabulu – Edward Zuma'. 2016, *News24*. 15 July 2016.

LA BIENNALE. 'Extraordinary success at the Biennale Arte 2013', news release, 2013.

'From the post-war period to the reforms of 1973'. www.labiennale.org/en/biennale/history/vb2.html?back=true. 5 November 2015.

Laduke, Betty. 'Sue Williamson: The Artist's Struggle toward Freedom in South Africa'. *Journal of Social Theory in Art Education*, vol. 7 (1987): 39–48.

Lapsley, Michael. 'Testimony'. Truth and Reconciliation Commission, 1996. www.justice.gov.za/trc/hrvtrans%5Ckimber/ct00654.htm. Accessed 3 July 2019.

Law-Viljoen, Bronwyn, and Angela Buckland. *Light on a Hill: Building the Constitutional Court of South Africa*. Johannesburg: David Krut Publishing, 2006.

Law-Viljoen, Bronwyn, and Ben Law-Viljoen, eds. *Art and Justice: The Art of the Constitutional Court of South Africa*. Johannesburg: David Krut, 2008.

Law-Viljoen, Bronwyn, and Karel Nel. 'Art and Justice'. In *Art and Justice: The Art of the Constitutional Court of South Africa*, edited by Bronwyn Law-Viljoen and Ben Law-Viljoen, 113–182. Johannesburg: David Krut, 2008.

Le Roux, Hannah. 'Hell/Whole: The Inversion of Constitution Hill'. *Art South Africa*, vol. 2, no. 4 (2004): 38–45.

Le Roux, Wessel. 'The Aesthetic Turn in the Post-Apartheid Constitutional Rights Discourse'. *Journal of South African Law*, vol. (2006): 101–120.

'Book Review: Linda Mulchay: Legal Architecture: Justice, Due Process and the Place of Law'. *Feminist Legal Studies*, vol. 21 (2013): 109–112.

'Descriptive Overview of the South African Constitution and Constitutional Court'. In *Transformative Constitutionalism: Comparing the Apex Courts of Brazil, India and South Africa*, edited by Oscar Vilhena, Upendra Baxi and Frans Viljoen, 135–175. Johannesburg: Pretoria University Law Press, 2013.

'Designs of the Times: The Remaking of South African and Dutch Courtroom Architecture during the 1990s'. *Fundamina: A Journal of Legal History*, vol. 13, no. 2 (2007): 50–74.

'Directory Provisions, Section 39 (2) of the Constitution and the Ontology of Statutory Law'. *SA Publiekreg (SA Public Law)*, vol. 21, no. 2 (2006): 382–401.

'War Memorials, the Architecture of the Constitutional Court Building and Counter-monumental Constitutionalism'. In *Law, Memory, and the Legacy of Apartheid: Ten years after AZAPO v. President of South Africa*, edited by Karin Van Marle and Wessel Le Roux, 65–92. Pretoria: Pretoria University Law Press, 2007.

Lederach, John Paul. *The Moral Imagination: The Art and Soul of Building Peace*. Oxford: Oxford University Press, 2004.

Lee, Taedong. *Global Cities and Climate Change: The Translocal Relations of Environmental Governance*. New York: Routledge, 2014.

Leslie, Robyn. 'Truth Will Set You Free: Implications of a Creative Narrative for the "Official" Discourse of the South African Truth and Reconciliation Commission'. In *Art and Trauma in Africa: Representations of Reconciliation in Music, Visual Arts, Literature and Film*, edited by Lizelle Bisschoff and Stefanie Van de Peer, 170–191. London: IB Tauris, 2013.

Levitt, Peggy, and Sally Merry. 'Vernacularization on the Ground: Local Uses of Global Women's Rights in Peru, China, India and the United States'. *Global Networks*, vol. 9, no. 4 (2009): 441–461.

Longair, Sarah. 'Unlocking the Doors of Number Four Prison: Curating the Violent Past in Contemporary South Africa'. In *Art and Trauma in Africa: Representations of Reconciliation in Music, Visual Arts, Literature and Film*, edited by Lizelle Bisschoff and Stefanie Van de Peer, 110–130. London: IB Tauris, 2013.

Louton, Bobbie, David Allen Still, Ian Pearson, Godfrey Sitholimela, Tirelo Mphahlele, and Esther Shaylor. 'Exploring the Issues around Rural On-Site School Sanitation in South Africa'. Water Research Commission, 2015.

Maart, Brenton. *Imaginary Fact: Exhibition Catalogue*. Grahamstown: National Arts Festival, 2013.

'Venice Distilled'. Archive and Public Culture, www.apc.uct.ac.za/news/venice-distilled.

Madra, Yahya M. 'From Imperialism to Transnational Capitalism: The Venice Biennial as a "Transitional Conjuncture"'. *Rethinking Marxism*, vol. 18, no. 4 (2006): 525–537.

Makin, Andrew, Janina Masojada, and Paul Wygers. 'The New Constitutional Court Building of South Africa: Part 1'. OMM Design and Urban Solutions, 1997.

'The New Constitutional Court Building of South Africa: Part 2'. OMM Design and Urban Solutions, 1997.

Mall, H, A Wilson, B Ngoepe, C De Jager, and S Khampepe. 'AC/99/0030: Amnesty Committee: Application in Terms of Section 18 of the Promotion of National Unity and Reconciliation Act, No. 34 of 1995. Jacques Hechter Applicant (AM 2776/96)'. 1999, Truth and Reconciliation Commission, www.justice.gov.za/trc/decisions%5C1999/99_hechter.html.

Mandela, Nelson. 'Speech by President Nelson Mandela at the Inauguration of the Constitutional Court'. 1995, www.constitutionalcourt.org.za/site/thecourt/mandelaspeech.html. 3 March 2016.

'Statement from the Dock at the Opening of the Defence Case in the Rivonia Trial'. Pretoria Supreme Court, 1964.

Manderson, Desmond. 'The Law of the Image and the Image of the Law: Colonial Representations of the Rule of Law'. *New York Law School Law Review*, vol. 57 (2012): 153–168.

Mani, Rama. 'Dilemmas of Expanding Transitional Justice, or Forging the Nexus between Transitional Justice and Development'. *International Journal of Transitional Justice*, vol. 2, no. 3 (2008): 253–265.

'Women, Art and Post-Conflict Justice'. *International Criminal Law Review*, vol. 11 (2011): 543–560.

Marchart, Oliver. 'The Globalization of Art and the "Biennials of Resistance": A History of the Biennials from the Periphery'. *World Art*, vol. 4, no. 2 (2014): 263–276.

Marikana Commission of Inquiry. 'Report on Matters of Public, National and International Concern Arising out of the Tragic Incidents at the Lonmin Mine in Marikana, in the North West Province'. 2015.

Marschall, Sabine. 'The Impact of the Two Johannesburg Biennales (1995 and 1997) on the Formation of a "New South African Art"'. *Social Dynamics*, vol. 25, no. 2 (1999): 119–137.

Martin, Andrew, Annie Kelly, Laura Turquet, and Stephanie Ross. *Hate Crimes: The Rise of "Corrective" Rape in South Africa.* London: Action Aid, 2009.

Martin, Marilyn. 'Death in Venice'. *Artthrob*, no. 73 (2003).

Martini, Federica, and Vittoria Martini. *Just Another Exhibition: storie e politiche delle biennali.* Milan: Post Media Books, 2011.

Marx, Gerhard, Maja Marx, and Philip Miller. 'REwind: Venice Monitor 2 Rewind HD/ Scene for Wawela Awards 2015'. 2007–2013, www.youtube.com/watch?v= XzdGruYiTyo. 5 March 2015.

'REwind: Venice Monitor 6 Mrs Plaatjies & Edward Juqu HD/Scene for Wawela Awards 2015'. 2007–2013, www.youtube.com/watch?v=6gya0j3w0PY. 5 March 2015.

'REwind: Venice Monitor 7 Calata/Scene for Wawela Awards 2015'. 2007–2013, www.youtube.com/watch?v=EcDBXvKZ6IA. 5 March 2015.

Mashatile, Paul. 'Speech on Occasion of the Opening of South African Pavilion at the 55th Venice Biennale'. 2013, www.dac.gov.za/content/speech-paul-mashatile-occa sion-opening-south-african-pavilion-55th-venice-biennale. 20 September 2015.

'Statement by the Minister Paul Mashatile on the Occasion to Announce Artists to Represent South Africa at the 55th International Art Exhibition – La Biennale di Venezia', 2013, Department of Arts and Culture, www.dac.gov.za/media_releases/ 2013/18-03-2013.html. 23 March 2013.

Masojada, Janina. 'Interview'. *Constitutional Court Trust Oral History Project* (2012).

'TedXUmhlanga'. 2014, YouTube, www.youtube.com/watch?v=FBEkvSC1sNc. 3 March 2016.

Mason, Judith. 'The Man Who Sang and the Woman Who Kept Silent (Triptych) 1998'. 2013, www.judithmason.com/assemblage/5_text.html. 23 March 2013.

Mcnamee, Eugene. 'Fields of Opportunity'. In *The Arts of Transitional Justice*, edited by Peter D Rush and Olivera Simić, 1–24. New York: Springer, 2014.

Meersman, Brent. 'An Imperfect Past and Its Impact on the Present'. *Mail and Guardian*, 2013, 4–5.

Melissen, Jan. 'The New Public Diplomacy: Between Theory and Practice'. In *The New Public Diplomacy*, edited by Jan Melissen, 3–27. Hampshire: Springer, 2005.

Meskell, Lynn. 'Trauma Culture'. In *Memory, Trauma and World Politics*, edited by Duncan Bell, 157–175. Hampshire: Springer, 2006.

Metz, Thaddeus. 'Ubuntu as a Moral Theory and Human Rights in South Africa'. *African Human Rights Law Journal*, vol. 11, no. 2 (2011): 532–559.

Mihai, Mihaela. 'Democratic "Sacred Spaces": Public Architecture and Transitional Justice'. In *Theorizing Transitional Justice*, edited by Claudio Corradetti, Nir Eisikovits, and Jack Volpe Rotondi. Oxford: Routledge, 2015.

'From Hate to Political Solidarity: The Art of Responsibility'. In *Hate, Politics, Law*, edited by Thomas Brudholm and Birgitte Schepelern, 192–212. Johansen: Oxford University Press, 2016.

Negative Emotions and Transitional Justice. New York: Columbia University Press, 2016.

Milton, Cynthia E. 'Images of Truth: Rescuing Memories of Peru's Internal War through Testimonial Art', in *Art from a Fractured Past: Memory and Truth-Telling in Post-Shining Path Peru*, Cynthia E Milton ed., 37–74. Durham: Duke University Press, 2014.

Miya, Eunice. 'Testimony'. Truth and Reconciliation Commission, Case No. CT/00818, 27 November 1996, 2. www.justice.gov.za/trc/hrvtrans%5Cpolls/ct00818.htm. Accessed 3 July 2019.

Modisane, Litheko. 'From Africa to America, and Back Again: Come Back, Africa (1959)'. In *South Africa's Renegade Reels: The Making and Public Lives of Black-Centered Films*, 25–69. New York: Palgrave Macmillan, 2013.

Mokoena, Lethole. 'Radio Interview: South African Pavilion'. 2011, www.spreaker.com/user/roma_radio_art_fair/south_african_pavilion_lethole_mokoena. 7 November 2015.

Möller, Frank. *Visual Peace: Images, Spectatorship and the Politics of Violence*. Hampshire: Palgrave Macmillan, 2013.

Moon, Claire. *Narrating Political Reconciliation: South Africa's Truth and Reconciliation Commission*. Lanham: Lexington Books, 2008.

Mooney, Christopher. 'Anri Sala'. 2013, http://artreview.com/features/feature_anri_sala/. 1 June 2016.

Moravčíková, Henrieta. 'Sensing the Common Ground'. 2013, http://commonpavilions.com/pavilion-czech-slovak-republic.html. 3 October 2015.

Mosely, Erin. 'Visualizing Apartheid: Re-framing Truth and Reconciliation through Contemporary South African Art'. In *Curating Difficult Knowledge: Violent Pasts in Public Places*, edited by Erica Lehrer, Cynthia E. Milton, and Monica Eileen Patterson, 128–141. New York: Palgrave Macmillan, 2011.

Muholi, Zanele. *Faces and Phases*. Munich: Prestel Verlag, 2010.

Mulcahy, Linda. 'Architects of Justice: The Politics of Courtroom Design'. *Social and Legal Studies*, vol. 16, no. 3 (2007): 383–403.

Legal Architecture: Justice, Due Process and the Place of Law. Oxford: Routledge, 2010.

Munro, Brenna M. *South Africa and the Dream of Love to Come: Queer Sexuality and the Struggle for Freedom*. Minneapolis: University of Minnesota Press, 2012.

Mutua, Makau. 'What Is the Future of Transitional Justice?' *International Journal of Transitional Justice*, vol. 9, no. 1 (2015): 1–9.

Mwambene, Lea, and Maudri Wheal. 'Realisation or Oversight of a Constitutional Mandate? Corrective Rape of Black African Lesbians in South Africa'. *African Human Rights Law Journal*, vol. 15, no. 1 (2015): 58–88.

Nagy, Rosemary. 'Transitional Justice as Global Project: Critical Reflections'. *Third World Quarterly*, vol. 29, no. 2 (2008): 275–289.

'Violence, Amnesty and Transitional Law: "Private" Acts and "Public" Truth in South Africa'. *African Journal of Legal Studies*, vol. 1, no. 1 (2004): 1–28.

Naidoo, Indres. *Island in Chains by Prisoner 885/63*. Harmondsworth: Penguin, 2012.

Nako, Nontsasa. 'The Memory Market: Black Women's Stories and the Legacy of the South African TRC'. In *Excavating Memory: Sites of Remembering and Forgetting*, edited by Maria Theresia Starzmann and John R. Roby, 265–289. Gainesville: University Press of Florida, 2015.

Ndevu, Thomaza. 'Body Maps'. 2002, https://ccac.org.za/thozama-ndevu-body-maps-2009-0037/. 17 April 2016.

Ndlovu, Sifiso Mxolisi. 'Sports as Cultural Diplomacy: The 2010 FIFA World Cup in South Africa's Foreign Policy'. *Soccer and Society*, vol. 11, no. 1–2 (2010): 144–153.

Noble, Jonathan Alfred. *African Identity in Post-Apartheid Public Architecture: White Skin, Black Masks*. Farnham: Ashgate, 2011.

O'doherty, Brian. *Inside the White Cube: The Ideology of the Gallery Space*. Santa Monica: University of California Press, 1999.

O'Toole, Sean. 'The Hanging Judge'. *Sunday Times Lifestyle*, 22 February 2004.

'The Venice Effect'. 2011, www.timeslive.co.za/lifestyle/2011/05/27/the-venice-effect. 3 November 2015.

Olsen, Tricia D, Leigh A Payne, and Andrew G Reiter. *Transitional Justice in Balance: Comparing Processes, Weighing Efficacy*. Washington, DC: United States Institute of Peace, 2010.

'On Vacation'. 2015, http://on-vacation.info/. 30 October 2015.

Papastergiadis, Nikos, and Meredith Martin. 'Art Biennales and Cities as Platforms for Global Dialogue'. In *Festivals and the Cultural Public Sphere*, edited by Gerard Delanty, Liana Giorgi, and Monica Sassatelli, 45–62. London: Routledge, 2011.

Parekh, Bhikhu. 'Non-Ethnocentric Universalism'. In *Human Rights in Global Politics*, edited by Tim Dunne and Nicholas J Wheeler, 128–159. Cambridge: Cambridge University Press, 1999.

Patel, Zarina, and Clinton David Van Der Merwe. 'Constitution Hill: Just Space or Space for Justice?' In *Architecture and Justice: Judicial Meanings in the Public Realm*, edited by Jonathan Simon. London: Routledge, 2016.

Payne, Malcolm. 'Chronology'. www.malcolmpayne.co.za/. 15 July 2013.

Perryer, Sophie. *10 Years 100 Artists: Art in a Democratic South Africa*. Cape Town: Bell-Roberts, 2004.

Phillips, Anne. 'Global Justice: Just Another Modernisation Theory?' In *Empire, Race, and Global Justice*, edited by Duncan Bell, 145–162. Cambridge: Cambridge University Press, 2019.

Pienaar, Gary, and Judith February. 'Twenty Years of Constitutional Democracy'. In *State of the Nation 2014: South Africa 1994–2014: A Twenty-Year Review*, edited by M Nkondo, M Sithole, F Nyamnjoh, T Meyiwa, and M Chitiga-Mabugu, 25–58. Cape Town: HSRC Press, 2015.

Piettre, Céline. 'France and Germany Will Trade Pavilions at the 2013 Venice Biennale'. 2012, http://blogs.artinfo.com/artintheair/2012/11/21/france-and-germany-will-trade-pavilions-at-the-2013-venice-biennale/. 15 June 2013.

Pissarra, Mario. 'Death to Venice! A South African Perspective on the Irrelevance of Representation at the Venice Biennale'. 2006, Africa South Art Initiative, http://asai.co.za/death-to-venice-a-south-african-perspective-on-the-irrelevance-of-repre sentation-at-the-venice-biennale/. 1 May 2016.

'Poetic World Politics'. *Alternatives: Social Transformation and Humane Governance*, vol. 25, no. 3 (2000).

Powell, Ivor. 'Venice: A Site of Memory'. 1995, http://mg.co.za/article/1995-06-09-venice-a-site-of-memory. 20 August 2013.

Ramirez-Barat, Clara, ed. *Transitional Justice, Culture, and Society: Beyond Outreach*. New York: Social Science Research Council, 2014.

Rancière, Jacques. *The Politics of Aesthetics*. Translated by Gabriel Rockhill. London: Continuum, 2006.

Reddy, Enuga S. 'The United Nations: Partner in the Struggle against Apartheid'. www.un.org/en/events/mandeladay/apartheid.shtml. 7 November 2015.

Reinhardt, Mark. 'Picturing Violence: Aesthetics and the Anxiety of Critique'. In *Beautiful Suffering: Photography and the Traffic in Pain*, edited by Mark

Reinhardt, Holly Edwards, and Erina Duganne, 13–36. Chicago: University of Chicago Press, 2007.

Resnik, Judith, and Dennis Edward Curtis. *Representing Justice: Invention, Controversy, and Rights in City-States and Democratic Courtrooms*. New Haven: Yale University Press, 2011.

Resnik, Judith, Dennis Curtis, and Allison Tait. 'Constructing Courts: Architecture, the Ideology of Judging, and the Public Sphere'. In *Law, Culture and Visual Studies*, edited by Richard K Sherwin and Anne Wagner, 515–545. Dordrecht: Springer, 2014.

Right to Know. 'What's STILL Wrong with the Secrecy Bill?' 2014, www.r2k.org.za/2014/09/11/whats-still-wrong-with-the-secrecy-bill/. 1 June 2016.

Roht-Arriaza, Naomi, and Javier Mariezcurrena, eds. *Transitional Justice in the Twenty-First Century*. Cambridge: Cambridge University Press, 2007.

Rorty, Richard. 'Human Rights, Rationality, and Sentimentality'. In *Wronging Rights?: Philosophical Challenges for Human Rights*, edited by Aakash Singh Rathore and Alex Cistelecan, 107–131. New Delhi: Routledge, 1993.

Roux, Theunis. 'Constitutional Courts as Democratic Consolidators: Insights from South Africa after 20 Years'. *Journal of Southern African Studies*, vol. 42, no. 1 (2016): 5–18.

Rush, Peter D, and Olivera Simić, eds. *The Arts of Transitional Justice: Culture, Activism, and Memory after Atrocity*. New York: Springer, 2014.

Russell, Barbara. 'The Woman Who Kept Silent: Remembering and Reconciliation in South Africa'. In *Violent Depictions: Representing Violence across Cultures*, edited by Susanna Scarparo and Sarah McDonald, 178–203. Newcastle: Cambridge Scholars Publishing, 2009.

Sachs, Albie. 'Interview'. *Constitutional Court Trust Oral History Project* (2011).

The Jail Diary of Albie Sachs. London: Sphere Books, 1969.

The Strange Alchemy of Life and Law. Oxford: Oxford University Press, 2009.

Sachs, Albie, and Vanessa September. *The Free Diary of Albie Sachs*. Johannesburg: Random House, 2004.

Sassatelli, Monica. 'The Biennalization of Art Worlds'. In *Routledge International Handbook of the Sociology of Art and Culture*, edited by Laurie Hanquinet and Mike Savage, 277–289. Oxford: Routledge, 2015.

Savage, Michael. 'The Imposition of Pass Laws on the African Population in South Africa 1916–1984'. *African Affairs*, vol. 85, no. 339 (1986): 181–205.

Schaap, Andrew. 'The Time of Reconciliation and the Space of Politics'. In *Law and the Politics of Reconciliation*, edited by Scott Veitch, 9–31. Oxford: Routledge, 2007.

Schneider, Cynthia P. 'Cultural Diplomacy: The Humanizing Factor'. In *International Cultural Policies and Power*, edited by J P Singh, 101–111. London: Palgrave Macmillan, 2010.

'Culture Communicates: US Diplomacy That Works'. In *The New Public Diplomacy*, edited by Jan Melissen, 147–168. Hampshire: Springer, 2005.

Schwartz-Shea, Peregrine, and Dvora Yanow. *Interpretive Research Design: Concepts and Processes*. New York: Routledge, 2012.

Segal, Lauren. *Number Four: The Making of Constitution Hill*. Johannesburg: Penguin, 2006.

Segal, Lauren, Clive Van Den Berg, and Churchill Madikida. *Mapping Memory: Former Prisoners Tell Their Stories*. Johannesburg: David Krut, 2006.

Shapiro, Michael J. *Studies in Trans-Disciplinary Method.* Oxford: Routledge, 2013.

Sherwin, Richard K. *Visualizing Law in the Age of the Digital Baroque: Arabesques and Entanglements.* Oxford: Routledge, 2011.

'Visual Jurisprudence'. *New York Law School Law Review,* vol. 57, no. 11 (2012): 11–39.

Siddiqui, Nadia, Hadi Marifat, and Sari Kuouvo. 'Culture, Theatre and Justice: Examples from Afghanistan'. In *The Arts of Transitional Justice,* edited by Peter D Rush and Olivera Simić, 113–134. New York: Springer, 2014.

Simić, Olivera, and Dijana Milosevic. 'Enacting Justice: The Role of Dah Theatre Company in Transitional Justice Processes in Serbia and Beyond'. In *The Arts of Transitional Justice,* edited by Peter D Rush and Olivera Simić, 99–112. New York: Springer, 2014.

Simić, Olivera, and Zala Volcic. 'In the Land of Wartime Rape: Bosnia, Cinema and Reparation'. *Griffith Journal of Law & Human Dignity,* vol. 2, no. 2 (2014): 377–401.

Smith, David. 'ANC's Secrecy Bill Seen as Assault on South African Press Freedom'. 2012, www.theguardian.com/world/2012/jun/06/south-africa-secrecy-bill-press-freedom. 1 June 2016.

'South Africa's "Secrecy Bill" Attracts International Condemnation'. 2012, www.theguardian.com/world/2012/jun/13/south-africa-secrecy-bill-un-condemnation. 1 June 2016.

Smith, Theresa. 'SA Art Back in Global Showcase'. 2013, www.iol.co.za/tonight/whats-on/western-cape/sa-art-back-in-global-showcase-1.1515423#.UouNJ2S4GLE. 3 November 2015.

Snyman, Cara. 'Constitutional Court Wins Again'. 2006, www.artlink.co.za/news_article.htm?contentID=2271. 3 March 2016.

Snyman, Johannes. 'Interpretation and the Politics of Memory'. *Acta Juridica,* vol. (1998): 312–337.

Soko, Mills, and Neil Balchin. 'South Africa's Quest for Leadership in Africa: Achievements, Constraints and Dilemmas'. In *Global and Regional Leadership of BRICS Countries,* edited by Stephen Kingah and Cintia Quiliconi, 225–242. Cham: Springer, 2015.

'South African Exhibition at the 55th International Art Exhibition – Venice Biennale 2013: Expression of Interest: Visual Arts Curators'. Newspaper advertisement, 25 January 2013.

South African Government. 'Census 2011 Listing Database'. 2011, www.census2011.co.za. 3 March 2016.

South African Government. 'Govt's Q&A Advertorial on the POSIB'. 2011, www.politicsweb.co.za/news-and-analysis/govts-qa-advertorial-on-the-posib. 1 June 2016.

South African Human Rights Commission. 'Report on the Right to Access Sufficient Water and Decent Sanitation in South Africa'. 2014.

South African Parliament. 'Superior Courts Act'. South Africa, 2013.

Staal, Jonas. 'Ideological Guide to the Venice Biennale'. 2013, http://venicebiennale2013.ideologicalguide.com/about/. 3 November 2015.

Stone, Maria. 'Challenging Cultural Categories: The Transformation of the Venice Biennale under Fascism'. *Journal of Modern Italian Studies,* vol. 4, no. 2 (1999): 184–208.

'Sue Williamson'. www.goodman-gallery.com/artists/suewilliamson. 11 April 2016.

Tang, Jeannine. 'Biennalization and Its Discontents'. In *Negotiating Values in the Creative Industries: Fairs, Festivals and Competitive Events*, edited by Brian Moeran and Jesper Strandgaard Pedersen, 73–93. Cambridge: Cambridge University Press, 2011.

Teitel, Ruti G. *Globalizing Transitional Justice*. Oxford: Oxford University Press, 2014.

Transitional Justice. New York: Oxford University Press, 2000.

'Transitional Justice and the Transformation of Constitutionalism'. In *Comparative Constitutional Law*, edited by Tom Ginsberg and Rosalind Dixon, 57–76. Cheltenham: Edward Elgar Publishing, 2011.

The Human Sciences Research Council. 'An Assessment of the Visual Arts in South Africa'. edited by Gerard Haag, 2010.

'The Index on Censorship'. www.indexoncensorship.org. 1 June 2016.

Thornton, Sarah. *Seven Days in the Art World*. London: Granta Books, 2012.

Truth and Reconciliation Commission. 'Amnesty Decision on Death of Steve Biko'. 1999, www.justice.gov.za/trc/media/pr/1999/p990216a.htm. 1 June 2016.

'TRC Final Report – Summary and Guide to Contents'. 1998.

'Truth and Reconciliation Commission of South Africa Report: Volume Five'. Cape Town: Truth and Reconciliation Commission, 1998.

'Truth and Reconciliation Commission of South Africa Report: Volume Two'. Cape Town: Truth and Reconciliation Commission, 1998.

United Nations General Assembly. 'Lifting of Sanctions against South Africa'. In Resolution 48/1, 1993.

'The Policies of Apartheid of the Government of South Africa'. In *Resolution 2396*, 1968.

Urban Works. 'Flame of Democracy at Constitution Hill'. http://urbanworks.co.za/flame-of-democracy/. 3 March 2016.

Van Den Berg, Niekie. 'Controversy Surrounds South Africa's Participation in the 2011 Venice Biennale'. 2012, www.da.org.za/archive/controversy-surrounds-south-africas-participation-in-the-2011-venice-biennale/. 25 September 2015.

Van Der Merwe, Hugo, and Audrey R Chapman. *Truth and Reconciliation in South Africa: Did the TRC Deliver?* Philadelphia: University of Pennsylvania Press, 2008.

Van Graan, Mike. 'Revised White Paper on Arts, Culture, Heritage: A Critique'. African Arts Institute, 2013.

'The Spear and the Marikana Massacre: Mirroring the Decline of South African Democracy'. *African Arts*, vol. 46, no. 2 (2013): 1–4.

Van Marle, Karin. 'The Spectacle of Post-Apartheid Constitutionalism'. *Griffith Law Review*, vol. 16, no. 2 (2007): 411–429.

Van Marle, Karin, Isolde De Villiers, and Eunette Beukes. 'Memory, Space and Gender: Reimagining the Law'. *Southern African Public Law*, vol. 27, no. 2 (2012): 559–574.

Vartanian, Hrag. 'Procedure for National Participations'. La Biennale di Venezia, 2015.

'Resistance to Turkey's Protest Violence Reaches the Venice Biennale'. 2013, http://hyperallergic.com/72413/resistance-to-turkeys-bloody-protests-reach-the-venice-biennale/. 30 October 2015.

Visual Arts Network of South Africa. 'VANSA Statement on the Venice Biennale'. 2011, http://vansa.co.za/voice/art-voice/copy_of_vansa-statement-on-the-venice-biennale. 10 June 2013.

Vladislavic, Ivan. *Portrait with Keys: The City of Johannesburg Unlocked*. London: W W Norton and Company, 2009.

Von Eschen, Penny. *Satchmo Blows Up the World: Jazz Ambassadors Play the Cold War*. Cambridge, MA: Harvard University Press, 2009.

Voparil, Christopher J. 'General Introduction'. In *The Rorty Reader*, edited by Christopher J Voparil and Richard J Bernstein, 1–52. Chichester: Wiley, 2010.

Vorster, Stacey L. 'Storytelling and Fraught Histories: Phila Ndwandwe's Blue Dress'. *Safundi: The Journal of South African and American Studies*, vol. 19, no. 2 (2018): 164–189.

Wagner, Anne, and Richard K Sherwin, eds. *Law, Culture and Visual Studies*. Dordrecht: Springer, 2014.

Wei, Chu-Chiun. 'From National Art to Critical Globalism: The Politics and Curatorial Strategies of the Taiwan Pavilion at the Venice Biennale'. *Third Text*, vol. 27, no. 4 (2013): 470–484.

White, Ben. 'Apartheid and Cultural Boycott'. 2015, www.middleeastmonitor.com/resources/reports-and-publications/20863-apartheid-a-cultural-boycott-then-and-now. 5 October 2015.

Whyte, William. 'How Do Buildings Mean? Some Issues of Interpretation in the History of Architecture'. *History and Theory*, vol. 45, no. 2 (2006): 153–177.

Williams, Kent Lindiwe. 'Dress as a Site of Multiple Selves: Address and Redress in Judith Mason's *The Man Who Sang and the Woman Who Kept Silent* and Wanja Kimani's *You Have Not Changed*'. *Image & Text*, vol. 29 (2017): 163–184.

Williamson, Sue. 'A Few South Africans'. www.sue-williamson.com/#!a-few-south-africans/cl06. 11 April 2016.

Resistance Art in South Africa. Cape Town: Double Storey, 1989.

South African Art Now. New York: Harper Collins, 2009.

'Sue Williamson's Diary: Venice and the World'. 2015, Artthrob, http://artthrob.co.za/2015/03/30/sue-williamsons-diary-venice-and-the-world/. 1 May 2016.

Wolff, Spencer. 'Human Dignity and Freedom of Speech in the Post Apartheid State'. *Macquarie Law Journal*, vol. 13 (2014): 99–127.

Wu, Chin-Tao. 'Biennials without borders'. *New Left Review*, vol. 57 (2009): 107–115.

Zaugg, Isabelle Alice, and Emi Nishimura. 'Angola and Kenya Pavilions in the 2013 Venice Biennale: African Contemporary Art and Cultural Diplomacy in the "Olympics of Art"'. *The Journal of Arts Management, Law, and Society*, vol. 45, no. 2 (2015): 134–149.

Zunino, Marcos. *Justice Framed: A Genealogy of Transitional Justice*. Cambridge: Cambridge University Press, 2019.

Archives

Archivio Storico delle Arti Contemporanee (ASAC), Venice, Italy

Constitutional Court Archives, Johannesburg, South Africa

South African History Archives, Johannesburg, South Africa

Index